THE STAR TREK®
COMPENDIUM

ABOUT THE AUTHOR

Allan Asherman is also the author of Titan Books' *The Star Trek Interview Book*, as well as *The Making of Star Trek II* and dozens of magazine and newspaper articles on films and television. An authority on the classic TV series *The Adventures of Superman*, he has worked in several capacities at DC Comics, was a film booker for Metro-Goldwyn-Mayer, and taught homebound students in the New York City school system. His other interests include studying music written for film and television; researching his favourite TV series (including *The Lone Ranger*, *The Untouchables*, *Science Fiction Theatre*, *Rocky Jones*, *Space Ranger* and *Men Into Space*); and uncovering new information about his favourite films (including *The Day the Earth Stood Still*, *Things to Come*, *This Island Earth*, *Jason and the Argonauts*, the 1959 *Ben Hur*, and various sound serials). He also provided the supplementary material for the Criterion Collection's special *Forbidden Planet* laser disc and the Titan Books Official Collectors' Magazine for *Batman Returns*. Allan and his wife, Arlene Lo (the proofreader at DC Comics), live in Long Island.

Allan Asherman welcomes any comments and can be reached at:

Allan Asherman
Box 1227
New York, NY 10185-1227
USA

For a complete list of Star Trek publications, T-shirts and badges please send a large stamped SAE to Titan Books Mail Order, 19 Valentine Place, London, SE1 8QH. Please quote reference STC.

THE STAR TREK® COMPENDIUM

BY ALLAN ASHERMAN

THE STAR TREK COMPENDIUM
ISBN 1 85286 472 9

Published by Titan Books Ltd
19 Valentine Place
London SE1 8QH

First edition August 1987
Second revised edition October 1989
Third revised edition May 1993
10 9 8 7

British edition by arrangement with Pocket Books, a division of Simon &
Schuster, Inc., under exclusive licence from Paramount Pictures Corporation,
the Trademark owner.

British Library Cataloguing-in-Publication Data.
A catalogue record for this book is available from the British Library.

Printed and bound in Great Britain by Hillman Printers (Frome) Ltd., Frome, Somerset.

ACKNOWLEDGMENTS

The author wishes to thank the following people, without whose aid and encouragement this book would not have been possible: Richard Arnold, Peggy Barilla, Ron Barlow, Diane Baron, Ruth Berman, Germaine Best, Cindy Casby, Wah Chang, Dave Cockrum, Cecilia Cosentini, Paula Crist, Madeleine Dale, Genny Dazzo, Linda Deneroff, Doug Drexler, Harlan Ellison, Jenny Ferris, Kelly Freas, Polly Freas, Adrian Fuentes, Carl Gafford, Gary Gerani, Joan Geruntho, Tom Geruntho, Mindy Glazer, David Gottlieb, Karen Gottlieb, Linda Harriman, Robert Harris, Sondra Harris, Lynn Holland, James Horner, Winston Howlett, Janet Ingber, Joyce Klanit, Andrea Kline, Ivan Kline, Devra Langsam, Howard Levine, Elan Litt, Jody McGhee, Shirley Maiewski, Michelle Malkin, Satoshi Matsubayashi, Ed Miarecki, Craig Miller, Teresa Minambres, Margie Nelson, Nichelle Nichols, P. S. Nim, Shannon O'Brien, Ray Pence, Fred B. Phillips, Mary Piero, Elyse Rosenstein, Steve Rosenstein, Jane Schmidt, Tom Sciacca, Kate Soenlehn, Phillip Soenlehn, Sally Steg, Fred Steiner, Leonard Suligowski, George Takei, William Theiss, Adrienne Tollin, Anthony Tollin, Bjo Trimble, Michael Uslan, Erwin Vertlieb, Steve Vertlieb, Howard Weinstein, Chuck Weiss, Barbara Wenk, Patrick White, Allison Whitfield, Joan Winston, Joyce Yasner; and special thanks to Sharon Jarvis and Lea Braff, my literary agents for the original edition and Sharon Jarvis, my literary agent for this revised edition; Eugene Brissie, editor of the original edition; Dave Stern, editor of this revised edition, David Hartwell, John Douglas, and Ellen Kushner formerly of Pocket Books; Helene Johnson, Howard Rayfiel, Tom Phillips and Kathy Mortensen of Paramount Pictures; "Star Trek's" Gene Roddenberry, Leonard Nimoy, Susan Sackett, and Harve Bennett.

The following organizations also provided assistance: The Star Trek Welcommittee, P.O. Box 12, Saranac, MI 48881; The Official Leonard Nimoy Fan Club, Rt. 3, Box 48, LaFayette, AL 36862, Sandra Keel, President; James Doohan International Fan Club, 1519 N.W. 204th St., Seattle, WA 98177; The George Takei Official World-wide Club, 62 Southbank Street, Leek Staffs, ST 13 FLN, England, Ena Glogowska, President; Grace Lee Whitney Fan Club, 2611 Silverside Road, Wilmington, DE 19810, Page Lewis, President; The William Shatner Fellowship, P.O. Box 1366, Hollywood, CA 90078, Helen Malloy, President.

Special thanks to my wife, Arlene Lo, for her invaluable assistance in preparing this revised manuscript, and for her wonderful confidence in this book and this writer.

For a catalog of Star Trek related souvenirs unavailable elsewhere write:

Lincoln Enterprises, Inc.
Box 691370
Los Angeles, CA
90069

Items are available from the television series as well as all the motion pictures.

ACKNOWLEDGEMENTS

This book is dedicated to Anne and Robert Asherman,
without whose initiative, guidance, and patience
the author could not have been produced.

This edition dedicated
to the enduring memory
of Robert Asherman.

CONTENTS

INTRODUCTION

When I was growing up in Brooklyn, New York, my parents' television set was a wondrous device. At the flick of a switch, and after a minute's warm-up time, the old set brought my favorite pals and heroes into my living room. As far back as I can remember, "Howdy Doody," "The Adventures of Superman," "Captain Video and His Video Rangers," "Captain Midnight," "Rocky Jones: Space Ranger," "Ramar of the Jungle," "Hopalong Cassidy," and "The Lone Ranger" were there to extend my horizons beyond reality.

One day, I noticed that the programs I liked best were those that featured spacemen and women and rocketships. I began to read books such as *By Spaceship to the Moon* and *Rocket Jets, Guided Missiles and Spaceships*. I learned that people could not breathe in space without space suits, and that in space there is no "up" or "down." On one especially magical day, my mother took me to Brooklyn's Abraham & Strauss department store to meet Willy Ley, a pioneer rocket scientist who had written some of the books on space I had read. I talked about nothing but rockets and space travel for days afterward.

I asked my school librarian if she had any books about spacemen and rockets and rayguns, whereupon I was led to a small bookcase marked "science fiction." I devoured the books, stories, and pictures from that bookcase, and I started to look elsewhere for more such wondrous things.

At about this time, I began to frequent the center section of my neighborhood movie theater, the Marboro, attracted by colorful posters that announced such films as *From the Earth to the Moon, The Mysterians, Rodan, Earth vs. the Flying Saucers,* and *This Island Earth*.

I saw *Forbidden Planet* on television and I loved it, and in 1960, *The Day the Earth Stood Still* was televised and I first saw this beautiful film. This was followed soon afterward by my first exposure to another classic science fiction movie, *Things to Come*.

After being exposed to more science fiction books and films, I began to attend science fiction conventions. When I heard about the annual *world* conventions, I determined that I would attend the next one. During the Labor Day weekend in 1966, I traveled by bus to Cleveland, Ohio, to attend "Tricon," that year's World Science Fiction Convention. During the bus ride I studied the convention's progress reports, which mentioned three special film events on the program. A new film, *Fantastic Voyage,* had been provided by 20th Century-Fox. The same studio's television division, with producer Irwin Allen, had also arranged to show the pilot episode of Allen's new series, "The Time Tunnel."

The third convention debut was to be another television pilot episode, the work of a producer with an unfamiliar name: Gene Roddenberry. The title of Roddenberry's new series: *Star Trek!*

Near the convention's registration area was a long table, behind which stood an attractive young woman wearing an intriguing costume. She said it was from a "Star Trek" episode that had already been filmed, "What Are Little Girls Made Of?" Maybe this show *would* be worth seeing; this costume did not look like something that had been designed for a children's audience.

Poised on a small stand in the middle of the table was a plaster model of what appeared to be a flying saucer with projecting tubes. The scale model bore the legend "NCC-1701," and was clearly not designed for travel within the Earth's atmosphere.

One of the several photos surrounding the little ship showed a man with pointed ears. He was holding the same model that was in front of me (the ship, *not* the woman), and he peered at me with an expression that encouraged me to find something else to stare at.

After my eyes had gone back to the woman for a while, I was surprised to see photos of William Shatner, whom I remembered from his "Twilight Zone" and "Outer Limits" appearances. He was clad in the same type of uniform as the fellow with the large ears.

Then I noticed the two little black objects on top of the photos. One looked like a small electric shaver. It had a grid, a metal wheel, and a small numbered gauge. It couldn't have been too important, I thought, because everyone was picking it up and examining it. I examined the object too, not knowing that I was holding one of the original hand phasers designed for "Star Trek."

Next to the "shaver" was another little black box covered with a gold grillework. (I didn't know how to open it, never having seen a "Star Trek" communicator before.)

I signed a form asking the studio to send me some of the photos on the table, and handed it to the woman in the android suit, who thanked me for showing interest in "Star Trek" (I recall wishing that I had bid on a group of original set drawings from "Star Trek" auctioned off earlier).

The next day, September 4, 1966, I awoke, dressed, ate, and stopped at the "Star Trek" table again where I was told that if I wanted to see something else about the show I'd better hurry: the films were about to start down the hall. I made my way into the room and found a seat. An assistant of Irwin Allen materialized with the "Time Tunnel" print, a 75-minute version that was never aired, and apologized that Mr. Allen could not be at the convention himself because of production deadlines. The lights went out, the film was shown, and we applauded after it was over.

A few minutes later, a tall man appeared at the front of the room. Although he looked formidable, his voice was contrastingly gentle. He sounded almost timid and nervous when he introduced himself as Gene Roddenberry, a lifelong science fiction fan. He told the audience that he had produced a new television pilot which would debut the following week on NBC-TV with a "sneak preview" episode. Even so, he stated, our opinion was still extremely important to him. With that, Roddenberry left the stage, and as the lights went out, the audience quieted down for one of the very first public airings of "Star Trek."

There was that funny spaceship again, with William Shatner's voiceover explaining the mission of the *Enterprise*. The weird guy with the pointed ears looked even stranger on film, with his slightly yellow complexion. I tried to spot the makeup seam on his ears and couldn't find any.

There was nothing childish about the episode, "Where No Man Has Gone Before." We waited for a kid or a wisecracking robot to enter the picture, but they never arrived. Even the music was somber, serious, and spectacular.

There must have been over 500 people in that audience. When the Enterprise hit the galactic barrier, 1,000 eyes opened wide. Five hundred respiratory rates accelerated with that wonderful pleasure that comes over lovers of all things when they see their favorite subject being treated well.

Then the whispers started. "He did say this was for television, didn't he?" Maybe we'd misunderstood. I recall wondering how Roddenberry could afford to do things

like this on a television budget. If he could have read our minds at any moment during that screening, he would have been the happiest producer in the world.

The audience continued to watch the episode intently. A very human captain was attempting to avoid killing a close friend. A satanic-looking first officer was pressuring the captain to liquidate the mutating individual. Someone noticed that Gary Mitchell's hair was gradually turning gray—one of the episode's many subtle touches.

We noticed people of varied races, genders, and planetary origins working together. Here was a future it did not hurt to imagine. Here was a constructive tomorrow for mankind, emphasizing exploration and expansion. This was the science fiction television series we all wanted to see. We were all extremely impressed.

Captain Kirk was a commander with guts, compassion, and a straightforward, no-nonsense manner. We liked him; we also liked Spock, the show's sparkling opticals, and that interesting starship. In fact, we liked everything about that episode more than anything else shown at the convention.

After the film was over we were unable to leave our seats. We just nodded at each other and smiled, and began to whisper. As the murmuring grew louder, Roddenberry returned to the stage. People quieted down again, waiting for him to say something. The producer, however, was waiting for *us* to say something. Roddenberry seemed to have no idea of the effect his show was having on us.

Finally, Gene Roddenberry broke the silence. He asked for the audience's opinion; we gave him a standing ova-

The man with pointed ears

tion. He smiled, and we returned the smile before we converged on him. We came close to lifting the man upon our shoulders and carrying him out of the room.

From that moment on, the convention was "divided" into two factions. Those of us who had seen "Where No Man Has Gone Before" were hooked. The unenlightened convention goers were convinced we were acting strangely to lavish so much attention on one television series episode.

Later, a group of "enlightened ones" asked Roddenberry if he had brought any other "Trek" film to the convention. Gene did have something else with him; the first "Star Trek" pilot that NBC had previously rejected. It wasn't in color, he explained; never mind, we assured him, we wanted to see it anyway. Shortly afterward, he showed "The Cage" for us.

"The Cage" *was* different from "Where No Man Had Gone Before," although not in a negative way. It showed the same attention to serious and imaginative detail. In addition there were the laser cannon opticals, the superb Talosian makeups, and another interesting musical score. Its most outstanding characteristics were the intelligence of its story, its polished production values, and the performances of its actors.

We were all excited, but we had no way of knowing that we had just witnessed the opening chapter of one of the most amazing stories in entertainment history—the birth of "Star Trek."

William Shatner in uniform

WILLIAM SHATNER

THE BEGINNINGS

"Star Trek *is a 'Wagon Train' concept—built around characters who travel to worlds 'similar' to our own . . . their transportation is the S.S. Yorktown, *performing a long-range exploration-science-security mission. . . .*"

—Series creator Gene Roddenberry, shown here with

1

THE FATHER OF "STAR TREK"

In the 1950's, the people who worked behind the cameras were usually overlooked in favor of those photographed by them. Only occasionally did a writer, director, or producer achieve personal fame as a result of Academy Awards or gossip-column scandals. Only rarely did a moviemaker emerge whose real-life exploits could match the fictional dynamism of his movies.

"Star Trek's" creator/producer Gene Roddenberry was an exception, with a background as colorful and exciting as the show that would bring him nationwide acclaim—and cause "Star Trek" fandom to nickname him "the Great Bird of the Galaxy."

Roddenberry was born in El Paso, Texas, on August 19, 1921. His father was a cavalry officer, stationed at Fort Bliss, Texas (the site of early U.S. rocket experiments). Roddenberry grew up in Los Angeles, and while in junior high school had his first exposure to science fiction. He majored in prelaw at Los Angeles City College, and three years later switched to engineering at U.C.L.A.

Gene was fascinated with flying and after earning his pilot's license left college to become a cadet in the U.S. Army Air Corps. The United States had just entered World War II, and after his Air Corps training Roddenberry was sent to Guadalcanal, where he flew 89 combat and reconnaissance missions. In the middle of all this excitement, Gene began to write stories for flying magazines.

After the war, he investigated airplane crashes for the Air Staff while living in Washington, D.C. Gene then went to work for Pan American Airlines, piloting flights to some of the most exotic places in the world.

While handling the Calcutta route, he lived in New York City and studied literature at Columbia University. At this point, Gene Roddenberry's life almost ended.

On a flight out of Calcutta, his plane crashed in flames in the Syrian desert. Roddenberry, the senior officer on the flight, directed two uninjured passengers to search for help while he stayed and talked with natives who had come to loot the plane. The two passengers reached a Syrian Army outpost, which sent a plane to pick up Roddenberry. Reaching the outpost, Gene broadcast a radio message that was relayed to Pan American. A rescue airliner was dispatched to the scene. Roddenberry and seven others were the only survivors of the India to Istanbul flight. Gene was later awarded a Civil Aeronautics commendation for his heroic behavior during and after the crash.

In 1949, having experienced sufficient drama in the air, Roddenberry moved to Los Angeles with the intention of creating drama for television. In Los Angeles, he was advised to find employment as either a newspaperman or a policeman because both of these jobs provided sufficient free time in which to write. Gene joined the Los Angeles Police Department.

But Patrolman Gene Roddenberry was still an adventurer. In addition to the relatively routine traffic detail, Roddenberry worked the jail wards and assisted in conducting investigations. He was then assigned the exotic (and dangerous) "skid row" beat, which brought him into contact with police informants, narcotics users, drug dealers, and prostitutes.

While Roddenberry was experiencing city life firsthand and gathering material for his later work on television crime shows, he was also developing an interest in the enormous narcotics problem plaguing American communities. He began to correlate his findings based on his on-the-job experiences, and supplemented these with research into police records and library sources. Promoted to the head of research in the office of Los Angeles' Chief of Police William Parker, Gene was easily able to prepare realistic and constructive studies on drug addiction.

By now, most of Roddenberry's time was spent in writing his studies and speeches for Chief Parker. At this time, he began to "moonlight" as a free-lance television writer, producing his first treatments and scripts under pseudonyms. In 1951, Roddenberry sold his first TV script. The following year he made his first science fiction script sale, "The Secret Defense of 117," (starring Ricardo Montalban) televised on Chevron Theatre."

Roddenberry's script ideas were attractive to such series as "Dragnet" because of his familiarity with police procedure and terminology. He was probably the most qualified script writer to dramatically recreate stories of crime in "the city, Los Angeles, California," as the original "Dragnet" introductions stated.

In 1954, Roddenberry left the Los Angeles police force and went to work as a full-time writer. His television sales included episodes for "Dr. Christian," "Dr. Kildare," "Four Star Theatre," "Highway Patrol," "The Jane Wyman Show," "The Kaiser Aluminum Hour," "The Naked City," and "Robert Taylor's Detectives." Roddenberry became head writer for "Have Gun—Will Travel," and also penned episodes for that series. Gene was a staff writer for the series "West Point" in 1956, and wrote episodes for that series including "The Brothers" and "Jet Pilot." His work in that series provided the inspiration for his first television show, "The Lieutenant."

Roddenberry first conceived the idea for "Star Trek" in 1960, and he was thinking about it even while producing "The Lieutenant," a series of hour-long episodes filmed at M-G-M Studios and telecast on the NBC network. "The Lieutenant" concerned life in the peacetime U.S. Marine Corps and starred Gary Lockwood as Lieutenant Bill Rice and Robert Vaughn as Captain Ray Rambridge. The show lasted for 29 episodes, and while these were being produced, M-G-M asked Roddenberry to come up with another series idea. At this time Gene prepared the first draft of his format for "Star Trek."

2
GENESIS

Dated March 11, 1964, the first printed work connected with the series was a 16-page booklet in which Roddenberry outlined his earliest ideas about the show:

The time is "somewhere in the future." It could be 1995 or maybe even 2995. In other words, close enough to our own time for our continuing characters to be fully identifiable as people like us, but far enough into the future for galaxy travel to be thoroughly established (happily eliminating the need to encumber our stories with tiresome scientific explanation). . . . The "parallel worlds" concept is the key to the "Star Trek" format . . . It makes production practical by permitting action-adventure science fiction at a practical budget figure via the use of available "Earth" casting, sets, locations, costuming, and so on.

As important (and perhaps even more so in many ways), the 'parallel worlds' concept tends to keep even the most imaginative stories within the general audience's frame of reference through such recognizable and identifiable casting, sets, and costuming.

Here's how Roddenberry first envisioned "Star Trek's" leading characters:

ROBERT M. APRIL
The "skipper," about 34, Academy graduate, rank of captain. . . . A short-hand sketch of Robert April might be "a space-age Captain Horatio Hornblower" . . . a colorfully complex personality, capable of action and decision which can verge on the heroic—who lives a continual battle with self-doubt and the loneliness of command. . . . His primary weakness is a predilection for action—but, unlike most early explorers, he has an almost compulsive compassion for the plight of others, alien as well as human, and must continually fight the temptation to risk many to save one.

THE EXECUTIVE OFFICER
Never referred to as anything but "Number One," this officer is mysteriously female—slim and dark in a Nile Valley way, one of those women who will always look the same between years 20 to 50. An extraordinarily efficient officer, "Number One" enjoys playing it expressionless, cool—is probably Robert April's superior in detailed knowledge of the multiple equipment systems, departments, and crew members aboard the vessel. When Captain April leaves the craft, "Number One" moves up to Acting Commander.

THE NAVIGATOR
José Ortegas, born in South America, is tall, handsome, about 25, and brilliant, but still in the process of maturing. He is full of both humor and Latin temperament. He fights a perpetual and highly personal battle with his instruments and calculators, suspecting that space, and probably God too, are engaged in a giant conspiracy to make his professional and personal life as difficult and uncomfortable as possible. José is painfully aware of the historical repute of Latins as lovers—and is in danger of failing this ambition on a cosmic scale.

SHIP'S DOCTOR
Phillip Boyce, an unlikely space traveler. At the age of 51, he's worldly, humorously cynical, makes it a point to thoroughly enjoy his own weaknesses. Captain April's only real confidant, "Bones" Boyce considers himself the only realist aboard, measures each new landing in terms of relative annoyance rather than excitement.

THE FIRST LIEUTENANT

The captain's right-hand man, the working-level commander of all the ship's functions from manning the bridge to supervising the lowliest scrub detail. His name is "Mr. Spock." And the first view of him can be almost frightening—a face so heavy-lidded and satanic you might almost expect him to have a forked tail. Probably half-Martian, he has a slightly reddish complexion and semipointed ears. But strangely—Mr. Spock's quiet temperament is in dramatic contrast to his satanic look. Of all the crew aboard, he is the nearest to Captain April's equal, physically and emotionally, as a commander of men. His primary weakness is an almost catlike curiosity over anything the slightest bit "alien."

THE CAPTAIN'S YEOMAN

Except for problems in naval parlance, "Colt" would be called a yeowoman; blond and with a shape even a uniform could not hide. She serves as Robert April's secretary, reporter, bookkeeper, and undoubtedly wishes she could also serve him in more personal departments. She is not dumb; she *is* very female, disturbingly so.

And here are excerpts Captain Robert M. April's from orders:

You are therefore posted, effective immediately, to command the following: the S.S. *Yorktown*.

> Cruiser Class—Gross 190,000 tons
> Crew Complement—203 persons
> Drive—space-warp (maximum velocity .73 of one light-year per hour)
> Range—18 years at galaxy patrol speeds
> Registry—Earth, United Space Ship

Nature and duration of command:

> Galaxy exploration and Class M investigation: 5 years

You will patrol the ninth quadrant, beginning with Alpha Centauri and extending to the outer Pinial Galaxy limit.

You will conduct this patrol to accomplish primarily:

(a) Earth security, via exploration of intelligence and social systems capable of a galaxial threat, and

(b) Scientific investigation to add to the Earth's body of knowledge of life forms and social systems, and

(c) Any required assistance to the several Earth colonies in this quadrant, and the enforcement of appropriate statutes affecting such Federated commerce vessels and traders as you might contact in the course of your mission.

Consistent with the equipment and limitations of your cruiser class vessel, you will confine your landings and contacts to planets approximating Earth-Mars conditions, life, and social orders.

The booklet also featured 25 episode synopses, many of which became actual "Star Trek" episodes. But Metro-Goldwyn-Mayer, though initially enthusiastic, did not buy Roddenberry's format.

Undeterred, Gene approached Desilu Studios, a production facility that had pioneered the filmed television series. An interested Desilu vice-president, Oscar Katz, submitted the "Star Trek" format to NBC (after being turned away at CBS), and Mort Werner, the network's vice-president in charge of programming, provided Roddenberry with $20,000 in development money to write three story ideas based upon the format. One of these three stories, "The Cage," was chosen as the series' first pilot.

The title of "Star Trek's" first pilot was changed to "The Menagerie" before it was completed, but since there is a two-part episode of the series that bears that name (as well as footage from the original pilot), this historic first episode is referred to as "The Cage" throughout this book.

3

"THE CAGE"

Dated September 8, 1964, the first draft of the story began with a rendezvous between the *Enterprise* and a space shuttle for the purpose of evacuating wounded starship personnel and replacing them with new crewmen. The technology expressed here is more primitive than anything seen in the television series, including an optically produced laser beam "track" for the approach and a hatchway connecting the two vessels. As represented in the draft, the entire operation seems to come right out of a 1950's space opera. Yet many of the key elements that would make "Star Trek" so successful were also present.

Here's how the ship's captain, Robert T. April (later Winter and finally Christopher Pike) was introduced:

DOLLY SHOT—BEGINNING AT ELEVATOR
The WHINE of the ship's high-speed turbo-elevator, then the door snaps open and ROBERT APRIL, Captain of the U.S.S. *Enterprise,* steps out into scene and crosses toward the docking hatch. A crewman is standing by with the captain's uniform coat and hat, April donning them as he crosses toward the docking hatch. Our first and most important impression is that he would not be completely out of place on the bridge of a naval cruiser in our own day. About 34, he is lean and capable both mentally and physically. In the next few scenes we'll also begin to see that this is a complex personality whose maturity and strong masculinity is combined with a sensitivity and warmth which the responsibility and loneliness of command often forces him to hide. He strides in to peer over the first crewman's shoulder, out the docking port.

The conflict on the alien planet which the *Enterprise* had just explored was attributed to the actions of one prejudiced officer. The first official duty being discharged by the captain concerned that crewman and explained the nature of April and Starfleet Command:

The last man in line, CROWLEY, is ex-navigator of the *Enterprise*. As April reaches him, neither man offers to shake hands.

CROWLEY
You send me back this way, April, they'll disqualify me as a navigator, break me as a ship's officer . . .

APRIL (interrupting)
You fired on friendly aliens, cost us four dead, three injured . . .

Number One (Majel Barrett) and science officer Spock

CROWLEY (interrupts angrily)
They looked like insects. How could I know they
were intelligent enough to have weapons?

APRIL (quietly)
Get off my ship, mister.

This respect for all life forms permeated the entire
series—and eventually developed into starfleet's Prime
Directive.

The script ends with a humorous little scene back on
the *Enterprise* bridge. Having heard the name "Eve"
mentioned, the ship's doctor, Boyce, chimes in:

BOYCE
Eve? As in "Adam"?

APRIL (snaps quietly)
As in "all ship's doctors are dirty old men." (whirls
toward Spock) What is this, Mr. Spock, a cadet
ship? Are we ready or not?

Spock, who has been leaning conspicuously toward
April to catch every word, now snaps back to his
position.

The strength of "Star Trek's" characters and its vision
of the future shone through clearly, even in this rough
draft, and NBC gave Roddenberry the go-ahead to begin
production on "The Cage." He began to gather together
the individuals who would bring the roles in his script to
life—the *Enterprise*'s first crewmembers.

To portray his starship's captain, Roddenberry chose

An unused makeup for Number One

Jeffrey Hunter. As a contract player for 20th Century-
Fox Studios during the 1950s, Hunter had the opportunity to play many diversified roles, but he is probably
best remembered for his performance as Christ in the
1961 M-G-M version of *King of Kings* and his role as
John Wayne's co-star in the classic western *The Searchers*.
He was also the star of the TV series "Temple Houston,"
which ceased production in September 1964—just in time
for him to accept the role of Captain Christopher Pike.

Pike's first officer, the mysterious Number One, was
played by Majel Barrett, who would later return to the
Enterprise as Nurse Christine Chapel. Born Majel Lee
Hudec. Majel married Gene Roddenberry on August 6,
1969, in a Buddhist-Shinto ceremony conducted in To-
kyo, Japan.

John Hoyt (Dr. Phillip "Bones" Boyce) created a character in "The Cage" who was very similar to Dr. McCoy.
With his acerbic observations and his role as Captain Pike's
analyst ("Sometimes a man will tell his bartender things
he'd never tell his doctor"), Hoyt (and Boyce) would have
fit right into the *Enterprise* family.

And for the role of ship's science officer Spock (the
only alien member of the *Enterprise*'s crew), Roddenberry
selected an actor who would eventually become as closely
identified with the series as himself—Leonard Nimoy.

"Star Trek" was not Nimoy's first exposure to filmed
science fiction. In 1952 the actor had donned strange
makeup that included upswept eyebrows when he appeared as Narab, an alien who visited Earth in the serial
Zombies of the Stratosphere (Republic). At the serial's
climax, Nimoy's character revealed the existence of a
superbomb and saved the Earth. Two years later in
Them (Warner Brothers) he appeared as a soldier who
indicated disbelief at a report of giant ants posing a threat
to civilization. Before being signed for "Star Trek," Nimoy
had appeared in an episode of Gene Roddenberry's series

Mr. Spock (Leonard Nimoy)

Vina (Susan Oliver)

"THE CAGE"

#1

WRITER: Gene Roddenberry
DIRECTOR: Robert Butler
PRINCIPALS: Captain Christopher Pike   Mr. Spock
Number One   Transporter Chief Pitcairn
Navigator José "Joe" Tyler   Vina
Dr. Boyce   Dr. Theodore Haskins
Yeoman Colt   The Keeper
Chief Petty Officer Garrison

◄ *Stardate Unknown:* The U.S.S. *Enterprise* is en route to the nearest Federation starbase for rest, recreation, repairs, and replacement of personnel lost during the exploration of Rigel VII. Despite the status of his ship, Captain Pike decides to investigate signs that a spaceship may have crashed on planet Talos IV. A landing party, including Pike, Lieutenant Spock, and Navigator José Tyler beams down and is startled to find an encampment created from makeshift tents and old spaceship parts. A band of ragged survivors comes forward, led by a man who introduces himself as Dr. Theodore Haskins. He explains that they are scientists who have been marooned on the planet since their ship, the S.S. *Columbia,* crashed almost twenty years before.

A beautiful young woman comes forward and is introduced as Vina, who was just a child when the ship crashed. Captain Pike is very much attracted to her. Watching his fascination are several aliens concealed underground who view the scene on a strange, television-like screen.

When Vina lures Pike to a rock formation to show him the secret of how the old scientists have survived in such perfect health, the aliens emerge from a concealed elevator, render Pike unconscious, and drag him into their underground chamber. Spock and Tyler reach the scene too late to help their captain. Meanwhile, the survivors and their encampment have vanished.

Pike awakens in a small enclosure, fronted by a super-strong, transparent material. The small aliens, led by the Keeper, approach his cage and converse telepathically, angering Pike by their references to him as a member of an inferior species. Pike is transported, by illusion, back to Rigel VII, where he once again sees Vina. After that illusion ends, both materialize in his cage again, where Vina tells Pike that she is the lone survivor of the S.S. *Columbia* crash.

When Captain Pike refuses to perform as the Talosians wish, the aliens try to get him interested in Vina by presenting her to him within various illusions designed to spark his masculine instincts: a medieval princess, a green-skinned Orion slave girl, and his "wife." The Talosians have lured the *Enterprise* to their planet so that Pike can

"The Lieutenant." Shortly before filming began on "The Cage," he was seen in two episodes of "The Outer Limits"—"I, Robot" and "The Production and Decay of Strange Particles."

Various tests were filmed before actual production on the episode got under way. In one, Majel Barrett appeared in an unused makeup for Number One. She had an extremely dark complexion, upswept eyebrows, and a facial expression that was devoid of emotion. Just as some characteristics were traded back and forth between Spock and Number One, apparently at one time their facial features were shared as well.

serve as a mate for Vina, enabling the Talosians to breed a race of humans they can use as slaves.

Meanwhile an *Enterprise* landing party prepares to have itself transported underground. Immediately before the transporter is activated, however, Number One and Yeoman Colt vanish, and the machine ceases to function.

The two females materialize within Captain Pike's cage. The Talosians reason that perhaps the captain will be more attracted to either of his crewwomen.

Examining Number One's laser pistol, Pike finds it completely drained of energy, but suspects that this is merely an illusion and that the weapon is actually functional. He has discovered that the Talosians cannot probe into hostile emotional moods, and deliberately assumes an attitude of mindless anger. Throwing the lasers to the floor near the concealed door of the cage, Pike sits and waits. As he anticipated, the Keeper attempts to remove the pistols. Pike quickly grabs the alien, and as Number One holds on to the tricky Talosian, Pike tries to shoot a hole into the wall of the cage. He threatens to shoot directly at the Keeper, and a hole instantly materializes in the wall. The Talosians have been keeping the *Enterprise* people from seeing the destruction their weapons had caused.

Using the Keeper as a shield, Pike and the others ascend in the elevator to the surface of Talos IV and learn the truth. Centuries before, the Talosians had wrecked the surface of their planet in a nuclear war and were forced to move their civilization underground, resulting in their increased mental abilities and their inability to produce children. After Number One threatens to commit suicide by setting the laser pistols to explode, the Talosians confide to him that they never wanted slaves; they only wished to perpetuate their heritage in the offspring of Pike and Vina.

Number One and Yeoman Colt are returned to the *Enterprise,* and the Talosians reveal the truth about Vina. She had actually survived the spaceship crash as an adult, but was horribly injured and disfigured. Without the aid of the Talosian illusions, Vina is a deformed, middle-aged woman. Pike sympathizes with her and asks the Talosians to give her back her illusion of beauty. Standing alongside the Keeper, Pike watches the full illusion that is the Keeper's gift to Vina; she is apparently walking happily away with an illusion of himself keeping her company. Back aboard the *Enterprise,* Pike refuses to discuss what has happened, and the *Enterprise* leaves Talos IV. ▶

Pilot segments of television series are usually very different from the rest of the episodes, but few are as different as "The Cage" is from the rest of "Star Trek." As an indication of this, it proved impossible to air "The Cage" as part of the "Star Trek" series until a story frame was created to form the outline of "The Menagerie." All traces of the starship's warp-drive sequences had to be gone because they were accomplished in a manner very different from that seen in the second pilot and the series.

Mr. Spock's decision to flee from Talos IV while the captain was still a captive of the Talosians (which presented the Vulcan in a most unfavorable light) was also edited out. Some footage was trimmed because it was too sensual for inclusion, although this film was produced almost two years before the first season started to take shape.

"The Cage" was the nucleus of what later developed into the "Star Trek" universe. The differences between the prototypes seen in this episode and their later refinement into the concepts we are familiar with can be seen in both the "production" (sets, decorations, backgrounds, and costumes) and "postproduction" phases (special effects, photographic effects, sound effects, and music). The men's shirts have round, ribbed necks and the women's collars are decoratively raised into V shapes that come to a point shortly below the neck. Both the males' and females' collars are the same colors as their garments.

The insignia are much plainer than the later versions. They are borderless, with no black outlines, and the interior shapes are crudely sewn. The backgrounds of the insignia are off-white, with interwoven gold threads.

All crew personnel wear trousers, a style that survives partially until "Charlie X." None of the trousers worn in "The Cage" have the interwoven "glitter" effect seen in the series' regular uniform trousers, but they *are* bell-bottomed like their later versions. Jackets are worn in the "outdoor" scenes on Talos IV.

Dr. Boyce wears a specialized medical tunic of the same color as Dr. McCoy's medical jacket. It is similar in design to the tunic worn by Nurse Chapel during operations in other episodes, and by occasional sick-bay patients. (This tunic shows up in "Where No Man Has Gone Before," in which Dr. Piper wears it over his regular shirt; patient Gary Mitchell wears a sleeveless version of the tunic.)

Spock and Captain Christopher Pike (Jeffrey Hunter) on the surface of Talos IV

Vina and Pike: A deadly illusion

Captain Pike's wardrobe also includes some special items, including his little-known *hat*. Although Pike never wore it in the final cut of "The Cage," the hat is seen resting atop his "TV set," near his laser pistol.

Pike's quarters would make even a claustrophobic person feel unconfined. The single room is huge and round, with a high, circular roof. Pike's cabin includes a soft bed, topped by a recessed bookcase cut into the wall. In the middle of the room is a large chair, next to which is a device that resembles a television camera, a small rectangular arrangement at the end of an extension. Most surprising is a large, wooden console containing a recognizable television screen.

The Talosians appear so convincingly alien for several reasons, none of which is accidental. To begin with, Roddenberry cast actresses in these roles, scouring Hollywood for short female performers with interesting faces. The women exhibit those subtle mannerisms that distinguish men from women, and because male voices had been dubbed for their characters, a conflict is created in the minds of the viewers. Crossing male and female characteristics produces an odd feeling, and the Talosians are therefore accepted as aliens. The bodily proportions of the actresses are concealed by the loose-fitting garments designed for them by William Theiss. The headpieces, with their bulging, pulsating veins and small, round ears, complete the illusion. Created for this episode by effects makeup artist Wah Chang, they are skillfully blended into the actresses' own features by Fred Phillips and his staff.

Guest star Susan Oliver (Vina) appeared in many Metro-Goldwyn-Mayer films of the 1950s. On television, she can be seen in episodes of many series, including "Route 66," "Longstreet," and "The Man from U.N.C.L.E."

One of her roles was astoundingly close to her part in "The Cage." On "The Twilight Zone," she starred in the episode "People Are Alike All Over," in which a space traveler from Earth arrives on Mars via a crash landing; he is the sole survivor and he finds himself welcomed by the Martians and romanced by young Teenya (Susan Oliver). Unknown to the spaceman, the Martians consider him an evolutionary inferior. Teenya encourages him to be happy in a mock-up of the astronaut's own home on Earth, which the Martians have provided. The astronaut finally discovers that he can't get out of his "house," which is in reality a cage designed to permit Martian families to visit the zoo and see an Earth creature in its natural habitat.

Roddenberry's script and Robert Butler's direction create an atmosphere of tension, and although there are action sequences within the film, the accent within the story is on the stress Captain Pike feels.

The music created for this episode by Alexander Courage adds to the claustrophobic atmosphere. Pike fears he cannot handle his job any longer and finds himself in a room too small for him, speaking to entities he towers over but whose mental abilities tower over his own. Courage uses a few common instruments, including the guitar, to produce melodic lines that emphasize the fears and anxieties present in the episode.

How much of the somber and contemplative content of "The Cage" is the result of Hunter's low-key portrayal of Pike? How would William Shatner have performed in that episode? When "The Cage" becomes available for home viewing, it will undoubtedly cause "Star Trek" fans to watch and wonder what the series would have been like had Jeffrey Hunter continued to portray the captain of the *Enterprise*.

"THE CAGE" PRODUCTION CREDITS

PRODUCER, WRITER Gene Roddenberry
DIRECTOR Robert Butler
ASSOCIATE PRODUCER Byron Haskin
DIRECTOR OF PHOTOGRAPHY William E. Snyder
CAMERA OPERATOR Jerry Finnerman
ART DIRECTORS Pato Guzman, Franz Bachelin
ASSISTANT ART DIRECTOR Walter M. Jefferies
USS ENTERPRISE DESIGN Gene Roddenberry, Walter M. Jefferies
MUSIC COMPOSED AND CONDUCTED BY Alexander Courage
COSTUMES CREATED BY William Ware Theiss
FILM EDITOR Leo Shreve
ASSISTANT TO THE PRODUCER Morris Chapnick
FIRST ASSISTANT DIRECTOR Robert H. Justman
SET DECORATOR Ed M. Parbers
SOUND MIXER Stanford G. Houghton
PHOTOGRAPHIC EFFECTS Howard A. Anderson Co.
SPECIAL EFFECTS Joe Lombardi
PROPERTY MASTER Jack Briggs
GAFFER Bob Campbell
PRODUCTION SUPERVISOR James A. Paisley
MAKEUP ARTIST Fred B. Phillips
HAIRSTYLES Gertrude Reade
RESEARCH Kellum DeForest
SPECIAL SCIENTIFIC CONSULTANT Harvey P. Lynn, Jr.

4

SECOND CHANCE

"The Cage" was delivered to NBC's New York offices in February 1965—and rejected. NBC felt the story was "too cerebral."

But "Star Trek" was not dead. After spending $630,000 on "The Cage," NBC felt the series format deserved a second chance. For the first time in television history, a second pilot was commissioned. Amid the chatter of disbelief within the industry, NBC let Roddenberry and Desilu know that some changes had to be made in the "Trek" format.

Much of the original cast was rejected; Number One, Navigator Tyler, and Dr. Boyce were among the casualties.

NBC reportedly wanted one other character dropped at this time. He was too inhuman, the network people thought, with no really likable trait; besides, he had those satanic, pointed ears. Would anyone really miss Mr. Spock if he were removed from the *Enterprise* duty roster? Gene Roddenberry thought so. He saw the Vulcan(ian) as the embodiment of "Star Trek's" exploration of the unknown—and insisted that Spock stay in the "Star Trek" format.

Roddenberry was given the go-ahead to commission three new script treatments, one of which would be accepted, developed into a finished script, and produced as the second "Star Trek" pilot.

The first story outline Roddenberry wrote was "The Omega Glory." Because of the "parallel evolution" idea included in this script, extensive use could be made of existing studio sets and stock wardrobes. Only one major guest star would be needed, and a minimum of costly new outer-space footage would have to be paid for. From an economic standpoint, "The Omega Glory" was extremely practical for a second pilot.

Roddenberry also wrote a story treatment called "Mudd's Women," centering around the aventures of a likable rogue named Harry Mudd, whose antics would cause the *Enterprise* to escape destruction by the narrowest of margins. The tale would have humor, drama, and a moral—

and it could be almost completely filmed using the existing *Enterprise* sets left over from "The Cage."

Samuel A. Peeples was called in to write the third outline, a quality science fiction tale with all the elements of a Greek tragedy, and all the opportunities for action-packed scenes and colorful opticals for which a network could ask: "Where No Man Has Gone Before."

Peeples had written novels and television scripts previously, and produced NBC's western series "The Tall Man" for two years. For Roddenberry, who has been quoted as saying that writing good science fiction is similar to writing any good "period" piece, he was ideal.

By early June 1965, all three treatments had been expanded into first-draft scripts and forwarded to NBC. For "Star Trek's" "second chance," the network chose to produce "Where No Man"—the most challenging and potentially expensive of the three scripts.

"Where No Man" was to begin shooting in July of 1965. But as Jeffrey Hunter had declined the role of Captain Kirk, the captain's chair was momentarily vacant. Gene Roddenberry, however, was already considering an actor who could capably fill it.

Canadian-born William Shatner had traveled to the United States in 1956 for an appearance on Broadway in *Tamburlaine*. When M-G-M featured him in their epic *The Brothers Karamazov* released the following year, the success of his career was assured. Stage appearances that followed included *L'Idiote, The World of Suzie Wong* (opposite France Nuyen and Sarah Marshall), and *A Shot in the Dark*. In 1964, Shatner was cast as Assistant District Attorney David Koster in the short-lived but critically acclaimed television series "For the People." The show was applauded for its relevance and courage, but unfortunately CBS had programmed it opposite "Bonanza," which at that time was the top-rated television series. William Shatner was therefore available to accept an invitation from Gene Roddenberry to attend a screening of "The Cage."

Shatner was no stranger to quality science fiction, fantasy, and horror produced for television. He had appeared twice in Universal's teleseries "Thriller" in "The Hungry Glass" and "The Grim Reaper." One reviewer dubbed him "the male Fay Wray" because of his talent for screaming. On two memorable occasions, Shatner entered "The Twilight Zone"—"Nick of Time" and "Nightmare at 20,000 Feet"—and in "The Outer Limits" episode "Cold Hands, Warm Heart" (1964) he appeared as an astronaut, the first person to travel to Venus as part of the space program called "Project Vulcan." In that episode his doctor was Malachi Throne (Mendez in "The Menagerie") and one of the mechanics at the space center was Lawrence Montaigne (who appeared in "Balance of Terror" and "Amok Time"). At one point in the story the astronaut's wife wanted him to leave his job: to end her objections concerning his work, Shatner delivered a monologue about a young man who had grown up watching the birds because he had always wanted to be "up there." The talk, which included phrases that would have been equally appropriate coming from the mouth of Captain James T. Kirk, could easily have begun with the words "The mission of this vessel, gentlemen, is to . . ."

Coincidentally Shatner had already worked with Leonard Nimoy in a 1964 "Man from U.N.C.L.E." episode, "The Project Strigas Affair." He played a double agent,

"Physicist" Sulu (George Takei)

working with Napoleon Solo and Ilya Kuriakin, while Nimoy appeared as an enemy operative.

"Where No Man" also introduced ship's engineer Lieutenant Commander Montgomery "Scotty" Scott, played by James Doohan, a skilled pilot who served in the Royal Canadian Air Force during World War II, began his career on Canadian radio, where he acted in over 3,500 radio shows.

Doohan, who has taught at New York's prestigious Neighborhood Playhouse, specializes in dialects. When he was first called in to read for the role of the *Enterprise* engineer, he recalls delivering his lines in a variety of accents until Roddenberry and director James Goldstone decided upon the Scottish. Scotty had very little dialogue in his first appearance, and there was no indication in this episode that "Star Trek's" audience would soon find a warm friend in the engineer.

Though Scotty's debut is hardly noticeable, Lieutenant Sulu's first appearance is both minuscule and atypical. "Physicist" Sulu had two significant lines of dialogue, and neither pointed to the adventure-loving, vital individual into which he would develop.

Born in Los Angeles in the opening days of World War II, actor George Takei and his family were relocated to Arkansas along with other Japanese-American families—an experience that made him determined to make himself known as an individual who cares about other human beings. An architecture major at the University of South-

Captain James T. Kirk (William Shatner)

ern California in Berkeley, George was first exposed to acting when he transferred to the Los Angeles campus, where he soon changed his major to theater arts. After a stint in the Desilu Actors' Workshop he obtained his Master's degree in theater and landed his first feature film assignment in the 1959 Warner Brothers film *Ice Palace*.

Though Scotty and Sulu both went on to become regular cast members, for actors Paul Fix (Dr. Mark Piper), Andrea Dromm (Yeoman Smith), and Lloyd Haynes (Communications Officer Alden), "Where No Man Has Gone Before" was to be both their first—and last—appearance as members of the *Enterprise* crew.

The first draft script of "Where No Man," dated May 27, 1965, began with a narration *not* indicated as a "Captain's Log" entry:

This is our galaxy—a gigantic cloud of suns and planets, in which our Earth is but a pinpoint, one speck of dust. The galaxy is so vast that even traveling at millions of miles per hour it would still take millions of years to cross through it . . . And yet, as incredible as it seems, our galaxy is itself only one of untold billions of other galaxies, separated by voids of emptiness so vast that time, matter, and even energy may not even mean the same out there . . . On stardate 1312.6 the massive space-warp engines of the U.S.S. *Enterprise* brought it to the edge of that black void. Until now, its missions of space law regulation, contact with

Lieutenant Commander Montgomery "Scotty" Scott (James Doohan) from "Where No Man . . ."

Earth's colonies, and investigation of alien life had always kept the vessel within our galaxy.

There was no introductory chess game between Kirk and Spock in this draft. Here the action started immediately on the *Enterprise* bridge, with a strange dialogue between Mitchell and Spock:

ANGLE—MITCHELL AND SPOCK
Clark Mitchell sees Elizabeth enter the bridge and looks at Mr. Spock. Quietly:

MITCHELL
Frigid Liz herself.

MR. SPOCK (dryly)
The human mechanism is capable of generating a surprising amount of energic heat—depending upon the skill of the operator.

MITCHELL
You speak like a man of experience, Mr. Spock.

MR. SPOCK (with dignity)
I have my moments.

MITCHELL (curious glance; smiles)
I'll bet you do.

This draft also featured a reference to the process of *returning* to normal space from warp drive, a procedure called "outwarp," and one of the fixtures on the bridge was an illuminated map table that indicated the area of space the starship was passing through.

The process of bringing the flight recorder aboard the *Enterprise* was more detailed than that eventually used for similar events within regular series episodes:

EXT. DEEP SPACE—ANGLE—U.S.S. *ENTERPRISE*
as a long thin, pencillike beam probes from the ship out into space.

EXT. DEEP SPACE—ANGLE—BEAM
as the probing beam locks onto a ship's recorder device, a metallic sphere, appearing somewhat charred and pitted. The beam begins to retract, pulling the sphere along with it.

INT. ENGINEERING DECK—CONFINED ANGLE—SPACE HATCH
as engineering officer, assisted by n.d. [no dialogue]

crewmen, check instruments and work controls. Outside we hear METALLIC SLIDING as the outer hatch opens, and a WHOOSH of air.

CLOSER SHOT—INSIDE HATCH
as the WHIRR of a motor slides it open, revealing the recorder device inside the compartment. Under the charred and pitted surface, we can dimly make out lettering: "U.S.S. *VALIANT*" and then in small lettering below it "Galactic Survey Cruiser." The engineering officer begins to attach thick electronic cables into receptacles provided on the surface of the recorder.

When Dr. Dehner defined the known varieties of ESP, there was a reference to Federation discoveries made on a world other than Earth:

. . . I did some postgraduate studies in ESP at the Vega IV Institute. As you know, the humanoids there are telepathically inclined. Actually, it's quite interesting. About the most we find on Earth is people who can read the backs of playing cards and that sort of thing, but there is an indication some Vegans can levitate objects, cause winds to blow, fires to start of themselves . . .

Such references to the history and science of other planets would become standard practice in "Star Trek" —one of the devices that made the series and the universe it depicted that much more believable.
But the *Enterprise*'s mission, jointly outlined in this "intercraft address" by Kirk and Spock, remained the same:

KIRK (Voice Amplified)
This is the captain speaking. We are now at the farthest reaches of our galaxy, the first Earth vessel to reach this point. (toward Mr. Spock) Science Officer, recap.

Mr. Spock is back at his library-computer section.

MR. SPOCK (Voice Amplified)
We would not be here, of course, unless we felt the *Enterprise* was capable of handling any force it meets. Or at least . . . any force we know of. I'm sure all departments are aware of the importance of this mission. Just as the first astronauts probed out beyond Earth long ago, today we probe out into regions beyond our galaxy. And for the same reason.

To seek out new life, and new civilizations—to boldly go where no man has gone before.

"WHERE NO MAN HAS GONE BEFORE"

▮▮▮▮▮▮▮▮▮▮▮▮▮▮▮▮▮▮▮▮▮▮▮▮▮▮▮▮▮▮ #2

WRITER: Samuel A. Peeples
DIRECTOR: James Goldstone
PRINCIPALS: Kirk   Lieutenant Commander Gary
             Spock   Mitchell
             Scott   Dr. Elizabeth Dehner
             Sulu   Lieutenant Lee Kelso
             Dr. Piper   Yeoman Smith
                            Lieutenant Alden

◄ *Stardate 1312.4:* While patrolling near the outer boundary of our galaxy, the *Enterprise* beams aboard the flight recorder of the *Valiant,* a galactic survey vessel that had visited this area almost two centuries before.

Upon attempting to leave our galaxy, the survey vessel had come in contact with an energy barrier which disabled the ship and killed some of the crew. One crewman, however, recovered from serious injuries sustained within the barrier. From this point, the tape's information is garbled; there are repeated requests for data on extrasensory perception (ESP), and a self-destruct order apparently given by the *Valiant's* captain.

Puzzled yet determined, Captain Kirk decides to move forward, only to contact the same energy barrier that had disabled the *Valiant.* Unknown radiations penetrate the ship, and Kirk orders the *Enterprise* to back out of the energy field. Several crewmen are dead and two have been knocked unconscious: Lieutenant Commander Gary Mitchell, a friend of Kirk's since their Academy days, and Dr. Elizabeth Dehner, a psychiatrist. Both recover and seem unharmed—though Mitchell's eyes now glow a bright silver. The ship's warp-drive engines are also severely damaged.

In sick bay, Kirk learns that Mitchell is feeling completely well. He is also reading material he never understood before with complete comprehension, and his reading speed is incredible. Showing off to Dr. Dehner, Mitchell "plays dead" by stopping all his bodily functions for almost a full minute. He is mutating into something beyond human.

Kirk and Mr. Spock discover Gary Mitchell's ESP quotient is extremely high, as is Dr. Dehner's. At a meeting of the *Enterprise* department heads, Sulu states Mitchell's powers are developing at an astounding rate. Spock suggests Kirk kill Mitchell now, while he still can; he cautions him not to wait too long, as the captain of the *Valiant* obviously did.

Unwilling to murder a man who was once one of his closest friends, Kirk sets course for Delta Vega, an uninhabited planet with an automated lithium-cracking station that can aid in repairing their damaged warp-drive engines. He intends to maroon Mitchell there. Mitchell is sedated and transported to the planet, where he's confined within a hastily built brig. But Gary has grown too strong to be held by a force field. Declaring that he has become a god, he escapes, taking along Dehner, who has also begun to mutate. Kirk follows with a phaser rifle, and Mitchell attempts to kill him with his psi powers. Dehner, realizing what Mitchell has become, helps Kirk overpower the mad superman, and is killed in the attempt.

Aboard the *Enterprise,* Kirk records that crewmen Mitchell and Dehner died in the line of duty. ▶

After NBC's reaction to "The Cage," Roddenberry was taking no chances: there is plenty of action in "Where No Man," most of it centering around Gary Mitchell.

When we first meet him, Mitchell is a capable officer whose friendship with Kirk goes back to their days together at Starfleet Academy. We know that on at least one mission he saved Kirk's life, that Kirk asked for him to be assigned to his first command, and that he once aimed "a little blond lab technician" at Kirk—whom the captain almost married!

The closeness of their relationship causes us to sympathize with Gary's fate at the end of the episode. He has not asked for what has happened to him, and when he slips back to normal for one brief instant in the brig, he looks at the captain and gently pronounces the name "Jim"—as though apologizing for all that he has done and will attempt to do.

But Captain Kirk has difficulty in deciding to eliminate his friend, either by marooning him on Delta Vega or by killing him outright, as Spock suggests. Only when Mitchell kills one of his crew does Kirk decide to take action.

Dr. Dehner is caught up in the middle of all this. Here,

Kirk and a transformed Dr. Dehner

she fills the role taken in the series by Dr. McCoy, observing and defining the medical situation and finally taking a hand in bringing it to a resolution. Since she was never slated to be a regular member of the *Enterprise* family, Elizabeth's solution to Gary Mitchell's problem is more drastic than any McCoy could take.

Guest star Gary Lockwood (Lieutenant Commander Gary Mitchell) had previously worked for Gene Roddenberry as the star of his 1962–63 MGM series "The Lieutenant." Though his science fiction experience began with "Where No Man," he went on to star as astronaut Frank Poole in Stanley Kubrick's classic *2001: A Space Odyssey.* Sally Kellerman (Dr. Elizabeth Dehner) made her TV debut on "The Outer Limits" (in the episode "The Bellero Shield") before she achieved stardom as the original Major Margaret "Hotlips" Houlihan in the feature film *M∗A∗S∗H.*

The only new weapon built for "Where No Man Has Gone Before" was the phaser rifle. Although it was mentioned in the writers' guide, the phaser rifle never appeared in any future "Trek" episodes.

In the wardrobe department, the jackets were discarded and the captain's hat was forgotten for the remainder of the series. The costumes were altered. Dr. Dehner wore a blue uniform. Mr. Spock's shirt was changed from blue to gold. The insignia had acquired their familiar gold background, black border, and finished appearance; they were still slightly smaller than those used in the regular episodes. Continuity had also started in reference to the insignia emblem. Kirk, Spock, and Mr. Alden wore stars. Gary and Scotty wore what would later become the "sciences" emblem. Dr. Piper, Mr. Sulu, Dr. Dehner, and Yeoman Smith wore the "ship's services" spiral.

The shirts still had their shoulder zippers; all except Mr. Spock's. To assist actor Leonard Nimoy, the collar was two separate halves that snapped together. This saved wear and tear on Spock's complex makeup.

The women still wore trousers.

Makeup artist Fred Phillips was temporarily replaced by another Desilu staffer, Robert Dawn (the son of M-G-M makeup great Jack Dawn, who created the makeup for hundreds of that studio's classic films, including *The Wizard of Oz,* 1939.)

Dawn's "Mr. Spock" was more severe than Phillips' Spock of "The Cage." His eyebrows swept sharply upward, and his shorter "bangs" made his head seem longer. His complexion was yellowish gold. Dawn's application of the ear tips was flawless. After Phillips returned to the "Star Trek" staff, Dawn was kept busy designing the many incredible makeup transformations featured in "Mission: Impossible."

Dawn did some very subtle things with the appearance of Gary Mitchell. To show the tremendous physical

Kirk on Delta Vega

stresses that Mitchell's body was experiencing, Dawn gradually added gray to actor Gary Lockwood's hair. By the last scenes of the episode, Mitchell's sideburns were completely gray.

There are actually *two* different versions of "Where No Man Has Gone Before," only one of which has been televised. The unaired variation is the one that Gene Roddenberry submitted to NBC.

It began with a view of our galaxy, accompanied by William Shatner's voiceover introducing the tale with dialogue that suggested the introduction of the episode's first-draft script.

The first interior scene was the chess game between Kirk and Spock. But when Kirk remarked how terrible it was that Spock had "bad blood" (*human* blood) in his veins, the captain added, "But you may learn to enjoy it someday."

When the disaster recorder materialized and began to flash off and on in the transporter room, the scene "froze," and over the picture the words "Star Trek" appeared in pink letters trimmed in silver-blue. In the same block-lettering style, the words "Tonight's episode: 'Where No Man Has Gone Before' " materialized as the opening theme was heard. This original theme was heard at various times throughout the series, usually before the end of an act.

The original opening credits were very short and were followed by a commercial break.

This version of "Where No Man" was divided into four acts, with a prologue and epilogue, in the same style as producer Quinn Martin's series (including "The Fugitive" and "The Invaders"). The end credits were backed by music that was never heard again in "Star Trek." A fast-moving, almost cheerful electronic melody, it accompanied the end credits that listed just the main performers.

"WHERE NO MAN HAS GONE BEFORE"
PRODUCTION CREDITS

PRODUCER Gene Roddenberry
WRITER Samuel A. Peeples
DIRECTOR James Goldstone
ASSOCIATE PRODUCER & ASSISTANT DIRECTOR Robert H. Justman
MUSIC COMPOSED AND CONDUCTED BY Alaxander Courage
DIRECTOR OF PHOTOGRAPHY Ernest Haller, ASC
PRODUCTION DESIGNER Walter M. Jefferies
ART DIRECTOR Roland M. Brooks
FILM EDITOR John Foley
SET DECORATOR Ross Dowd
COSTUMES CREATED BY William Ware Theiss
SOUND MIXER Cameron McCulloch
POST PRODUCTION EXECUTIVE Bill Heath

MUSIC EDITOR Jack Hunsaker
SOUND EDITOR Joseph G. Sorokin
PRODUCTION SUPERVISOR James Paisley
WARDROBE Paul McCardle
SPECIAL EFFECTS Bob Overbeck
MUSIC CONSULTANT Wilbur Hatch
MUSIC COORDINATOR Julian Davidson
MAKEUP ARTIST Robert Dawn
HAIRSTYLES Hazel Keats
SOUND Glen Glenn Sound Co.
PHOTOGRAPHIC EFFECTS Howard A. Anderson Co.
EXECUTIVE IN CHARGE OF PRODUCTION Herbert F. Solow
A Desilu Production in association with Norway Corp.

Robert Dawn's version of Mr. Spock

5
THE SERIES TAKES SHAPE

By October 1965, Gene Roddenberry had been involved in the production of two other Desilu television pilots.

The first was "Police Story," a contemporary crime series written and produced by Roddenberry. Because of the producer's real-life police experiences, "Police Story" (not to be confused with the later NBC-TV series of the same title) combined action with the scientific realities of a well-run crime-fighting agency. It featured DeForest Kelley as a lab specialist and Grace Lee Whitney as a judo instructor. Although this pilot did not sell as a series, it was broadcast during September 1967 on NBC.

The other pilot produced by Gene at this time was a western. Created and written by Sam Rolfe, "The Long Hunt of April Savage" was a somber study of a tragic, vengeance-seeking hero whose humanity vanished when his family was killed in 1871. The pilot episode was called "Home Is an Empty Grave." It did not make it to series status either.

After finishing work on these two projects, Roddenberry was free to attend to postproduction work on "Where No Man Has Gone Before." The second "Trek" pilot was reworked, its optical effects devised, photographed, and edited in, as were the sound effects. Once again Alexander Courage was commissioned to compose the episode's musical score, recorded on November 29, 1965.

"Where No Man Has Gone Before" was delivered to NBC's New York headquarters in January 1966. In the middle of the following month Roddenberry was notified of the network's acceptance of the pilot. At last, "Star Trek" was to be a television series.

The first thing that happened after NBC's acceptance was another series of changes in the crew of the starship *Enterprise*. Yeoman Smith, Dr. Piper, and Communications Officer Alden were dropped from the format. Physicist Sulu became Helmsman Sulu, and George Takei signed on for the five-year mission along with William Shatner and James Doohan.

These changes did not come about immediately: in fact, one piece of publicity was prepared while Smith, Piper, and Alden were still on the active-duty roster. Prepared by the network sales planning division of NBC in New York, the 12-page booklet was entitled "Advance Information on 1966–67 Programming: 'Star Trek.' "

In that booklet the series' regular crewmembers are identified as Captain Kirk (William Shatner), Mr. Spock (Leonard Nimoy), Mr. Scott (James Doohan), Mr. Alden (Lloyd Haynes), Mr. Sulu (George Takei), Dr. Piper (Paul Fix), and Yeoman Smith (Andrea Dromm).

The description of Mr. Spock mentions his logical way of thinking and attributes this to his father, a native of the planet "Vulcanis." People from Vulcanis, the booklet states, are called "Vulcanians," and, it elaborates, they do not lack emotions: they just don't believe in revealing their emotions in public. This description seems to be the earliest acknowledgment that Spock is a "split personality," exhibiting his Vulcan stoicism, denying his human emotions, and functioning within an environment in which his emotions *should* be expressed.

We now come to the booklet's most significant feature, which reflects NBC's displeasure regarding Mr. Spock's presence in the "Star Trek" format. Two pictures of the Vulcan are included, and in each one his eyebrows have been restored to their human contours. One of the photos has Spock's ears shortened so that their pointed tips are barely noticeable. The other picture shows the Vulcan with completely human ears. Though responsibility for these altered photos was traced back to a minor official in the network's art department, it is highly unlikely that such a thing would be done without the permission of someone higher up in the corporate structure.

Chief Officer of Medicine Dr. Mark Piper is established in the booklet as the oldest person aboard the *Enterprise*. His duties, itemized in the publication, include all those later assumed by Dr. McCoy, including being physician and psychological "watchdog" to the *Enterprise* crew.

In addition, the booklet reveals that planetary explora-

The infamous airbrushed photo

In this draft, as in the "Where No Man" first draft, the opening was a narration concerning the mission of the *Enterprise* and was not indicated to be a "Captain's Log" entry.

The starship crew, which numbered 604, contained only two familiar individuals, Captain Kirk and Mr. Spock.

Spock, in this draft, was still referred to as a "Vulcanian" with one Terran ancestor. He also possessed abilities that were either present to lesser degrees in the series, or not at all. Among these was a hypnotic ability where women were concerned. This survived into the final draft of "The Omega Glory" and is seen in the filmed episode as Spock compels the female Yang to bring him his communicator.

The other *Enterprise* crewmen mentioned in the script did not appear in "The Omega Glory" or any other series episode. Lieutenant Commander Piper was the youthful male navigator, a position not regularly filled by one individual until Chekov joined the crew. Lieutenant Phil Raintree was the helmsman, and died during the script's climactic action, the ship's doctor, named Milton Perry, was also killed during the episode.

Two significant members of the *Enterprise* crew were different in the earliest version of "The Corbomite Maneuver" script. The navigator was Ken Easton, who never appeared, and the communications officer was Dave Bailey, who appeared in the finished episode but not in this capacity.

tion would largely depend upon Dr. Piper's evaluations of alien life forms—a duty later assigned to Mr. Spock.

Communications Officer Alden is described as an efficient, respected, and vital young technician who performs duties vital to the ship's welfare, and who also contributes constant computations and speculations. The emphasis on both mathematics and scientific guesswork suggests other talents later added to Spock's characteristics.

Sulu's title in this publication is chief of the Astro Science Department. Like Dr. Piper, he was required to aid in determining whether or not newly discovered planets should be explored. Traces of these responsibilities are found in the episode "Man Trap," in which Sulu appears to be in charge of a collection of alien plants. In Theodore Sturgeon's earliest drafts of "Shore Leave," Sulu beamed down with a portable biological analysis apparatus, although in the final script this tool does not appear.

Yeoman Smith, on her first assignment into outer space, was described as "popular." Her qualifications are specifically identified as (1) secretarial capabilities; (2) a talent for making coffee; and (3) providing an attractive target for the eyes of spacemen everywhere. The yeoman was intended to be little more than "window dressing" aboard the U.S.S. *Enterprise*.

For Roddenberry, although the task of selling "Star Trek" had been accomplished, his real labors were only just beginning. His show was on the road; now he had to get his starship off the ground. Some of this task had already been accomplished, including the refinement of the series format after "The Cage" had been rejected.

The first-draft script of "The Omega Glory" was written as one of NBC's choices for the second "Trek" pilot. It contains some interesting differences from the "Star Trek" with which we are familiar.

Yeoman Janice Rand (Grace Lee Whitney)

One of the series' earliest publicity photos

The earliest photos taken for "Star Trek" after it reached series status feature only William Shatner, Leonard Nimoy, and Grace Lee Whitney, who was to portray the captain's new yeoman, Janice Rand.

A native of Detroit, Michigan, following her graduation from high school Grace moved to Chicago, where she placed second in the Miss Chicago contest.

On a vacation in New York City, Grace auditioned for a role in the Broadway musical *Top Banana*. She won the role, understudied the star, and accompanied the play's cast to Hollywood to appear in the film version of the play. She duplicated this success in the play and film versions of *Pajama Game*. Her appearance in "Police Story" (as policewoman Libby Monroe) first brought her to Gene Roddenberry's attention, and led to her being signed for the role of Janice Rand.

These early publicity shots feature Shatner and Nimoy in costumes that were trial concepts for the series' wardrobe. Closer to the final uniforms of the series than they were to those used in the two pilots, they are still not the final designs. The most important difference is that Spock wears a command insignia instead of a ship's sciences circle. Yeoman Rand wears the ship's services spiral symbol.

The majority of these early shots feature a painted backdrop of a planet and starfield, with a three-foot *Enterprise* miniature suspended between the drop and the performers. Kirk and Spock held blueprints, flasks, retorts, and other scientific paraphernalia. Yeoman Rand joined her two fellow crewmembers in brandishing a large flashlight with colored reflectors. The phaser rifle from "Where No Man Has Gone Before" was also in evidence—the last time it was seen. The phasers, communicators, and tricorders for the series were unavailable when these photos were taken.

While the designs of the costumes and the show's props were still being finalized, so was the rest of the *Enterprise* crew. Actor DeForest Kelley was the next to sign on for the five-year mission, cast in the role of ship's surgeon Dr. Leonard "Bones" McCoy.

DeForest Kelley was born in Atlanta, Georgia, where he obtained his first performing experience singing in his church choir. His singing progressed to solo work, and after completing an engagement at the Atlanta Paramount Theatre, working with the Lew Forbes Orchestra, DeForest moved to California.

A Paramount talent scout saw Kelley in a U.S. Army training film during World War II, and after a screen test he was given a contract with Paramount that lasted two and a half years. Ironically, one of the first film roles he played was for *Variety Girl*, in which he portrayed . . . a Paramount talent scout. DeForest appeared in many westerns, including *Gunfight at the O.K. Corral* (1957, Paramount), *Warlock* (1959, 20th Century-Fox), and *Gunfight at Comanche Creek* (1963, Allied Artists).

On television, he appeared in "Y.O.R.D.," an episode of "Science Fiction Theatre" in which he portrayed a doctor in communication with a in distress UFO. Kelley was also a doctor in the "Bonanza" episode "The Decision" —costarring John Hoyt, who played the *Enterprise* chief medical officer in "The Cage."

With his portrayal of Dr. Leonard "Bones" McCoy, DeForest's distinguished career of screen villainy came to an end as he swiftly developed McCoy into a powerful, likable and lovable individual.

After DeForest Kelley was cast, the Desilu sales department issued a brochure to inform the television industry about "Star Trek." The brochure features three photos, all from "Where No Man Has Gone Before." William Shatner is listed as the star of the series and Leonard Nimoy as the costar. Under the "also starring" category are Grace Lee Whitney, Kelley, and George Takei. One of the photos is the shot of Spock that had been retouched in the NBC booklet previously mentioned. In this brochure, the photo remained untouched.

The Desilu booklet emphasized that "Star Trek" was not based upon gadgetry but the human drama resulting

Leonard "Bones" McCoy (DeForest Kelley)—just an old country doctor

from the concentrated excitement man will experience in space.

The brochure also mentions something NBC did not include in its initial booklet: that "Star Trek" would be part fantasy and part fact, as a result of the assistance of scientists from the Rand Corporation (described as "America's space think factory").

Although the series was sold and its initial publicity was being distributed, one important member of the *Enterprise* crew was not yet on board. As late as the beginning of May 1966, the month the series' first regularly produced episode began filming, there was no Lieutenant Uhura.

It is difficult to imagine the *Enterprise* without her. In her role as the ship's spokesperson, Uhura is a living extension of the starship—and it is difficult to imagine any actress other than Nichelle Nichols portraying the beautiful lieutenant.

At the age of 16, Nichelle wrote a ballet for a musical suite by Duke Ellington. She toured with Ellington's band performing her own work and later singing as well. She gained her experience in the performing arts in Chicago, Los Angeles, and New York. Twice nominated for the Sara Siddons Award as best actress of the year (for her roles in the plays *The Blacks* and *Kicks and Company*), Nichelle understudied the lead in the Broadway play *No Strings*. While in New York City she also appeared as a singer at two famous landmarks, the Blue Note and the

Playboy Club. Continuing her singing with Lionel Hampton's band, Nichelle toured the world before returning home to resume her acting career. In California, Ms. Nichols was highly praised by the critics for her work in James Baldwin's play, *Blues for Mr. Charlie,* and began to appear in movies and television productions.

In 1964, she guest-starred in an episode of "The Lieutenant," an appearance that first brought her to the attention of producer Roddenberry.

Since her success as Uhura, Nichelle has lived the real-life equivalent of the "Star Trek" dream more than any other performer connected with the show; while listening to a presentation by a scientist from the National Aeronautics and Space Administration at a "Star Trek" convention, she became deeply interested in the space program. After the convention, Nichelle toured the Ames Space Center near San Jose, California. She then flew an eight-hour, high-altitude astronomy mission aboard the C-141 Astronomy Observatory (analyzing the atmospheres of Saturn and Mars), was a guest at the Jet Propulsion Laboratory witnessing the Viking Probe's soft landing on Mars, and wrote an article about Viking for the National Space Institute.

Since then, Nichelle has been appointed to the institute's board of directors, and joined the space-shuttle astronaut-recruiting program. She has also formed her own company, Women in Motion, which continues to attract women and minorities into the space program. For the company's promotional film, "What's in it for Me?", Nichelle functioned as producer and star, and provided two of her own pieces of music as well.

Uhura (Nichelle Nichols), whose name means "freedom"

THE EPISODES

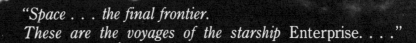

*"Space . . . . the final frontier.
These are the voyages of the starship Enterprise. . . ."*

6
FIRST SEASON

Even before the first "Star Trek" episode was televised, there was a significant behind-the-scenes change of command. In August 1966 Gene Roddenberry stepped down as the series producer and became the executive producer. Writer Gene L. Coon assumed the post of producer and functioned in that capacity for the remainder of the first season.

The "Star Trek" episodes were not aired in their original production order. After a television episode is filmed, it enters its "postproduction" phase, during which the soundtrack is completed and the photographic effects are added. Due to the amount of work that must be completed during postproduction, some episodes are ready before others. This determines the order in which episodes are completed, delivered to the network, and televised. Episode numbers within this book refer to production number.

"The Man Trap," the sixth "Star Trek" episode in terms of the series' production schedule, progressed from first- to final-draft script status in the middle of June 1966, and was filmed during the remainder of that month. Alexander Courage was commissioned by the series' associate producer, Robert H. Justman, to compose the music for the episode. On August 19, 1966, Courage conducted an orchestra of approximately 25 musicians in the first recording session for a "Star Trek" series episode.

NBC aired "The Man Trap" as their special "sneak preview of a new, hour-long series, 'Star Trek' " beginning at 8:30 P.M., E.S.T. on Thursday, September 8th, 1966.

The September 14 issue of *Variety* contained a negative review of "Star Trek," stating that the series "won't work." The reviewer called it dreary and confusing, though he conceded the leading performers were trying very hard to appear credible. He concluded that "Star Trek" would be "better suited to the Saturday morning kidvid bloc," and said he was stumped how "Star Trek" had made it to television. The *New York World Journal-Tribune* called "Trek" "dubious science fiction," but added

that it had "a weird, comic strip appeal and no doubt will earn a high rating." The paper referred to Mr. Spock as "half-Earthling, half-Vulcan, and all spook." *TV Guide,* in its September 10–16 "Fall Preview Issue," observed "the sky's not the limit on this 'Trek.' "

Though not an overnight success with the press and the Nielsens, "Star Trek" almost immediately became something very special to its fans. Science fiction clubs in universities throughout the country held meetings to discuss the series after each episode. The fans, however, did not supply the "big numbers" statistics that networks and sponsors equate with the commercial success of television series. Within three months after its television debut, "Star Trek" was in danger of cancellation.

On December 10, 1966, a form letter was sent from Los Angeles, California, with no return address on the outside of the envelope. Inside was a message from an impressive array of science fiction writers, including (in alphabetical order) Poul Anderson, Robert Bloch, Lester del Rey, Harlan Ellison, Phillip José Farmer, Frank Herbert, Richard Matheson, Theodore Sturgeon, and A. E. van Vogt. They called themselves "the Committee" (no relation to the group of fans who would later start the first annual "Star Trek" conventions), and had sent their letter to everyone on the mailing list of the 1966 World Science Fiction Convention.

Harlan Ellison mentioned that convention and the special citation that "Star Trek" had been awarded there by convention personnel. A brief passage followed that discussed the television ratings system, and how it was unfair to judge "Trek" against "the competition" ("Lost in Space") which had a year's head start at attracting an audience.

Worse than the thought of "Star Trek" being cancelled, the letter stated, was the possibility of the series' format being converted into something closer to a kiddie show. At that point, a "lobotomy" for "Star Trek" was a distinct possibility—provided the show was not canceled first. "WRITE LETTERS," the message urged. Complain to television stations, sponsors of "Star Trek," television columnists and magazines, such as *TV Guide*. Let the world know that "Star Trek" has an audience and that its fate matters to many individuals. It had to be done *now*, before it was too late!

The first letter-writing campaign to save "Star Trek" was a success, with enough noise being made to generate the attention of prospective sponsors and NBC. "Star Trek" was renewed—but its problems were far from over.

"THE CORBOMITE MANEUVER"

||||||||||||||||||||||||||||||||||||||||||||| #3

WRITER: Jerry Sohl
DIRECTOR: Joseph Sargent
PRINCIPALS: Kirk   Uhura
            Spock   Lieutenant Dave Bailey
            McCoy   Balok
            Sulu   Yeoman Rand
            Scott

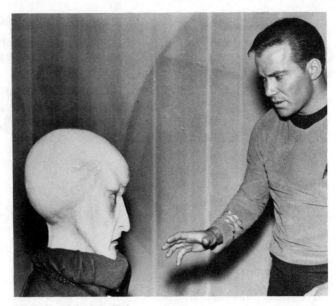

"Balok" and Captain Kirk

◄ *Stardate 1512.2:* While attempting to explore an uncharted area of space, the U.S.S. *Enterprise* is confronted by an alien "warning buoy." The starship's phasers destroy the radioactive buoy. Soon afterward, a gigantic spherical spaceship—the *Fesarius*—traps the *Enterprise,* and an alien voice promises destruction in ten minutes. Spock's reference to acknowledging defeat in the game of chess leads Kirk to recall the game of poker. The captain stages a desperate bluff, telling the alien commander Balok that Federation ships are equipped with a self-destruct system called "corbomite," which would also destroy any attacker. The destruction of the *Enterprise* is temporarily averted. Later, when the alien separates from the main body of his ship and seems to be in distress, Kirk goes to his rescue. Finally, the frightening alien is revealed to be a puppet operated by a childlike entity who has been testing them to determine whether Kirk and company are truly peaceful. Diplomatic relations are established, and Mr. Bailey, who had lost his nerve awaiting Balok's "death threat," volunteers to remain on board the alien's ship as an "exchange student." ►

In this episode, almost all the familiar "Star Trek" characters are still developing. This is most evident with Dr. McCoy, who makes his debut here. In "The Corbomite Maneuver" McCoy appears to be more psychologist than practicing physician. He lurks on the bridge most of the time, menacing and short-tempered.

Nichelle Nichols once complained about saying nothing but "Hailing frequencies opened, sir"; she must have

been referring to this episode. In "The Corbomite Maneuver" she is simply a leggy attraction seated sensuously on the bridge, a futuristic switchboard operator with no other talents. In the briefing room, everyone else seated at the table is actively participating in the discussion; Uhura just sits there looking kittenish and detached.

Yeoman Janice Rand fares even worse. She doesn't have any hailing frequencies to open and makes her debut as a glorified maid, serving the captain's salad and bringing hot coffee to the bridge. In a scene filmed but ultimately edited out of the final print she enters Kirk's empty quarters, gets a clean uniform from his wardrobe drawer, and lays it out on his bed.

Mr. Spock's half-human characteristics are present, but their effects on his individuality are inconsistent. Spock accuses Mr. Bailey of being too emotional when the young man shouts. Later, however, the Vulcan shouts about the superheating of the engines. Once, when Spock can supply no helpful suggestions, he starts to say "I'm sorry" to Captain Kirk.

The camera angles emphasize Spock's alien aspects. At one point the camera shoots toward the ceiling over his station as Spock suddenly rises into the frame. His hair is still jaggedly banged, his eyebrows pushed upward more than in later episodes. His shirt collar is higher than anyone else's to further set him apart from the rest of the crew.

All references to Spock's parents are in the past tense. He compares the *Fesarius*'s commander to his father and also tries his hand at black comedy, advising the nervous Mr. Bailey to have his adrenal glands removed.

Mr. Sulu, progressing from ship's physicist in "Where No Man" to helmsman, here acquires some of Spock's characteristics. His voice never wavers; his judgment and actions are swift and purposeful.

Some of the costumes made for "The Corbomite Maneuver" were heavy velour that shrank after it was cleaned, giving the appearance of being too small for the actors. These shirts have higher collars than usual, with the zippers sewn in more visibly than in the later uniforms. In "The Corbomite Maneuver" and "Mudd's Women," Uhura wears a gold uniform fashioned from velour.

Composer Fred Steiner's score for this episode was heavily utilized throughout most subsequent episodes, as were Alexander Courage's scores for the two pilot films. For this reason, many "Star Trek" fans regard this (and other themes written by Steiner for other "Trek" segments) as the definitive musical representations of "Star Trek's" individuals and adventures.

The miniatures and composite photography supplied by Howard Anderson Company are extremely effective, especially the shot of the *Fesarius* "growing" until it dwarfs the *Enterprise,* and the revolving cube with its reds, yellows, and blues reflecting on the faces of the bridge personnel. Similar effects are reflected off the sculpted Balok puppet head, the work of artist Wah Chang. The Anderson people also added a wavering animation effect, also used over the Thasian in "Charlie X."

There are several "bloopers" in "The Corbomite Maneuver": toward the end of the episode we see Mr. Bailey in front of a completely blank main viewing screen. The large lucite screen, backed with pulsating light patterns (which were used as cues to alert the cast and crew that a matte would be inserted over this footage), has no optical inserted at this point.

Another omission in this episode has Mr. Sulu observing that there is only a minute left to destruction. He then looks up at the viewing screen, glances back toward Kirk, and announces, "I knew he would." Ted Cassidy's voiceover for Balok was supposed to have been dubbed in, saying, "You now have one minute," but for some reason the line was never added to the composite sound track.

The voice of the real Balok was dubbed by Vic Perrin, perhaps best known as the "Control Voice" that introduced every episode of "The Outer Limits." His vocal talents are also heard in "Arena" and "The Changeling," and in "Mirror, Mirror" he portrayed the alien leader Tharn.

Director Joseph Sargent's feature films include *The Taking of Pelham 1-2-3, The Man, MacArthur,* and the science fiction thriller *Colossus: The Forbin Project.* He also directed the TV movie *The Night That Panicked America* (cowritten by *ST II: TWOK* director Nicholas Meyer).

Writer Jerry Sohl worked on two other "Trek" episodes: "This Side of Paradise," under his pseudonym of Nathan Butler, and "Whom Gods Destroy," with Lee Erwin.

"MUDD'S WOMEN"

#4

WRITER: Stephen Kandel (story by Gene Roddenberry)
DIRECTOR: Harvey Hart
PRINCIPALS:
Kirk	Eve McHuron
Spock	Magda Kovas
McCoy	Ruth Bonaventure
Scott	Ben Childress
Sulu	Lieutenant John Farrell
Uhura	Gossett
Harry Mudd	Benton

◄ *Stardate 1329.1*: Harry Mudd, with his cargo of three beautiful women, is beamed aboard the *Enterprise* just as his ship is destroyed in an asteroid field. In rescuing Mudd and his women, the *Enterprise* burns out its dilithium crystals. The starship proceeds as quickly as it can to a mining planet to replenish its supply. Mudd, against whom Kirk has filed criminal charges, makes advance contact with the miners, promising them his women in exchange for his freedom. The miners, led by Ben Childress, agree to the deal—only to discover that the women are using a highly illegal Venus drug to make themselves beautiful. The marriages work out nonetheless, and Kirk gets Harry—and the crystals he needs to run his ship. ►

After "The Cage" was rejected by NBC, Gene Roddenberry included "Mudd's Women" as one of the three candidates for the second pilot. Writer Stephen Kandel then adapted Roddenberry's story line into a full script after preparation of "Star Trek's" first season had begun, combining a fast-talking con man with elements from vintage space opera and the western plot device of "wiving settlers" to produce an offbeat but extremely popular adventure.

Roger C. Carmel does a masterful job in bringing Harry Mudd to life. He emerges as a likable lost soul, a greedy scoundrel who's also a bit of a child and has difficulty in accepting responsibility for his actions. Mudd never really hurts anyone in any manner that causes lasting physical or mental harm—the thought of him brandishing a phaser is laughable; he'd be frightened out of his wits just *looking* at such a weapon.

It is somewhat surprising that NBC never eliminated the drug angle from this script. Perhaps the setting was so far removed from reality the network never realized what they were dealing with. It's also possible the network was happy with the ending, which proved the drug was not really that potent after all. It was the "magic feather" that enabled Dumbo to fly, or the "wizard" who was going to get Dorothy home to Kansas. Yet when Harlan Ellison handled the problem of drug addiction in a far more serious and direct manner in his first-draft script

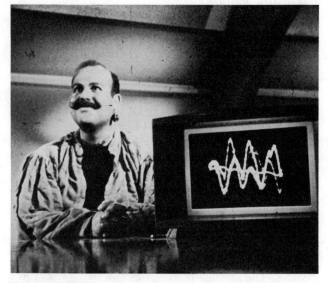

His name is Mudd

for "The City on the Edge of Forever," it was necessary to rewrite the entire tale.

Mr. Spock still suffers from "growing pains" in this episode, retaining his special raised collar to segregate him from the other crewmembers. Mudd calls him a "Vulcanian." And in one scene, as Eve leaves Kirk's cabin, Spock can be seen standing against the wall, arms folded across his chest, cocking his head to one side and affecting a mischievous smile worthy of any "elf with a hyperactive thyroid." This rather strange sense of humor was soon written out of his character.

Jerry Finnerman's soft-focus photography of "Mudd's Women" became a standard practice for all female guest stars throughout the series.

Gene Dynarski (Ben Childress) also appears as a council member in "The Mark of Gideon." Susan Denberg (Magda) was the beautiful and unlikely choice for the "monster" in the British feature film *Frankenstein Created Woman* shortly after she appeared as a centerfold Playmate of the Month in *Playboy* magazine.

"THE ENEMY WITHIN"

 **#5**

WRITER: Richard Matheson
DIRECTOR: Leo Penn
PRINCIPALS: Kirk   Yeoman Rand
           Spock   Lieutenant John Farrell
           McCoy   Technician Fisher
           Scott   Technician Wilson
           Sulu

◀*Stardate 1672.1:* In orbit around Alpha 177, the *Enterprise* experiences a momentary transporter malfunction, caused by a magnetic ore accidentally brought on ship. Scotty checks the equipment, finds nothing wrong, and beams aboard Captain Kirk. After they leave the transporter room, a duplicate Kirk materializes. The malfunction has split Captain Kirk into two people, each physically complete but lacking mentally and emotionally. The "good" Kirk is compassionate, intelligent, and deliberate. The "bad" Kirk is violent, amoral, and savage.

An animal beamed aboard the *Enterprise* shortly thereafter is divided into two creatures as well—and after Yeoman Rand accuses the captain of assaulting her, Spock realizes the same thing has happened to Kirk. The transporter malfunction must be repaired shortly or a stranded landing party, led by Sulu, will freeze to death on the planet's surface.

The captain, meanwhile, is dying—neither half can survive alone. Scotty rigs the transporter to run through the impulse engines, and after capturing the "bad" Kirk, beams both captains down—and back as a single person. The restored Kirk then orders the landing party rescued. ▶

This episode, the only "Star Trek" segment written by Richard Matheson, is a cornerstone of the Kirk-Spock-McCoy relationship. It is also the first time McCoy says, "He's dead, Jim."

The success of "The Enemy Within" is primarily the result of Richard Matheson's treatment of the old Jekyll-Hyde theme: he explored the problems of one man being divided into two in a fresh, exciting way (significantly, it is the evil Kirk who possesses the captain's command attributes).

Matheson's script lacked two important details pertaining to McCoy and Spock. He suggested that Spock "slug" the double with a phaser. The direct violence would not have done Spock credit as a unique character. Leonard Nimoy suggested the answer and, with the assistance of William Shatner, improvised the first Vulcan Nerve Pinch. The script also had Spock announcing the death of the "space spaniel." This was changed to a job for Dr. McCoy, and the classic "he's dead, Jim" was born.

William Shatner uses his considerable stage training

Yeoman Rand faces "The Enemy Within"

very well in this episode. One of his favorite devices is to enter a scene facing away from the audience. He will suddenly pivot, then gesture and begin to say something; at that very instant the audience is compelled to watch *him*, no matter who else is in the scene. In the episode's teaser, Shatner materializes with his back to the audience, and then pivots rapidly. The camera cuts to focus on the "bad" Kirk's bestial expression, exaggerated makeup, and underlit face. The effect is thoroughly successful.

The sensitive score of composer Sol Kaplan also assures the quality of "The Enemy Within." Kaplan would also score "The Doomsday Machine" and his music for both these scores would be used throughout other "Trek" episodes.

When Kirk and the double confront each other on the bridge, the main viewing screen can be seen in back of them. In one scene the screen is completely blank, just a large piece of white plastic sheeting upon which no scene was rear-projected.

One of the most blatant continuity errors of the entire series occurs in this episode. For the only time during the series, Kirk has no insignia when he materializes in the transporter; neither does the double. Later, Kirk is seen before he has a chance to change uniforms, and the insignia has suddenly returned. This was due to the fact that the shirts were dry-cleaned, but the insignia (being non-dry-cleanable) was removed before the garments were cleaned. On this one occasion someone forgot to sew the proper one back on.

The scratches on Kirk's face and the double's change sides when they confront each other on the bridge. This was the result of some close-ups of Shatner's face being printed backward to conform to the needs of the film editor.

"THE MAN TRAP"

▯▯▯▯▯▯▯▯▯▯▯▯▯▯▯▯▯▯▯▯▯▯▯▯▯▯▯▯▯▯▯▯▯▯ #6

WRITER: George Clayton Johnson
DIRECTOR: Marc Daniels
PRINCIPAL:
Kirk	M113 Monster
Spock	Yeoman Janice Rand
McCoy	Professor Robert Crater
Sulu	Darnell
Uhura	Green
Nancy Crater	

◄ *Stardate 1531.1:* The *Enterprise* visits planet M-113 to give archeologists Robert and Nancy Crater supplies and medical checkups. Years ago, Nancy was romantically involved with Dr. Leonard McCoy—whom she nicknamed "Plum." Now she is literally a different woman. Each member of the landing party sees Nancy differently because the real Nancy is dead, killed by a shape-changing alien which has assumed her identity. The creature, the last surviving native of this planet, has been enjoying a symbiotic relationship with Professor Crater. Crater supplies the salt that sustains the entity, and the creature provides Crater with companionship. The arrival of the *Enterprise* party upsets the delicate balance of this strange alliance. Craving additional salt, the creature kills two crewmen and boards the *Enterprise* disguised as one of its victims. The creature assumes Dr. McCoy's appearance and identity before Kirk eventually tracks it down and kills it with the aid of Spock and the real McCoy. ►

"The Man Trap" is a haunting tale, a study in loneliness and tragedy with elements of horror and mystery. Dr. McCoy once remarked (in "Court-Martial") that all his old friends look like doctors; Nancy Crater was apparently the exception. Whatever unhappy marriage Leonard McCoy experienced, he clearly held very special memories of Nancy.

A man of science, Crater prevented himself from harming the creature when it killed Nancy for her body salts. To avoid the solitude of being the only living human on M-113, Crater and the creature came to an understanding.

Unfortunately for the creature, it attempts to invade Kirk's domain and kills two people left in the captain's charge. Disregarding the exceptional gifts the creature obviously possesses, and the intelligence that goes along with them, Kirk only tries to hunt it down and kill it. There is never any talk of communicating with it, except for one remark from Crater.

If all "Star Trek" episodes were structured in this manner, the series would not have been the same. One of the most uplifting aspects of the show is the appreciation shown for all life forms. Throughout the series, Kirk crossed paths with various living things and destroyed them, e.g., "Obsession," "The Immunity Syndrome,"

"Operation: Annihilate!" and "The Lights of Zetar." The creatures in those episodes threatened entire civilizations. In "The Man Trap", though, it is difficult to believe that we are dealing with the same Captain Kirk who would later try to communicate with the Horta despite Spock's recommendation to kill the creature.

Kirk also hints that he thinks the "arrangement" between the creature and Crater is unnatural. In "Metamorphosis" he talks Cochrane out of believing this of the Companion's attraction to him. The only differences between the two relationships are that the Companion was acting out of love, not out of self-preservation, and the Companion did not kill. The Horta, however, killed, and Kirk was *still* determined to communicate with it.

"The Salt Vampire" (as it is usually referred to by "Trek" fans) was portrayed (in all its various incarnations) by the greatest number of performers ever called upon to represent one entity in "Star Trek." To maintain continuity between its transformations, the entity was seen sucking its knuckle when thinking. The most effective use of this mannerism is seen as the camera pans between Jeanne Bal and DeForest Kelley as the two successively portray the creature. Kelley turns in his strangest performance of the entire series in his scenes as "the unreal McCoy," altering his mannerisms to convey a furtive presence rather than his usual likable one.

Alexander Courage's eerie score for this episode combines strings, woodwinds, and organ chords to produce alien sounds. This score, of all the "Trek" music Courage composed, is the closest to his work on "The Cage."

Professor Crater uses an old-style phaser originally seen in "The Cage" and "Where No Man Has Gone Before" and later in "What Are Little Girls Made Of?" When Kirk shoots Crater, the working phaser can be seen: its grillework is raised and a light shines on the pistol-grip weapon's front.

As Crater is shot he lurches back: the accompanying sound effect is that of a ricocheting gunshot. Accompanied by a bright animated effect, the sequence is enhanced by slowing down his voice to suggest he has been stunned.

McCoy's medical tools and the ship's turbo-lifts have different sound effects in this episode. When Kirk activates his communicator, the "flip open" sound effect is used instead of the "call" sound. On two occasions there is no sound at all as Kirk opens his communicator.

Mr. Sulu's botany hobby indicates that his areas of expertise were being developed even before the next episode, "The Naked Time." His interest in botany is also apparent in "Shore Leave."

The botany room is a redress of the sick-bay set. When McCoy performs the autopsy, the "dead man's" heartbeat is distinctly heard.

This episode is also the origin of McCoy's medical tools. Because of the creature's craving for salt, various scenes were planned to include saltshakers. Futuristic saltshakers were gathered, but at the last minute it was feared they would not be recognized for what they were, and the specially gathered shakers were customized into medical sensors instead.

Alfred Ryder (Professor Crater) deserves much of the credit for making the episode as believable as it is. Ryder, an accomplished director in addition to his performing talents, also starred in segments of "Voyage to the Bottom of the Sea," "One Step Beyond," "Land of the Giants," and "The Man from U.N.C.L.E."

The unreal McCoy

"THE NAKED TIME"

▭▭▭▭▭▭▭▭▭▭▭▭▭▭▭▭▭▭▭▭▭▭▭▭▭▭▭▭▭▭ **#7**

WRITER: John D. F. Black
DIRECTOR: Marc Daniels
PRINCIPALS: Kirk   Chapel
             Spock   Dr. Harrison
             McCoy   Lieutenant Kevin Riley
             Scott   Joe Tormolen
             Sulu   Lieutenant Brent
             Uhura

Spock's human half surfaces

◀ *Stardate 1704.2:* The scientific research team on planet Psi 2000 reports that the planet is due to be destroyed. Arriving to evacuate the scientists, the U.S.S. *Enterprise* discovers that the researchers have frozen to death after someone in the camp turned off the life-support systems. To add to the mystery, the positions of the bodies indicate that the researchers went berserk before they died. The riddle is solved when Lieutenant Tormolen, who lands to investigate with Mr. Spock, spreads a strange germ he has contracted on the planet. As the *Enterprise* crew begins to become infected, strange things happen. Mr. Sulu threatens the bridge crew with a sword while Lieutenant Riley locks himself in engineering and turns off the ship's engines. The disease must be conquered and control regained of the starship in time to prevent the *Enterprise* from being destroyed when its orbit decays around the doomed planet. A last-minute attempt succeeds in hurling the ship back in time to make an escape. ▶

Whatever the "Star Trek" viewer is in the mood to see, "The Naked Time" has it. And the episode's script was crucial in the development of "Star Trek's" most important characters.

We had seen Kirk split into two parts in "The Enemy Within": in that same episode we heard Spock explain that he too is actually two halves sandwiched together. In "The Naked Time" we do not *hear* about this division, we *see* it.

Beneath his quiet exterior Spock seethes to express his emotions openly, and yet he stays far away from Christine Chapel's admission that she loves him. His first impulse is to "lock himself away" so that no one (especially the woman who loves him) will see him with his defenses down, a confused child's mind locked within the brain of a technological genius. Once again, Spock mentions his parents in the past tense, expressing sympathetic regard for his human mother, resentment toward his Vulcan father.

The U.S.S. *Enterprise,* we learn, makes Kirk just as divided. The captain is simultaneously resentful of his ship because it keeps him from living a "normal" existence, and fearful because he may someday lose her. He sees the ship in much the same way as a frightened bridegroom readies himself for his wedding, mourning his lost independence while unable to conceive of an existence without the focal point of his love.

In their confusion, Kirk and Spock aid each other. Even with the *Enterprise* in danger, Kirk has great difficulty in recovering from his nightmare. It is only the sight of Spock caught up in *his* confusion that forces Kirk to recover. And only the realization that his captain is ill enables Spock to fight the virus.

William Shatner and Leonard Nimoy do superb jobs of bringing their characters to life. Several other episodes of "Trek" afforded Nimoy chances to emote; this was his first. In addition to his subtle flair for comedy, Nimoy exhibits a clear ability for serious drama. A simple smile from Spock would later be enough to bring tears to our eyes in "This Side of Paradise." The admission of his great unhappiness does the same thing here.

Shatner's intense gazes directed at "his" *Enterprise* are also very effective. Much of this success may be attributed to director Marc Daniels, but the final triumph belongs to Shatner. His Kirk is a tragic subject, whose possessive gestures toward the ship and plaintive pleas to be released from her spell are classically powerful.

George Takei had his first chance to shine in this episode. Armed with a sword, endless energy, his chest smeared with oil, Lieutenant Sulu roams the corridors of the *Enterprise* menacing security men—and parrying his way into the hearts of "Star Trek" fans forever.

"The Naked Time" also marks the first appearance of Lieutenant Kevin Thomas Riley, played by actor Bruce Hyde. During his two "Trek" appearances, Riley became one of the most well-liked *Enterprise* crewmen. His zany antics in "The Naked Time" account for only a small part of his appeal; most of the credit must go to Hyde for

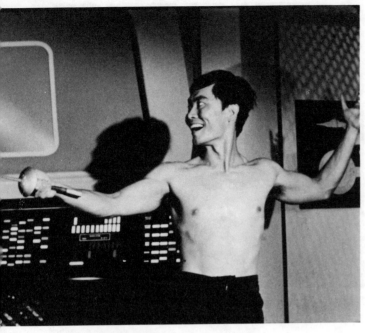

Sulu the swashbuckler

adding so much dimension to a character with so little to do.

The trip of the *Enterprise* backward through time is wonderfully executed. Originally, Roddenberry had intended the *Enterprise* to become transparent when in warp drive. The effect was abandoned, but in "The Naked Time" we see how it would have appeared. The Howard Anderson opticals are aided by Alexander Courage's tremendously effective music (also used in "Errand of Mercy" as the Organians abandon their human appearance), and the glimpse of Sulu's chronometer moving backward.

The environmental suits created for this episode were never seen in "Star Trek" again, although in several early episodes crewmen can be seen in corridors wearing similar outfits.

"CHARLIE X"

#8

WRITER: D. C. Fontana (story by Gene Roddenberry)
DIRECTOR: Lawrence Dobkin
PRINCIPALS:
Kirk	Charlie Evans
Spock	Thasian
McCoy	Yeoman 3/C Tina
Uhura	Lawton
Yeoman Janice Rand	Captain Ramart

◄ *Stardate 1533.6:* The cargo ship *Antares* docks with the *Enterprise* to deliver young Charlie Evans, the lone survivor of a crash on the planet Thasus 14 years before. The personnel of the *Antares*, Captain Ramart and Tom Nellis, seem unusually eager to leave—and when the *Antares* is destroyed, suspicion falls on Charlie. Aboard the *Enterprise*, Charlie begins to work "miracles." At first these are harmless pranks, kept in check by Kirk, whom Charlie comes to regard as a father figure, but when Yeoman Rand spurns his advances, she is erased from existence by the youngster. Various other ship personnel are victimized, and in his eagerness to arrive at Colony Alpha Five, Charlie assumes control of the *Enterprise*. In an attempt to tax Charlie's control abilities, Kirk switches on the starship's interior systems to their fullest extent. Then a shimmering alien face materializes on the *Enterprise* bridge and identifies himself as a Thasian, come to take Charlie back. Despite Charlie's pleas, he vanishes along with the alien, doomed to spend the rest of his life alone on the bleak planet Thasus. ►

"Charlie X" is a study in tragedy; people suffer and sometimes die because of his actions. But Charlie remains a sympathetic character. An especially dramatic moment comes when his last word, a plea to "stay," is echoed several times, gradually decreasing in volume as he disappears. This effect is also heard in "The Squire of Gothos" and "Who Mourns for Adonais?"

It is illogical that Charlie goes on so long before he is suspected of having "the power," especially after he produces the perfume and the photos of Janice from out of nowhere.

In the final version, Charlie is definitely not to blame for what he does. He was never taught to curb his powers, and he was not disciplined to tame his destructive urges because those urges could do the insubstantial Thasians no harm. Charlie was never taught to deal with people because the Thasians were careful to avoid any people except Charlie. Likewise, the Thasians are not really to blame either. They gave Charlie his power simply so that he could survive.

Charlie and the *Antares* crewmen both wear shirts left over from "The Cage" and "Where No Man Has Gone

Before." In some scenes, Charlie wears a brown suede wraparound tunic that is much too large for him. This appears to be a rejected version of Kirk's fatigue shirt; a command insignia is visible on the belt of the garment. The color portraits of Yeoman Rand which Charlie produces on the backs of the playing cards are actually publicity photos of Grace Lee Whitney.

The first-draft script for "Charlie X" is virtually the same in concept as the final draft, with some interesting differences. In the first draft, Charlie forced a young female yeoman to her knees, disappointed because she does not resemble Janice. McCoy betrayed great glee at the prospect of Jim Kirk's trying to teach young Charlie the facts of life. Uhura, in this draft, was a talented mimic, who parodied all the crewmembers in the recreation room.

Robert Walker, Jr. (Charlie) turns in a powerful and fascinating performance. His father was a brilliant performer, equally able to tackle comedy (as in *See Here, Private Hargrove*) or play a psychopath (in *Strangers on a Train*). The younger Walker's portrayal of Charlie Evans is every bit as effective and polished as any part his father ever played.

There is a continuity error in this episode as well: during McCoy's examination of Charlie in sick bay, a reflection of Robert Walker standing up is clearly visible on the monitor above Charlie's bed—even though the camera pans back to find Charlie lying down.

Lawrence Dobkin, the director of "Charlie X," began his career as an actor. In *The Day the Earth Stood Still* [20th Century-Fox, 1951] he was one of the doctors who took care of the wounded Klaatu.

Charlie and Spock get acquainted

"BALANCE OF TERROR"

#9

WRITER:	Paul Schneider	
DIRECTOR:	Vincent McEveety	
PRINCIPALS:	Kirk	Romulan Commander
	Spock	Decius
	McCoy	Centurion
	Scott	Lieutenant Andrew Stiles
	Sulu	Specialist Robert Tomlinson
	Uhura	Specialist 2/C Angela Martine
	Yeoman Rand	Commander Hanson

◄ *Stardate 1709.1:* The *Enterprise* is patrolling along the Romulan Neutral Zone, a border between the Federation and the Romulan empire. As Captain Kirk is performing the wedding ceremony of crewmembers Angela Martine and Robert Tomlinson, an Earth outpost announces that it is under attack from the Romulans. Kirk witnesses the destruction of the outpost, but is helpless to assist. The Romulans have perfected an invention that renders their ships invisible, and Kirk reasons he must overtake and destroy the enemy vessel before it can return home. To the surprise of all, transmissions intercepted from the Romulan ship reveal that they look almost exactly like Vulcans, which causes Lieutenant Stiles to express his distrust of Mr. Spock. When the Romulan commander is finally cornered, he self-destructs his ship rather than surrender—and Stiles, whose life has been saved by Spock, realizes his prejudicial attitude is wrong. ►

"Balance of Terror" is one of the few "Trek" episodes that deals straightforwardly with prejudice. Lieutenant Stiles, coming from a family who had fought the Romulans, distrusts Spock because of the Vulcan's Romulan-like features. Prejudice is not an accepted characteristic for a space traveler; we learn from Uhura later in the series that racial prejudice in "Star Trek's" time era is indeed an obsolete relic of the past.

The Romulans we see do not fit the "faceless" picture the Federation has of them: each has his own motivations, his own understanding of the empire's policies. The young soldier Decius is impulsive, eager to confront the Federation vessel; the commander is tired of hostilities, and questions what his true duties really are. The old Centurion, aboard as an observer, communicates with his commander in much the same manner that Kirk communicates with McCoy.

Significantly, the actions of both Captain Kirk and the Romulan commander are totally devoid of prejudice. The final conversation between the two, in which the Romulan admits that he and Kirk could have become friends under different circumstances, is the episode's most eloquent editorial against the act of waging war.

Many "Star Trek" episodes were written from an initial inspiration, a preexisting literary or motion-picture concept expressed in terms of the world of tomorrow. Usually, those ideas were reworked so thoroughly it was difficult to spot the original inspiration. This segment is a notable exception. Its dramatic situations are drawn largely from two motion pictures about submarine warfare, *Run Silent, Run Deep* and *The Enemy Below*. "Balance of Terror" is a war movie translated into science fiction terms: a confrontation between a "surface vessel" (the *Enterprise*) and a "submarine" (the Invisible Romulan ship).

The cramped quarters of the Romulan bridge suggest a submarine-type environment; there is even a monitor device that resembles a periscope (the *Enterprise* chapel is just a redress of the transporter-room set).

The Romulan warship was designed and constructed by artist Wah Chang, who never received screen credit for his work in "Star Trek." No additional shots were ever taken on this miniature after this episode's effects photography was completed. All views of the Romulan ship seen in "The Deadly Years" were stock footage taken from this episode (thereafter, the Romulans began to use Klingon vessels).

The Romulan "energy bolts" were animated effects double-exposed against a background of stars; although Kirk and Sulu specify that phasers are being used, the optical effect of photon torpedoes is shown.

Mark Lenard (the Romulan commander) made his "Star Trek" debut in this episode. He is better known to "Trek" fans as Sarek, Spock's father, a role he first portrayed in "Journey to Babel." Lenard has the distinction of being the only performer who has appeared in "Star Trek" as a Vulcan, a Romulan, and a Klingon (in *ST-TMP*). He has also appeared at many "Star Trek" conventions, where he's always a welcome guest.

Lawrence Montaigne (Decius) returned to "Trek" as Stonn in "Amok Time."

Kirk's Romulan counterpart

"WHAT ARE LITTLE GIRLS MADE OF?"

▮▮▮▮▮▮▮▮▮▮▮▮▮▮▮▮▮▮▮▮▮▮▮▮▮▮▮▮▮▮▮▮▮▮▮▮ #10

WRITER: Robert Bloch
DIRECTOR: James Goldstone
PRINCIPALS: Kirk   Dr. Roger Korby
             Spock   Ruk
             Uhura   Dr. Brown
             Christine Chapel Matthews
             Andrea   Rayburn

◀ *Stardate 2712.4:* The *Enterprise* arrives at planet Exo III to learn the fate of Dr. Roger Korby, the "Pasteur of archeological medicine." On board is Nurse Christine Chapel, Korby's fiancée, who has given up a bioresearch career on Earth to find him. Korby contacts the *Enterprise* and confirms that he is living in underground caverns he discovered while suffering from severe frostbite five years before. At his request, only Kirk and Christine beam down. The doctor shows them ancient machines left behind by the long-dead Exoites—the "Old Ones"—which Korby used to create his aides, Dr. Brown and young Andrea— now revealed as androids. Korby fashions an android duplicate of Kirk, intending to capture the *Enterprise* and "seed" the universe with androids. But Kirk plants false memories in his duplicate's brain—and Spock realizes something is wrong. Kirk then turns the androids against Korby, who, now aware that his own android body has made him more machine than man, embraces Andrea and fires a stolen phaser between them, killing them both. Spock arrives with a landing party moments later; Nurse Chapel announces that she is staying with the *Enterprise* crew. ▶

This episode presented Kirk with another threat to his identity. In "The Enemy Within," the "other" Kirk was an extension of himself; here, it is an android armed with Kirk's memories. As his memory patterns are being copied, Kirk forces anti-Spock sentiments to flow from his mind; this clever "distress signal" alerts the Vulcan and helps foil Korby's plans.

When "Kirk" joins Chapel at the dinner table, we are as shocked as Christine to learn that the dynamic young man is actually the android duplicate. The android's comment, "Androids don't eat, Miss Chapel," is one of the eeriest moments in the series.

Nurse Chapel had been introduced in "The Naked Time," but here we learn her reason for signing on the *Enterprise*. Her love for Korby helps explain her attraction to Spock— the epitome of a scientific researcher.

Most of this episode's overtones of horror are the result of author Robert Bloch's affection for the work of H. P. Lovecraft. Lovecraft's classic horror stories speak of "the Old Ones," ancient, all-powerful entities that dominate the human race. Bloch has the android Ruk refer to *his* creators as "the Old Ones," and the pyramid-shaped doors in the caverns fit Lovecraft's descriptions of the dwellings of his creatures.

Sherry Jackson (Andrea) steals the show with her smooth performance and her William Theiss costume—clearly designed to accentuate her natural resources. TV viewers first saw her as Terry Williams, Danny Thomas's daughter in "Make Room for Daddy."

Ted Cassidy (Ruk) was one performer who did not have to worry about having a show stolen from him. His first exposure on television, as Lurch in "The Addams Family," brought him instant recognition. Cassidy appeared in Gene Roddenberry's TV pilot movies *Genesis II* and *Planet Earth*.

Danger on a frozen world

Makeup artist Fred Phillips accentuated the natural planes of Cassidy's face with grease pencil and covered the performer's hair with a latex headpiece. The makeup, together with William Theiss's imaginative costume, made Cassidy appear more formidable here than anywhere else.

In one of "Star Trek's" best split-screen effects, Captain Kirk is shown conversing with his duplicate at a dinner table. In this technique, two separate pieces of film are sandwiched together to form one image; the same process was used to show both Kirks lying side by side on the android table.

The captain's brother, George Samuel Kirk, is spoken of here for the first time. He is said to have three sons, instead of the one featured in "Operation: Annihilate!"

"DAGGER OF THE MIND" #11

WRITER:	Shimon Wincelberg (S. Bar-David)	
DIRECTOR:	Vincent McEveety	
PRINCIPALS:	Kirk	Dr. Tristan Adams
	Spock	Dr. Simon Van Gelder
	McCoy	Dr. Helen Noel
	Uhura	Lethe
	Ensign Berkeley	

◄ *Stardate 2715.1:* The *Enterprise* is delivering supplies to Tantalus Five, a "progressive" penal colony directed by Dr. Tristan Adams. A Tantalus inmate escapes to the starship and demands asylum. An apparent raving madman, the patient is subdued and taken to sick bay. There he is identified as Dr. Simon van Gelder, Dr. Adams's assistant. Kirk and psychiatrist Dr. Helen Noel beam down to Tantalus to make sure all is well there. After they have left, Mr. Spock uses a Vulcan mind meld on Dr. van Gelder and determines that Adams has turned Tantalus into a chamber of horrors, using a "neural neutralizer"—a device responsible for Van Gelder's incoherent state. Kirk and Helen experience the device firsthand when Adams uses it to convince Kirk that the captain is hopelessly in love with Dr. Noel. Helen risks her life to cut the colony's power so that Spock and a landing party can beam down through the planet's defensive force field. During the attack, Dr. Adams accidentally perishes in his own machine, and Dr. van Gelder becomes the new director of Tantalus, where his first act is to dismantle the neural neutralizer. ►

The script for "Dagger of the Mind" required a device to provide access to Van Gelder's mind. Earlier drafts contained a lengthy scene in which a machine containing colored lights is used to hypnotize the patient. Before "Star Trek's" staff writers were through reworking this sequence they had devised the Vulcan mind meld—one of the most important developments in Spock's character.

As late as the final-draft script, it was Janice Rand, not Dr. Helen Noel, who accompanied Captain Kirk to Tantalus Five. It is interesting that although Rand would enjoy two other appearances in "Star Trek," she was not permitted to appear in this episode as a woman the captain falls (however artificially) madly in love with. This may be the clearest indication of why Rand was soon to be written out of the "Trek" format. After backing Kirk into a corner by creating the possibility of a relationship between the two (the attempted rape in "Enemy Within"; Janice wanting to show Kirk her legs in "Miri"), someone probably decided that such a relationship would not only limit the series but the range of Kirk's entanglements as

The exterior of the Tantalus complex

"MIRI"

||||||||||||||||||||||||||||||||||| **#12**

WRITER: Adrian Spies
DIRECTOR: Vincent McEveety
PRINCIPALS: Kirk   Miri
            Spock   Jahn
            McCoy   Lieutenant John Farrell
            Yeoman Rand

◄ *Stardate 2713.5:* The *Enterprise* discovers a planet that looks amazingly like Earth, where they find a ruined, deserted city. Its only inhabitants are "children," all centuries old, the product of life-prolongation experiments. After exposure to the results of that research, the adults of the planet died horrible deaths, acquiring scar tissue and going berserk. When the children's slowed-down metabolism finally allows them to reach puberty, they too will sicken and die. Kirk and the entire landing party—except Spock—are infected with the disease. McCoy must find an antidote before they go mad and die from the illness. The children, who mistrust all adults (they refer to them as "grups") harass the intruders, stealing their communicators and abducting Yeoman Rand. Kirk enlists the aid of one—Miri, who has a crush on the captain. She assists in recovering the kidnapped yeoman and the party's communicators. McCoy, having synthesized an experimental antidote, uses it on himself and proves its effectiveness, saving his shipmates and the planet's "youthful" inhabitants. ►

"Miri" includes one of the most chilling moments in the series as Kirk is hit, kicked, and otherwise pummeled by the children while the camera focuses on one little girl's diabolical smile.

The first-draft script of "Miri" depicted more of a relationship between Miri and Jahn, a distorted "Peter Pan" type of environment with Jahn as Peter, Miri as Wendy, and the "onlies" as the lost boys. The children's society was filled with ritualism: when it was discovered that Miri's childhood was nearing an end, the "onlies" individually announced they could no longer regard her as their playmate.

The "city street" section of the studio where this episode was shot was redressed to look old and neglected. These exteriors also appear (in a less dilapidated state) in "The Return of the Archons" and "The City on the Edge of Forever."

An effective camera angle was used when McCoy passed out after taking the antidote. Part of the "lab" set was built on a raised platform so that the camera could shoot the scene level with McCoy's prone figure.

The fading blemishes on McCoy's face were photographed by steadying the head of actor DeForest Kelley, exposing

well. Kirk comes to a similar conclusion in "The Naked Time" when he states he has "no beach to walk on."

James Gregory's lovingly diabolical portrayal of Dr. Adams makes up for many defects in the story, but it is Morgan Woodward's Van Gelder who steals the show. Woodward's pain and intensity are frightfully convincing, and the actor's operatic training gave him great vocal projection and control. Woodward also appeared as Captain Tracy in "The Omega Glory."

"Dagger of the Mind" suffers from an illogical premise. Given the technical and sociological level of development within the United Federation of Planets, it is impossible that Dr. Adams's sadistic nature could have gone unnoticed before he assumed command of Tantalus. If he was sane before his assignment there, his staff should have seen something happening to his mind. His presence, position, and psychological state do not speak well either for the Federation—or this episode's credibility.

"Dagger of the Mind" features doorways, corridors, consoles, and furniture used throughout "Star Trek": the chair in the neural neutralizer room is also seen in "Operation: Annihilate!" and in an altered form in "Whom Gods Destroy."

Character names in "Star Trek" episodes are usually significant. Here, "Lethe" (in mythology the "river of forgetfulness") is an inmate who has forgotten her past criminal life. This reference is a lot more subtle than introducing a character who met Kirk at a Christmas party and calling her "Dr. Noel."

a few feet of film, and slowly peeling away his special makeup—the same time-consuming process used to give Vina her "true appearance" in "The Cage."

Terminology was still not settled on at this point: there is a reference to "Space Central" rather than the standard "Starfleet Command."

Kim Darby (Miri), best known for her role opposite John Wayne in *True Grit*, also costarred with William Shatner in the 1972 TV movie *The People*, concerning peaceful aliens who must settle on Earth. Also appearing in this episode among the "oldies" were Grace Lee Whitney's two sons and William Shatner's daughter—who is shown walking away with Captain Kirk at the end of the episode.

Kirk, McCoy and Rand examine a familiar relic

"THE CONSCIENCE OF THE KING"

▮▮▮▮▮▮▮▮▮▮▮▮▮▮▮▮▮▮▮▮▮▮▮▮▮▮▮▮▮▮ **#13**

WRITER: Barry Trivers
DIRECTOR: Gerd Oswald
PRINCIPALS: Kirk   Lenore Karidian
     Spock   Lieutenant Leslie
     McCoy   Lieutenant Kevin Riley
     Uhura   Lieutenant Matson
     Yeoman Rand   Martha Leighton
     Anton Karidian   Dr. Thomas Leighton

◄ *Stardate 2817.6:* Kirk receives a message summoning the *Enterprise* to the home of Dr. Thomas Leighton, a brilliant research scientist whom Kirk knew many years before. The summons is a trick to lure the captain to planet Q so that he could see and meet actor Anton Karidian. Leighton thinks that Karidian is actually Kodos, the ex-governor of Tarsus IV, who initiated a massacre there that killed the doctor's entire family and part of Kirk's as well. When Leighton is killed, Kirk investigates and decides to transport the Karidian troupe on the *Enterprise* so that he can study the enigmatic actor. In an effort to discover the truth Kirk romances Karidian's daughter, Lenore. During the voyage Lieutenant Kevin Riley, another survivor of the massacre, is poisoned, and nearly dies. A phaser explodes, almost killing Kirk and Spock. Riley recognizes Karidian as Kodos, but a shocked Kirk discovers the insane murderer of the survivors is Lenore—who accidentally kills her father. ▶

The elements that make this episode so successful are timeless. Tales of vengeance and justification have formed the basis of dramas that span the centuries—including many of William Shakespeare's plays. "Conscience of the King" writer Barry Trivers used *Hamlet* and *Macbeth* as points of identification for both his audience and the characters within his story.

In a brief scene, omitted from the episode's final cut, Karidian returned from a late-night walk around the *Enterprise* decks and addressed Lenore, stating "I am thy father's spirit, doomed for a certain term to walk the night." This quotation from Act I of *Hamlet* includes the dialogue that Karidian, as the ghost of Hamlet's father, recited as Kevin Riley aimed his phaser at the actor: "I could a tale unfold whose lightest word would harrow up thy soul; freeze thy young blood . . ."

In another cut sequence, as Spock and McCoy discussed what was happening aboard the ship, Karidian was discovered wandering around the corridor outside sick bay, again suggesting comparison with the ghost in *Hamlet.*

Kodos, in becoming Karidian, has condemned himself to a kind of hell, forcing himself to relive his past life in his performances. It is no wonder that Lenore Karidian is insane. She would have little choice in the matter, growing up with a brooding, guilt-ridden father taking refuge in Shakespeare's characters. Karidian, the actor, was never really alive at all. A private man who never permitted himself to be seen offstage, he regarded his sole purpose in life as raising his daughter in a guilt-free environment that he knew he was not providing.

Much of the credit for the story's effectiveness must go to actors William Shatner and Arnold Moss. Shatner's training was in Shakespearean theater, and he was able to use it to full advantage here. "Conscience of the King" was the first "Star Trek" episode to include moods and situations so clearly derived from the work of the Bard.

To offset the power of Shatner's performance, someone recommended that a performer with a powerful delivery and a strong sense of drama portray Karidian. Casting director Joseph D'Agosta and director Gerd Oswald were jointly responsible for choosing Arnold Moss.

"Conscience of the King" marked the second and last appearance of Lieutenant Kevin Thomas Riley. In the final-draft script, his dialogue was delivered by a "Lieutenant Robert Daiken." It wasn't until actor Bruce Hyde

was cast for this role, and someone recalled that he had appeared in "Star Trek" before, that the change was made.

This episode also marked the final appearance of Grace Lee Whitney as Yeoman Janice Rand. She was finally removed at network pressure to enable Kirk to have a succession of romantic interests. Roddenberry has stated many times over the years that he should have retained Grace in the cast (she eventually returned in *Star Trek— The Motion Picture*).

Composer Joseph Mullendore's music adds to the drama's somber tone. Unfortunately, he never returned to score another "Star Trek" episode, although his music for this segment can be heard edited into other shows.

"Conscience of the King" featured only three planetside sets: a darkened theater stage, a small living room, and a brief planet exterior. The need to conserve costs is evident in the view from Dr. Leighton's window. The window frame came from the lithium-cracking station set in "Where No Man Has Gone Before," and the painted backdrop behind it was initially used for the picnic scene in "The Cage."

The shuttle-bay observation deck consisted of a narrow walkway, a porthole, and a window overlooking the hangar. The hangar itself is never seen in this episode, though when it was designed, it included overhead windows intended to conform in size, shape, and location to the observation deck. The deck itself, however, does not appear in any other "Star Trek" episodes.

Kirk shows Lenore (Barbara Anderson) the shuttlecraft observation deck

"THE GALILEO SEVEN"

▪▪▪▪▪▪▪▪▪▪▪▪▪▪▪▪▪▪▪▪▪▪▪▪▪▪▪▪▪▪▪▪▪▪▪ #14

WRITERS: Oliver Crawford, S. Bar-David (Shimon
Wincelberg) (story by Oliver Crawford)
DIRECTOR: Robert Gist
PRINCIPALS: Kirk   Lieutenant Boma
Spock   Gaetano
McCoy   Latimer
Scott   Lieutenant Commander Kelowitz
Sulu   Yeoman Mears
Uhura   High Commissioner Ferris

◀ *Stardate 2821.5:* En route to planet Makus III, the *Enterprise* encounters a giant quasarlike formation, Murasaki 312. When Kirk orders the starship's shuttlecraft *Galileo* to investigate the phenomenon, Galactic High Commissioner Ferris objects to the delay in the *Enterprise*'s mission to deliver important medical supplies. When the *Galileo* crash-lands on planet Taurus II with Spock, McCoy, Scotty, and others aboard, Ferris demands the *Enterprise* abandon its search and continue its original mission. On the planet, Spock must keep everyone alive, a task complicated by Neanderthal-like natives, and find a way to return to the *Enterprise*. His greatest challenge, however, is to win the respect of the men under his command: although all his decisions are logical, the Vulcan is looked upon as a cold-blooded leader. After Mr. Scott uses the crew's phasers as an emergency fuel supply, the shuttle is able to achieve lift-off. In orbit, the Vulcan makes a last-minute emotional decision to jettison the shuttlecraft's fuel tanks, resulting in a flare that alerts *Enterprise* to her position—and saves the *Galileo* and its remaining crewmembers. ▶

This script is a very special one in terms of Mr. Spock's evolution. At first he fails miserably because he cannot accept the fact that the apelike creatures' reactions are based upon illogical, bestial motivations. The Vulcan behaves in a cold-blooded fashion, concealing the anxiety he feels on the occasion of assuming his first command. He is fully (and logically) prepared to leave the three dead crewmen behind unburied so that the rest of the *Galileo*'s crew can return in the damaged shuttle. Though Spock stubbornly denies that his decision to jettison the *Galileo*'s fuel was emotionally inspired, his denial fools no one, least of all Captain Kirk and Dr. McCoy. He is, at least tacitly, acknowledging his membership in the human race.

The role of Yeoman Mears was created to replace Yeoman Janice Rand, who was written out of the "Star Trek" format before this episode was filmed. In the script's first draft Mears's lines were delivered by Rand. A set of revised blue script pages contains a notice that "Rand" has been changed to "Mears" throughout the script.

The starship's shuttlecraft, included in the August 1966 revision of *The Star Trek Writers' Guide,* was mentioned in "The Conscience of the King" before its debut in this episode.

In addition to the miniature hangar deck set (later supplemented with a full-scale portion of the set to allow people to be seen boarding or leaving the craft), two *Galileos* had to be built: a miniature and a full-scale exterior mockup. The full-sized mockup was built by AMT Corporation workers, supervised by automotive designer Gene Winfield (who later constructed the full-size vehicles used in *Bladerunner*). The interior of the shuttlecraft was a separate set, constructed on wooden foundations with a removable wall to allow for various camera angles. There are some inconsistencies, such as the windows visible on the exterior's doors, which were omitted in the interior. The ceiling of the interior is also considerably higher than that of the full exterior mockup.

To convey the illusion of the craft's lift-off, the shuttle set was tilted up a few feet, so that the actors and chairs leaned back.

The apelike alien was portrayed by actor Buck Maffei concealed behind a mask, gloves, and a heavily padded fur costume. He held a shield and spear proportionate to his height, but when Spock handles these objects, we see oversized props that make the aliens seem much larger.

When the phaser-two units are fired in one scene, the "cue lights" of the working models can be seen. The performers "freeze" while firing to make it easier for animators to insert the beams after production.

The small rectangles of light that sometimes surround the shuttle are the dim outlines of "garbage mattes" inserted by the opticals lab to eliminate wires, lights, and other details of the miniatures soundstage.

Guest star Don Marshall (Lieutenant Boma) later became a regularly featured performer on "Land of the Giants."

Scotty works another miracle

"COURT-MARTIAL"

WRITERS: Don M. Mankiewicz, Stephen W. Carabatsos (story by Don M. Mankiewicz)
DIRECTOR: Marc Daniels
PRINCIPALS: Kirk
Spock
McCoy
Sulu
Uhura
Captain Chandra
Commodore Stone
Samuel T. Cogley
Jamie Finney
Timothy
Lieutenant Areel Shaw
Lieutenant Commander
   Benjamin Finney
Lieutenant Hansen
Captain Krasnowsky
Space Command
   Representative
Lindstrom

James T. Kirk: unwavering in the face of impossible odds

◄ *Stardate 2947.3:* During an ion storm, the *Enterprise* takes a severe buffeting and Records Officer Ben Finney enters the starship's ion pod to take important readings. When the storm makes it necessary to jettison the pod, Kirk follows normal procedures and warns Finney to evacuate. The pod is jettisoned, with Finney apparently inside. At Starbase 12, Commodore L. T. Stone institutes a court-martial against Kirk after discovering that *Enterprise* computer records show that the captain did not give Finney an adequate chance to escape from the pod. Lieutenant Areel Shaw, the prosecuting attorney and an old girlfriend of Kirk's, retains the brilliant but eccentric lawyer Samuel Cogley to defend the captain. Although all the evidence is against Kirk, Mr. Spock refuses to believe that his captain did not go by the rules. The Vulcan decides that the *Enterprise* computer's evidence is wrong. He plays chess with the computer, winning several games, and thereby discovers the machine's programming has been altered. Finney is actually *alive*, in hiding aboard the *Enterprise:* due to an old grudge, Finney had hoped to fake his own death to discredit Captain Kirk. ►

"Court-Martial" is definitely Captain Kirk's episode. All of the action and dialogue revolve around him, and we get the impression that Starfleet Command will think twice before questioning his command abilities again.

The audience is manipulated along with McCoy into perceiving Spock as a cold-blooded, emotionless alien. When we follow him to play chess with the ship's computer as the captain is fighting for his professional life, we hate the Vulcan for his unfeeling attitude. Dr. McCoy puts the audience's reaction into loud, accusing words . . . only to be efficiently silenced by Spock's logical motive of testing the computer's memory banks.

Still, McCoy is not cured of his repeated urge to pick on Mr. Spock. In court, when Cogley denounces computers for infringing upon human dignity, McCoy shoots an acid look toward the Vulcan.

The scene between Commodore Stone and Captain Kirk at the end of Act One is beautifully charged with doubt, tension, and disbelief; the final freeze-frame on Kirk's angered face effectively completes the exchange. The reluctant personal friction between Kirk and Stone finally resolves itself when Stone hears the single remaining heartbeat aboard the starship—and exclaims "Finney!"

"Court-Martial" boasts not one but two beautiful optical paintings of Starbase 12. A close and distant view were prepared for the base, one suggesting a daylight view, the other an evening landscape.

The commodore's office also appears in "The Menagerie," complete with the same building cutouts positioned outside the window. The furniture in Kirk's quarters includes a couch with a rear panel attached to the wall, not directly to the furniture. A similar piece is evident in "Journey to Babel."

One of the least imaginative props designed for a "Star Trek" episode is the "white sound device" used by Dr. McCoy to single out the sound of Finney's heartbeat. It is obviously a 20th-century microphone.

In the starbase bar, several walls from Balok's ship in "The Corbomite Maneuver" can be seen. And the crucial scenes where Kirk is shown abandoning Finney are viewed on the screen used as the *Enterprise*'s main viewing screen in "The Cage" and "Where No Man. . ." This screen had rounded corners: the screen used throughout the series is rectangular. When Kirk greets someone during this sequence, he says he hasn't seen him since "the Vulcanian expedition." This is one of the last times "Vulcanian" is heard in "Star Trek."

"Court-Martial" contains three well-cast secondary

McCoy listens impassively as the charges against Kirk are read

characters: Elisha Cook, Jr. (Cogley), best remembered as Wilmer, the "fall guy" in *The Maltese Falcon,* has played an impressive number of murderers, crazies—and an occasional good guy. In *The House on Haunted Hill* he had the last word on Vincent Price. His television appearances date back to 1949 and the pilot episode of the "Dick Tracy" teleseries (as an eccentric criminal, "Coffeehead").

Percy Rodrigues (Stone) was Dr. Miles, the resident physician of "Peyton Place," and appeared regularly as Jason Hart in "The Silent Force" (1970–71). Richard Webb (Finney) is famous as TV's "Captain Midnight" and also starred in the 1958 teleseries "U.S. Border Patrol" as Patrolman Don Jagger.

WRITER:	Gene Roddenberry	
DIRECTOR:	Marc Daniels	
PRINCIPALS:	Kirk	Captain Christopher Pike
	Spock	Number One
	McCoy	Dr. Phillip Boyce
	Scott	Yeoman Colt
	Uhura	Commodore José Mendez
	Sulu	José Tyler
	Miss Piper	The Keeper
	Lieutenant	Dr. Theodore Haskins
	Hansen	Vina
	Chief Humbolt	C.P.O. Garison

◄ *Stardate 3012.4:* A call supposedly sent by former *Enterprise* Captain Christopher Pike diverts the starship to Starbase 6. Pike, crippled, scarred, and completely paralyzed in a recent accident, is abducted and brought aboard the *Enterprise* by Spock. Starbase Commodore Mendez and Captain Kirk overtake the starship when it warps out of orbit—locked on course for the forbidden planet Talos IV. To visit this world demands the death penalty, and Kirk is forced to convene a court-martial against his Vulcan friend. The entire proceeding, however, is meaningless—for after a series of surprises, it is revealed that Mendez was never actually aboard the *En-*

The crippled Captain Pike

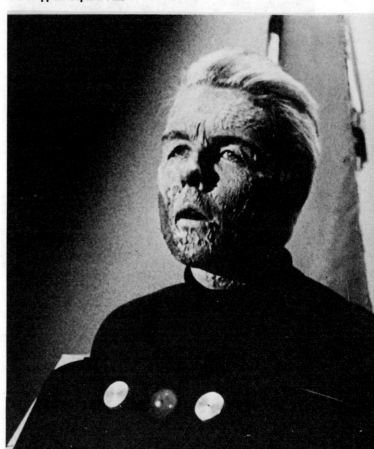

terprise. His presence on the ship and in the shuttlecraft with Kirk had been an illusion caused by the Talosians working in league with Spock. The mystery is explained as an attempt to get Pike to Talos IV. Once there, the benevolent inhabitants intend to use their powerful mental abilities to enable Pike to lead a happy life despite his deformities and paralysis. Kirk allows Pike to beam down to the planet—and Starfleet Command drops all charges against Spock. ▶

"Star Trek" was an expensive series to produce. Although the second pilot, "Where No Man Has Gone Before" had featured many visual discrepancies from the series format and did not include the characters of Dr. McCoy, Uhura, and Yeoman Rand, there was never any question that it would be included in the series' network run. The first pilot was another story. "The Cage" included so many discrepancies that at first it seemed there was no way to make use of it on the air. Roddenberry's solution was to create a "frame" around the original footage that would preserve the series' continuity while making it possible to utilize the first pilot's footage.

"The Menagerie" is also one of the most interesting "Trek" episodes produced. The inclusion of the original pilot's footage accounts for much of its appeal.

Captain Pike's ill fortune is a tragic reminder that starship captains are not immortal. Add to this shock the further suggestion that Spock may be going insane, and Captain Kirk finds his strengths and his friendships at stake.

Spock, of course, is not insane. On the contrary, the Vulcan and the Talosians succeed in staging an elaborate charade in their "fiction of a court-martial." Kirk is kept busy trying to defend his friend, and Spock accomplishes what he has set out to do without confiding in his captain.

Would Kirk have aided his first officer if he had been told all the facts? In more than a passing sense, what Spock does here for Pike will later be duplicated by Kirk working on behalf of Spock and McCoy in *Star Trek III*.

We also see a rare instance of Kirk's off-duty life catching up with him (in a commodore's office, of all places) as Miss Piper announces that her friend Yeoman Helen Johannson "simply mentioned that she knew you" (from Miss Piper's expression it is doubtful that was all she mentioned).

The matte painting of Starbase 6, executed in blues, grays, and white, makes excellent use of perspective. We not only see the area adjoining the beam-down point, but we also see around the corner where, many blocks away, there are still some buildings under construction. The muted colors give a peaceful look to the complex, and are similar to those used in creating the city for "A Taste of Armageddon."

When "The Menagerie" was filmed, actor Jeffrey Hunter was both unavailable and unaffordable for what amounted to a minor supporting role. Everything we see of the healthy Captain Pike was filmed for the original pilot in 1964 (including the ending in which Pike and Vina stroll off arm in arm). The crippled Pike was portrayed by actor Sean Kenney, who bears more than a passing resemblance to Hunter. Kenney can also be seen as the navigator in "Arena" and "A Taste of Armageddon." Guest star Malachi Throne (Commodore Mendez) also provided the voice of the keeper for both "The Cage" and "The Menagerie."

Spock on trial

"SHORE LEAVE"

`▯▯▯▯▯▯▯▯▯▯▯▯▯▯▯▯▯▯▯▯▯▯▯▯▯▯▯▯▯▯▯▯▯▯` **#17**

WRITER: Theodore Sturgeon
DIRECTOR: Robert Sparr
PRINCIPALS: Kirk
Spock
McCoy
Sulu
Uhura
Caretaker
Finnegan
Don Juan
Ruth
Alice in Wonderland
Yeoman Tonia Barrows
Lieutenant Esteban Rodriguez
Specialist 2/C Angela Martine-
Teller

◄ *Stardate 3025.3:* Captain Kirk decides to give his men shore leave on an inviting Earth-like planet—but trouble begins when McCoy sees a giant, talking white rabbit being chased by a little girl. Sulu is menaced by a Samurai warrior; other crewmen are strafed by aircraft, chased by tigers, and threatened by swordsmen. Kirk meets Finnegan, an old nemesis from his Academy days, and Ruth, an old flame. Then McCoy is killed by a black knight on horseback, and as the perils become progressively deadlier, Spock and Kirk realize their thoughts are being brought to life. A kindly old man appears, identifying himself as the planet's Caretaker and explains they are in an "amusement park" where advanced alien science synthesizes the "entertainment" from the thoughts of the "vacationers." McCoy appears, alive and well in the company of two Rigel cabaret girls. Kirk decides that, with the proper mental precautions, this can be a good shore leave planet after all—just as Ruth reappears. ►

In Theodore Sturgeon's final story outline—written before any of the "Trek" episodes had been telecast—there was more emphasis on technical and personal aspects of the adventure. In his original opening, Sulu and McCoy gathered specimens on the planet, with Sulu using a tool containing a folding microscope, binoculars, and a slide-mounting attachment. During this sequence Sulu referred to McCoy as "sawbones," and discovered that all cellular materials on the planet were identical, suggesting an artificially constructed environment. They also determined that the entire world was barren, except for the one fertile area where the *Enterprise* people had arrived.

McCoy faced the black knight to prove that a crewman's "mother," who suddenly materialized, was an illusion—and he died denying the reality of the situation, with a circus calliope playing as Kirk arrived on the scene. The outline also included an eerie scene in which McCoy's body was shown being dragged down into the planet by mechanical arms that emerged through trapdoors in the surface.

The communicators stopped working because they op-erated on power broadcast from the *Enterprise,* and the starship had started to lose all power. At one point the *Enterprise* was drawn down into the planet's atmosphere and daylight was visible through the ship's observation ports.

When Kirk realized what was happening, he concentrated on his wish to know everything about the situation, and in answer to his thoughts, the Caretaker materialized. The planet, he disclosed, was over 1,000 years old and completely automated (implying he was not a human being, but a constructed device). Originally programmed for a smaller number of guests than the *Enterprise* crew, it had automatically siphoned off energy from the vessel to compensate.

Characterization is well handled in the finished episode much of which was rewritten on location (Roddenberry recalls sitting under a tree and rewriting as the episode was shot): McCoy is a true Southern gentleman, Sulu grins like a kid with a new toy when he acquires his "police special" pistol, and Kirk is seen recalling a romantic entanglement of his youth, one of our few glimpses into the captain's past.

The young woman who beams down with Mr. Rodriguez is referred to in the script as "Mary Teller," and is called "Teller" by Kirk at one point in the episode even though as Rodriguez cradles her after she's been shot he calls her Angela. Actress Barbara Baldavin, who plays this role, also appears as Angela Martine in "Balance of Terror." After the actress was signed for "Shore Leave," someone recalled she had been on the ship before. The decision was made to refer to her by her original character's name, but the credits and scene with Kirk were not changed.

Guest star Bruce Mars (Finnegan) played his part with such energy that many fans wished to meet the genuine article in a later episode. Unfortunately such a meeting never came about, although Mars did return for a brief role as a policeman in "Assignment: Earth."

Much of "Shore Leave" was filmed outdoors at "Africa USA," a privately owned facility that served as the location of many Hollywood productions. To render the landscape more alien, exotic plants and feathers were scattered around and red paint sprayed on nearby trees. The area available for shooting was not a large one; in the chase between Kirk and Finnegan we pass the same fallen tree more than once.

Gerald Fried's music adds greatly to the flavor of the story. His suspense and chase themes succeed in building tension, and his theme for Finnegan was sprightly enough to be edited into many later episodes (usually in connection with Scotty or an unusual and funny moment, such as the encounter with the policeman in "The City on the Edge of Forever").

The late Theodore Sturgeon, who also wrote "Amok

Kirk and Spock examine the mysterious Black Knight

"THE SQUIRE OF GOTHOS"

WRITER: Paul Schneider
DIRECTOR: Don McDougall
PRINCIPALS: Kirk   Uhura
    Spock   Trelane
    McCoy   Lieutenant Karl Jaeger
    Scott   Lieutenant DeSalle
    Sulu   Yeoman Teresa Ross

◀ *Stardate 2124.5:* In Space Quadrant 904, eight days away from Colony Beta Six, the *Enterprise* is trapped in orbit around an uncharted planet. There, Kirk and company are confronted by Trelane, an illogical but extremely powerful alien. Although he appears to be an adult humanoid fascinated with the history of the planet Earth, Kirk reasons there is more to him than his outward appearance—and challenges him to a duel. When Trelane loses, he sentences Kirk to hang. In the nick of time, the alien's parents appear to rescue Kirk and the Enterprise from their playful son. ▶

Time," was born in 1918 (real name: Edward Hamilton Waldo) in New York City. He sold his first science fiction story in 1939 and was one of the central writers of the years sometimes referred to as the golden age of science fiction. Most of his magazine contributions were for *Astounding Science Fiction* and *Galaxy*. His books include *More Than Human* (1953), *A Touch of Strange* (1958), and *The Cosmic Rape* (1958).

"The Squire of Gothos" is an enjoyable and original episode, but it never develops into anything beyond a lighthearted adventure.

At first glance, Trelane appears to be a hobbyist studying the Earth with a super-telescope and controlling the *Enterprise* crew with sophisticated machines. He enjoys music and dancing, and has an eye for the ladies.

Kirk treats Trelane as he would cope with Harry Mudd: he plays off the man's idiosyncrasies while searching for weaknesses with which to save his ship. Kirk erroneously reasons that Trelane's power is dependent upon a machine. He destroys the mechanism and promptly realizes Trelane's incredibly powerful alien nature.

The implications of his encounter with Trelane are staggering to Kirk. This "boy" has created a planet out of nothingness, in the same manner that a human boy might make a mudpie in a sandbox. The captain also suffers the indignity of being called a "primitive creature" by Trelane's mother. Although Trelane is in reality an insubstantial creature, his parents have male and female voices (supplied by James Doohan and Barbara Babcock).

The budget of "Squire" was kept as low as possible by furnishing the interior of Trelane's castle with a large store of furniture, paintings, and other *objets d'art* from Paramount's extensive prop department. Many of these items appeared in the films of Cecil B. DeMille, including *The Buccaneer;* one of the "decorations" was the full body costume of the salt vampire from "The Man Trap," which can be seen propped up in an alcove near the front door of Trelane's home.

Guest star William Campbell (Trelane) has appeared in feature films including *The High and the Mighty* (1954) and *Battle Cry* (1955). On television, he and character actor Paul Birch starred as truckdrivers in the series "Cannonball." Campbell also appeared as Koloth, the Klingon captain in "The Trouble with Tribbles."

Kirk and Sulu—trapped by Trelane

"ARENA"

▭▭▭▭▭▭▭▭▭▭▭▭▭▭▭▭▭▭▭▭▭▭▭▭▭▭▭ #19

WRITER: Gene L. Coon (from a story by Frederic L. Brown)
DIRECTOR: Joseph Pevney
PRINCIPALS:

Kirk	Metron
Spock	Lieutenant O'Herlihy
McCoy	Lieutenant Commander Kelowitz
Scott	Lieutenant Harold
Sulu	Lieutenant Lang
Uhura	Lieutenant DePaul

◄ *Stardate 3045.6:* Captain Kirk receives a request from Commodore Travers to visit Starfleet base Cestus III. Upon arriving, Kirk finds the base completely destroyed. Suddenly Kirk and his landing party are ambushed; Lieutenant Harold, the lone survivor of the Cestus personnel, testifies that his base was destroyed by a sudden and merciless attack. His people did *not* have time to request the presence of the *Enterprise*. The call was a trap, set by the attackers. Returning to the *Enterprise*, Kirk follows the enemy spaceship. When the two vessels intrude upon the territory of the powerful Metrons, the Metrons decide to settle the conflict by having Kirk fight the alien commander, a Gorn, in single combat. The loser's ship will be destroyed. The Gorn is a man-size, immensely strong reptile, as resourceful as Kirk in battle. The captain constructs a weapon with which he conquers the Gorn—and his refusal to kill his defeated opponent impresses the Metrons. Perhaps one day, they inform Kirk, their race and the Federation may meet as friends and equals. ►

"Arena," the short story by Frederic L. Brown, was too good a prospect to be turned down by either "The Outer Limits" or "Star Trek" ("The Outer Limits" version was called "Fun and Games").

Writer Gene L. Coon's "Star Trek" scripts (especially "Devil in the Dark" and "Metamorphosis") share a common theme: a firm conviction that prejudice must be conquered if mankind is ever to take its place alongside other intelligent civilizations. This conviction is one of the greatest reasons for "Star Trek's" continued popularity: Kirk's victory, achieved after we have shared his fear and his weaknesses (including an instinctive fear of reptiles) increases our faith in "Star Trek's" principles. He is severely tested during this episode, and although his ship is directly threatened by the Gorn and the Metrons, he never forgets himself sufficiently to act like a predatory animal instead of an intelligent individual. "Arena" makes us acutely aware that the *Enterprise* is not always on time to save UFP outposts, and that the starship itself is vulnerable (especially to technology as powerful as that possessed by the Metrons).

The opening scene, detailing the destruction on Cestus III, is extremely effective. The outpost was filmed on location at Paramount Ranch in Agoura, CA. The most important "prop" of this episode is the Gorn itself, constructed by Wah Chang.

Two familiar but usually unsung faces are visible in "Arena." Grant Woods (Mr. Kelowitz) appears in this same role in "The Galileo Seven" and "This Side of Paradise." Sean Kenney (Mr. DePaul, the helmsman) appears as the crippled Captain Pike in "The Menagerie." He is also seen aboard the *Enterprise* in "A Taste of Armageddon."

The voice of the Metrons (the warning message and the entity itself) was supplied by Vic Perrin. His first bit of dialogue here is strongly reminiscent of his introductory speech for each episode of "The Outer Limits" (". . . we will control all that you see and hear").

The grenade launcher sound effect was also used for the photon torpedoes, and the glare of the weapon's detonation was provided by an animated overlay.

A moment of dire peril for Kirk

"THE ALTERNATIVE FACTOR"

#20

WRITER: Don Ingalls
DIRECTOR: Gerd Oswald
PRINCIPALS: Kirk | Lazarus
Spock | Lieutenant Charlene Masters
McCoy | Commodore Barstow
Uhura | Lieutenant Leslie

◄ *Stardate 3087.6:* Orbiting a lifeless planet, the *Enterprise*'s instruments detect a moment of "nonexistence" experienced throughout the universe. Starfleet Command believes it to be the prelude to an invasion, and Kirk must determine its cause. When Spock's sensors detect the sudden presence of a humanoid life form on the planet, Kirk beams down and meets Lazarus. The stranger is actually two different people: one rational, the other a madman from an anti-matter universe. The "nonexistence" effect is the result of the irrational Lazarus passing through a dimensional corridor between universes. The sane Lazarus steals the ship's dilithium crystals to prevent his mad counterpart from using them to open the rift between the parallel universes. When he discovers the truth, Kirk aids Lazarus in trapping his insane counterpart within the dimensional corridor, thus assuring the safety of both universes. The two Lazaruses will remain locked in combat throughout eternity. ►

The first-draft script of "The Alternative Factor" told the same story as the completed episode, involving two universes and one man who is actually two very different individuals. This early version, however, contained one vital element missing from the filmed version. In this draft, the sane Lazarus was depicted as a dynamic and desperate man. While attempting to stop his counterpart from destroying both universes, he fell in love with Engineering Lieutenant Charlene Masters, a relationship the insane Lazarus then abused to help obtain the ship's dilithium crystals.

This is one of the strangest "Star Trek" adventures. It starts out to tell a simple story with elements of mystery, suspense and horror. It emerges as a confusing and fragmentary study in what can go wrong with an episode. This is especially surprising considering its director, Gerd Oswald, whose only other "Trek" episode, "Conscience of the King," is one of the most compelling installments of the series.

Actor John Drew Barrymore was scheduled to portray Lazarus, and there are some surviving publicity materials that credit him. Shortly before the episode was to start filming, Barrymore became unavailable. Robert Brown was obtained as a last-minute replacement.

As we watch the episode, it is difficult to tell whether

the sane or insane Lazarus is on the scene. No other "Star Trek" episode is edited in such an ambiguous manner. Instead of connecting scenes in a continuous rhythm of action, we are left with a variety of scenes joined together with little or no visual or dramatic symmetry.

Much of the episode's footage is repetitive, such as Lazarus's tendency to fall off cliffs, acquire bloody facial wounds, and go wandering off by himself. But his wanderings on the planet's surface are still more understandable than those he takes aboard the *Enterprise*. Kirk has received orders of a most vital nature. The universe is experiencing something very dangerous and frightening and Starfleet has seen fit to put its forces on invasion alert. Kirk has followed through on this by calling for his crew to assume battle stations.

Why, then, does he allow Lazarus to have free run of the ship to the extent that McCoy has to needle the captain about it? At one point in the episode Lazarus even finds his way to the ship's bridge, makes it known that he disagrees with the captain, and vowing revenge, is al-

lowed to leave with one security man following him. To make matters worse, Lazarus eludes his security shadow and finds his way to one of the most vital areas of the ship, the engineering section, where he proceeds to steal the vessel's source of power.

This is the only time in the series that we see where the dilithium crystals are recharged and tied in to the *Enterprise* engines. In "Mudd's Women" we see crystals (completely different in appearance from the ones seen in this episode) that have burned out. Later in the series we will see Scotty installing yet another variety of the crystals.

The transitional footage of Lazarus entering the dimensional corridor was produced by double-exposing a rotating abstract shape over an astronomical photograph and combining this with color negative footage of two stuntmen slugging it out. The actual set used for this area was a small, bare room with orange and purple walls and a smoke-covered floor that hid a safety mattress.

Kirk and Spock searching for Lazarus

"TOMORROW IS YESTERDAY"

▮▮▮▮▮▮▮▮▮▮▮▮▮▮▮▮▮▮▮▮▮▮▮▮▮▮▮▮▮ **#21**

WRITER: D. C. Fontana
DIRECTOR: Michael O'Herlihy
PRINCIPALS: Kirk   Colonel Fellini
           Spock   Technician Webb
           McCoy   Captain John Christopher
           Scott   Air Police Sergeant
           Sulu   Transporter Chief Kyle
           Uhura

Sulu on old Earth

◀ *Stardate 3113.2:* After an encounter with the gravitational forces of a "black star," the *Enterprise* is hurled backward in time to the twentieth century. Flying over Nebraska, the starship is sighted and classified as a UFO. Air Force pilot Captain John Christopher photographs the *Enterprise* with his jet's wing cameras. When his jet is accidentally destroyed by the starship's tractor beam, he is transported aboard. After first deciding that it would not alter history if Captain Christopher never returned to Earth, Spock then discovers that Captain Sean Jeffrey Christopher (their guest's as-yet-unborn son) will lead an important expedition into space.

This leaves Kirk and company with three large problems: (1) retrieving the film that shows the *Enterprise* in Earth orbit; (2) getting the pilot back where he belongs, and (3) returning to their own time without changing history. After Sulu, Kirk, and Spock surreptitiously obtain the film, Scotty duplicates the "slingshot effect" responsible for their time-accident, Christopher is returned to his jet, and the *Enterprise* returns home. ▶

"Tomorrow Is Yesterday" is one of the most popular "Star Trek" episodes. The high opinion most fans have of this adventure is easily understandable: it is the answer to a Trekker's daydreams. We would all like to visit the U.S.S. *Enterprise,* but here we have the next best thing: we follow someone else from our own era as he beams aboard and discovers what life on a starship is all about. Of course, there are complications. Captain Christopher did not ask for his visit; he wants to go home.

Yet he weathers his first visit to a UFO (complete with strangely clad aliens who speak our language, employ beautiful women as crew personnel, and do not believe in little green men) with great aplomb. The single aspect of the *Enterprise* that seems to impress him most is his first view of Lieutenant Uhura, perhaps the most eloquent testimony to his mental (and physical) health.

D. C. Fontana's script ties in neatly with contemporary mythology. Spock almost expresses amusement at the *Enterprise* being dismissed as a mirage or as a mass of swamp gas.

Spock also takes definite delight in shocking the poor

Air Force security man who is accidentally beamed aboard. This same hapless visitor is astounded to receive a bowl of chicken soup from the exotically attired and accented transporter chief Kyle (John Winston).

Lieutenant Sulu finally gets to visit Earth in a relatively barbaric time period. George Takei wears the delighted expression of a child discovering a closetful of new toys while touring the Omaha installation. Captured by the security people, Kirk knows that his predicament is no laughing matter, but it is evident that he, too, regards this as a unique adventure.

One would think that after 200 plus years, science would have produced smaller and more powerful flashlights; not so with the one Kirk uses in this episode. Perhaps a conventional flash was used for the same reason we see contemporary saltshakers in "The Man Trap."

The only disappointing feature of this episode is an *Enterprise* flyby in which the starship is matted against a globe of Earth. Parts of the ship seem to "wink out," because of technical problems with the matte.

"THE RETURN OF THE ARCHONS"

▭▭▭▭▭▭▭▭▭▭▭▭▭▭▭▭▭▭▭▭▭▭▭▭▭▭ **#22**

WRITER: Boris Sobelman (story by Gene Roddenberry)
DIRECTOR: Joseph Pevney
PRINCIPALS: Kirk   Lindstrom
        Spock   Tula
        McCoy   First Lawgiver
        Sulu   Tamar
        Scott   Hacom
        Uhura   Bilar
        Reger   Lieutenant Leslie
        Marplon   Lieutenant O'Neil
        Landru

◀ *Stardate 3156.2:* The U.S.S. *Enterprise* visits planet Beta III in Star System 6–11 to learn the fate of the U.S.S. *Archon,* a Federation ship that had visited the planet a century before. After beaming down to explore the planet, Mr. Sulu is hit by a strange ray. Transported back aboard the *Enterprise,* he is found to be under the influence of a controlling force. A landing party beams down and sees the planet's populace suddenly begin an orgy that lasts exactly twelve hours. Reger, a native whose daughter Tula was a participant in "the Red Hour" orgy, tells them that monklike Lawgivers roam the planet serving the ruling mystical figure Landru. Outsiders—such as the crew of the *Archon* and Sulu—are "absorbed" and transformed into a part of "the body." Reger and Marplon, two members of the anti-Landru underground, prevent Kirk and Spock from being absorbed. Kirk then learns that Landru is a computer, programmed by a scientist and leader thousands

A stranger from the hills

of years ago to protect his people. Kirk destroys the computer, freeing the people of Beta III to rule themselves. ▶

Captain Kirk's concerns for the rights of the individual over those of the machine have generated extensive debate as to whether his antimachine acts ever constitute violations of the Prime Directive. This issue is clouded because Kirk usually induces the machines to destroy themselves, as in this episode, the first to spotlight Kirk's talents as a computer destroyer. The dialogue usually sounds something like "You have failed to fulfill your prime directive, and you must therefore destroy yourself" (it's a good thing the machines never tried to reverse this tactic against Captain Kirk . . .).

"The Return of the Archons" contains some interesting character bits. It has one of the few episode teasers to fade out on Mr. Sulu, and gives George Takei a chance to go berserk, although his transformation here is much quieter than that in "The Naked Time."

Mr. Spock is seen for a short time apparently sleeping with his eyes open. Although the Vulcan may have been in deep meditation rather than asleep, Spock's behavior in this episode is decidedly strange, partly because of his motivation to conform to "the body" to avoid the wrath of the Lawgivers. Spock has ample opportunity here to deliver his effective, brow-raising, ironic stares. He also throws a good, old-fashioned punch instead of using his customary Vulcan Nerve Pinch.

The final draft of this script featured a very human subplot to offset the nonhuman behavior of Landru and the Lawgivers. Sociologist Luster (changed to Lindstrom in the final draft) falls in love with Reger's daughter, Tula. Although Lindstrom's protest about Tula's fate in "the Red Hour" was left in, the attraction between the two was edited out.

The episode's first act opens with three different angles of *Enterprise* flybys dissolved into each other—a beautifully edited sequence. Most glimpses of the *Enterprise* are short or only involve one point of view.

Another of the episode's most effective moments has Reger explaining that before Landru was in power, things were different. He reverently uncovers a self-contained lighting panel to a background of heavy shadows and eerie music (lifted from "The Corbomite Maneuver").

The phaser blast that vaporizes the wall of the computer room is a well-done combination of double exposure (Landru's fading image), animated overlays (the phaser beams and heat effect), and a substituted wall (with and without holes).

Landru's materializations are accompanied by the same sound effect later used for sensor and tricorder sounds. Guest star Charles MaCauley (Landru) later appeared as Jaris in "Wolf in the Fold."

"A TASTE OF ARMAGEDDON"

▮▮▮▮▮▮▮▮▮▮▮▮▮▮▮▮▮▮▮▮▮▮▮▮▮▮▮▮ **#23**

WRITERS: Robert Hamner, Gene L. Coon (story by Robert
              Hamner)
DIRECTOR: Joseph Pevney
PRINCIPALS: Kirk   Sar 6
             Spock   Mea 3
             McCoy   Ambassador Robert Fox
             Scott   Yeoman Tamura
             Uhura   Lieutenant Galloway
             Anan 7   Lieutenant DePaul

◀ *Stardate 3192.1:* The *Enterprise* journeys to planet Eminiar VII to establish diplomatic contact. Although the Eminians warn Kirk against visiting, at the insistence of Federation Ambassador Robert Fox, a landing party beams down. They discover Eminiar has been at war for centuries with its neighboring world, Vendikar. Suddenly, Kirk is informed that the *Enterprise* has been declared a "casualty," and all aboard her are considered dead. Through Eminiar's council head Anan 7 and a young woman named Mea 3, Kirk learns that the "war" is fought with computers: "casualties" on both planets willingly enter antimatter chambers and die to prevent all-out destruction. After the landing party is imprisoned, Ambassador Fox beams down and learns of the situation—whereupon Kirk and Spock escape and destroy Eminiar's computers. Now, Kirk says, you will have to fight your war for real. To escape the horrors of material destruction the two worlds, with the aid of Ambassador Fox, begin to talk peace. ▶

This episode is the perfect follow-up to "The Return of the Archons." Whereas a machine had rendered the followers of Landru emotionless and stopped the progress of their society, the people of Eminiar VII have turned themselves into mechanical monsters, killing their own kind with the aid of computers.

Ambassador Robert Fox is one of the most irritating examples of Federation stubbornness (along with Galactic High Commissioner Ferris from "The Galileo Seven") ever to grace the series. After being exposed to the Eminiar government's policies, though, even Fox can stand things no longer. It is rewarding indeed to see Fox finally take up a sonic disruptor and follow Kirk on his rounds of computer demolition.

Steven W. Carabatsos ("Trek's" script consultant at the time) and Robert Hamner are credited with writing the first-draft script. The *Enterprise,* damaged and in need of repair materials found on Eminiar *VII,* was denied permission to orbit and make repairs. Kirk beamed down anyway and learned that Eminiar had been at war with the planet Verikan III for over 1,000 years. The principles of the "war" were explained to Kirk by Mea, as she was

declared a casualty. Mea and Sar were to be married; Kirk attempted to persuade them that life was preferable to death. Spock beamed down and, in the computer room, overheard a distress call from Kirk. Using his Vulcan strength, Spock swatted guards aside like flies to get to Kirk. He then destroyed the antimatter chamber (with a rewired tricorder bomb) and fled with Kirk and Mea. Learning that a planetary defense mechanism was absorbing the *Enterprise*'s power, Kirk surrendered. When the chance presented itself, Kirk risked radiation burns and destroyed the computer. At the end of the first draft, no mention was made of the *Enterprise*'s leaving diplomats behind to help with the negotiations.

The Eminiar beam-down is greatly enhanced by the beautiful optical painting of an alien city. The style of this illustration is similar to the rendering of the starbase in "The Menagerie." In fact, the same wall built for the set in "The Menagerie" (in front of which the actors stand) is also included in this matte with the same circle (also featured as the council platform in "Mirror, Mirror") and a different piece of sculpture.

The Eminiar corridors contain doorways that were originally constructed for "What Are Little Girls Made Of?" Eminian furnishings include ultramodern office furniture, stock furniture, and specially made futuristic chairs. The small monitors from the *Enterprise* bridge in the pilot episodes show up in the council room here, (they're also in Mendez's office in "The Menagerie") as do the computer

Spock telepathically arranges an escape

banks from "Menagerie." Excellent use of colored lights made the few sets seem like many.

The sonic disruptor pistols were used as the basis for the Klingon sidearms; the front sections were removed and reworked.

The Eminiar costumes resembled those featured in "What Are Little Girls Made Of?" Also present in Anan's wardrobe are the black turtleneck shirts that are in evidence throughout "Star Trek's" universe.

Guest star David Opatoshu (Anan 7), best remembered for his roles in such movies as *The Naked City* and *Exodus,* appeared in many science fiction and fantasy tales on television, including roles in "Voyage to the Bottom of the Sea," "The Time Tunnel" "One Step Beyond," "The Twilight Zone," and "The Outer Limits." Barbara Babcock (Mea) also appears in "Plato's Stepchildren." Her vocal talents are heard in "The Squire of Gothos" and "Assignment Earth."

"Star Trek" familiars appear here, too. Sean Kenney is Lieutenant DePaul and David L. Ross is Galloway. Although Eddie Paskey does not appear here as "Mr Leslie," he does play one of the citizens of Eminiar VII.

The optical painting of Eminiar 7

"SPACE SEED"

#24

WRITERS:	Gene L. Coon, Carey Wilbur (story by Carey Wilbur)
DIRECTOR:	Marc Daniels
PRINCIPALS:	Kirk Khan Noonian Singh
	Spock Lieutenant Marla McGivers
	McCoy Lieutenant Spinelli
	Scott Joaquin
	Uhura Transporter Chief Kyle

◄ *Stardate 3141.9:* The *Enterprise* discovers a "sleeper ship" from the late twentieth century. The crewmembers are found in a state of suspended animation, and the leader, a magnetic individual named Khan, is revived. Ship's historian Marla McGivers is strongly attracted to the man—whom Spock identifies as Khan Noonian Singh, the most dynamic and dangerous of the artificially bred men of the 1990s—and once absolute ruler of more than a quarter of Earth. With Marla's aid, Khan, supremely contemptuous of the *Enterprise* crew—especially Kirk—revives his crew and takes the ship. But when she realizes Khan intends to kill those who will not aid him Marla rescues the captain. Kirk then unleashes anesthetic gas throughout the occupied sections of the ship and recaptures the *Enterprise.* He gives Khan and his people the choice of facing arrest or colonizing a virgin and hostile planet. Khan chooses to be a colonist, and Marla elects to go with him. Spock wonders what will come from these "seeds" the *Enterprise* has planted. ►

The character of Khan is one of the most magnetic to appear in "Star Trek," and it was no wonder that producer Harve Bennett chose him as the central figure of his first "Star Trek" feature film. Carey Wilbur began his story for "Space Seed" by explaining how out of place in today's world a man from Renaissance times would be. The same was true, he theorized, for a man of this century transported into "Star Trek's" era. Drawing a parallel with the 18th-century British custom of deporting undesirables, Wilbur postulated "seed ships" that would take unwanted criminals from overpopulated Earth into outer space. The *Botany Bay* was said to have left Earth in the year 2096 and traveled for 500 years before being discovered by the *Enterprise.* On board the ship in this draft were 100 criminals (males and females) and a volunteer crew of a few lawmen.

The outline's "Khan" was "Harold Ericcson," a man reminiscent of the ancient Vikings. His first act was to assault Captain Kirk; he was then subdued and placed in the *Enterprise* brig with the other survivors. The *Enterprise* people at first knew nothing about the *Botany Bay* being a convict ship, and Ericcson committed a murder to pre-

and TV shows for over three decades, and after he left Mexico in the 1950s was under contract to Metro-Goldwyn-Mayer. The present generation knows him best as Mr. Roarke, the mysterious manager of "Fantasy Island" and Zach Powers on "The Colbys."

Madlyn Rhue (Marla) has appeared in many Warner Brothers TV episodes, and in vintage 20th Century-Fox teleseries including "Adventures in Paradise" and "Peyton Place." Blaisdell Makee, who appears as Mr. Spinelli in this episode, is also seen in "The Changeling" as an *Enterprise* crewman named Mr. Singh.

The Botany Bay miniature (refitted as a freighter) is also seen in "The Ultimate Computer." The pressure chamber in this episode became part of McCoy's medical lab. One of the sleeper units' doorframes was salvaged from "Space Seed" and incorporated into the set for McCoy's research lab, where it became an overhead unit of unspecified function.

As Kirk bends over the sleeper unit containing Khan, you can see his phaser slip off his Velcro belt and fall to the ground. You can also see actor DeForest Kelley's eyes glance back and forth between Khan and the floor, wondering whether the "take" was going to be used.

Khan Noonian Singh

vent them from learning the truth. Ericcson captured the *Enterprise* and intended to become a pirate using the starship. When Marla was in danger of being shot during a phaser fight involving Kirk, Ericcson surrendered and accepted his fate.

In the final draft Khan is not a criminal but a fanatic who had left Earth by his own choice. He is a challenge for Kirk and company not because of their ignorance of the criminal mentality but because of his greater physical and mental ability. Fortunately for Kirk, Khan proved to have an ego that caused his downfall.

In a startling show of chauvinism, Khan takes advantage of historian Marla McGivers' attraction to him. She has been studying brawny historical types for her entire professional life, fantasizing about meeting them, and when she confronts one in the flesh, her fantasies take precedence over her Starfleet loyalties and everything she has ever worked to achieve. She chooses to become an outcast and crawls to him on her hands and knees. All this is surprising considering that "Star Trek" is known as a series that preached equality between the sexes.

Ricardo Montalban (Khan) has appeared in feature films

Rendezvous with the sleeper ship

"THIS SIDE OF PARADISE"

☐☐☐☐☐☐☐☐☐☐☐☐☐☐☐☐☐☐☐☐☐☐☐☐ #25

WRITER: D. C. Fontana (story by Nathan Butler [Jerry Sohl] and D. C. Fontana)
DIRECTOR: Ralph Senensky
PRINCIPALS: Kirk   Leila Kalomi
Spock   Elias Sandoval
McCoy   Lieutenant Commander Kelowitz
Sulu   Painter
Uhura   Lieutenant DeSalle
Leslie

For the first time, Spock knows happiness

◄ *Stardate 3417.3:* The *Enterprise* arrives at planet Omicron Ceti III, where Kirk expects to find all the colonists dead because of the deadly Berthold rays to which they have been exposed for three years. But when a landing party beams down, colony leader Elias Sandoval informs them that everyone on the planet is quite well— including Leila Kalomi, a young botanist with whom Spock had worked six years before. Leila leads Spock to a clump of plants that spray him with their spores, liberating the Vulcan's emotions. Spock expresses his long-suppressed love for Leila. Other members of the landing party are exposed, plants are beamed up to the *Enterprise,* and before long everyone except Kirk is affected. The captain discovers that violent emotional reactions are the antidote to the spores' effects, and tricks Spock into coming back aboard the Enterprise. He goads him into a fight, and barely avoids being killed by the Vulcan's superior strength. The conflict restores Spock to normal, and he assists Kirk in constructing an apparatus that frees the *Enterprise* crew and the colonists from the spores. ►

Fans of Mr. Spock had wanted him to show emotion ever since Harry Mudd insulted him in "Mudd's Women"— his joking with Yeoman Rand at the close of "The Enemy Within" and his bout with temporary insanity in "The Naked Time" only increased that desire. Here, at last, their wishes came true. Leila Kalomi had known Spock before, and had fallen in love with the Vulcan.

But under the influence of the spores, Spock looks at Leila and admits "I can *love* you" as his barriers melt away. We share his happiness because he is the embodiment of our fear of alienation.

In the midst of all this, Kirk is being deprived of the *Enterprise* by the spores. But *nothing* can separate Kirk from his responsibilities, and in attempting to take him over the spores sign their own death warrant. Kirk's love is the *Enterprise;* he has no peace without his ship and crew.

Spock is released from the spores' influence partially by guilt. The Vulcan first demonstrates his superhuman strength in "The Naked Time," when one blow sends the captain hurtling over the briefing room table. This time around he comes close to bashing Kirk's head in. The shock frees him from the spores' effects—and imprisons him once again within himself.

The final scenes between Spock and Leila are tremendously effective, thanks not only to the rapport between Leonard Nimoy and Jill Ireland but the retracked music of Alexander Courage.

The story outline and earliest first-draft script for "This Side of Paradise" were called "The Way of the Spores," and were very different from the final episode. In these early drafts Mr. Sulu was the central figure in love with the Eurasian beauty Leila. McCoy discovered an internal condition that would have necessitated Sulu's resignation from Starfleet service, had the spores not cured his condition. His illness gave Sulu a will to develop a relationship with Leila (just as similar circumstances would later affect McCoy's judgment in "For the World Is Hollow and I Have Touched the Sky").

The spores in the early drafts were a communal intelligence; when someone was possessed by them, that individual was granted telepathic abilities to link up with other possessed minds. The abilities of the spores to restore health were complete enough to enable them to return the dead to life.

The antidotes for the spores were either the possession of a certain blood type or the introduction of alcohol into the affected person. Kirk literally leaped upon Spock and forced liquor down his throat to restore the Vulcan to normal.

In a surprise ending, the spores were revealed to be benevolent, conscious entities who never intended to act against anyone's will.

"This Side of Paradise" marks one of the few occasions in which DeForest Kelley functions as a Southern gentleman, sipping mint juleps, letting his full accent show, and treating the audience to his endearing smile.

This is also one of the few times actor Eddie Paskey delivers dialogue as "Mr. Leslie." His recurring appearances help convey the impression that the *Enterprise* has a constant crew.

Jill Ireland (Leila) appeared in four episodes of "The Man from U.N.C.L.E.," as well as segments of "Night Gallery" and "Voyage to the Bottom of the Sea." Ms. Ireland is married to international movie star Charles Bronson.

Frank Overton (Elias Sandoval) appeared in one of the most memorable segments of "The Twilight Zone," "Walking Distance." He appeared with William Shatner in "Dick Powell Theater's" pilot "Colossus" in 1963, and can also be seen in episodes of "One Step Beyond," "Thriller," "The Invaders," and "The Twilight Zone."

Kirk—alone on the bridge

"THE DEVIL IN THE DARK"

#26

WRITER: Gene L. Coon
DIRECTOR: Joseph Pevney
PRINCIPALS: Kirk   Chief Engineer Vanderberg
            Spock   Lieutenant Commander Giotto
            McCoy   Ed Appel
            Scott   Schmitter
            Horta

◀ *Stardate 3196.1:* The pergium miners on planet Janus VI are being killed by an unknown creature that can burrow through stone. Chief mining engineer Vanderberg summons the *Enterprise* to assist in locating and killing the monster. When the creature steals a vital part of the PXK reactor, which regulates the mining colony's life-support functions, Spock realizes that they are dealing with an intelligent life form. After Kirk wounds the entity, Spock performs a Vulcan mind meld. He learns that the creature, which calls itself a "Horta," is killing only to prevent the destruction of its thousands of silicon eggs. McCoy using construction materials, heals the wounded Horta. The miners attack with the intention of killing the creature, but when they learn "she" is only a defensive mother and they have been killing her unborn children, they calm down. Vanderberg and his people agree to form a symbiotic relationship with the Horta. The freshly hatched children will dig the pergium—while the miners will sit back and become rich. ▶

The last "Outer Limits" episode produced was called "The Probe," and concerned an alien space probe that landed on Earth. The script called for an overgrown "microorganism" that was designed and built by artist Janos Prohaska, an expert in makeup and costume effects. Prohaska had done work for STAR TREK before he visited the office of producer-writer Gene L. Coon. Upon seeing the "monster suit," Coon wrote "The Devil in the Dark" for which Prohaska created the Horta ("The Outer Limits" costume had the suggestion of head and limbs; the Horta was constructed without such details, and allowed Prohaska to move more freely than he could in his earlier creation). Although the script progressed from first to final draft in only three days, "The Devil in the Dark" is one of the most intriguing and important episodes of "Star Trek."

"Trek" repeatedly explored the problem of prejudice and how we will deal with it when we venture out into space. "Xenophobia" (the fear of different life forms), "Trek" tells us, will be a thing of the past by the *Enterprise*'s era; at least applying to creatures with recognizable intelligence and technology. Suppose, however, a definitely hostile and dangerous life form is discovered. If

Tunnel of terror

its chemical structure and physical shape are sufficiently different from ours, would anyone (including Captain Kirk and Mr. Spock) care whether the entity's actions were rational, or would it be treated as a monster, hunted down and destroyed without any attempt to communicate with it?

We had already seen the bipedal "salt vampire" of "The Man Trap" treated in that manner. Like that creature, the Horta kills during the course of this episode and despite evidence that it possesses intelligence, no one questions its motivations. Even Mr. Spock, who has a hatred for violence and an expert's idea of how it feels to be different and unaccepted, has a surprising initial reaction as Kirk tells him he is alone with the creature. "Kill it, Captain," he shouts, "kill it quickly." Here, it is Kirk who makes the decision to give the creature the benefit of the doubt. When the Vulcan sees that his friend and commander is not in danger, he agrees to the "terrible, personal lowering of mental barriers" and communicates with the Horta. The dramatic device of the Vulcan mind meld, devised to allow Spock to perform "hypnosis" in "Dagger of the Mind," is transformed in this encounter with the Horta into one of the most magical attributes of the Vulcan: the ability to converse with and understand any life form he can trust and touch. This is the Vulcan credo of "infinite diversity in infinite combinations" in its first true appearance, which sets the stage for another magical episode—"Metamorphosis" (also written by Coon).

Although Leonard Nimoy's performance during the mind meld sequence is noteworthy, William Shatner's acting during the last half of this episode is one of the most amazing displays of the man's talents. While the scenes involving the hunt for the Horta were being shot, Shatner received a phone call informing him that his father had just passed away. Despite suggestions that production of the episode be halted, the actor insisted upon finishing his scenes for the day.

There are at least two different versions of the optical painting created to represent the underground mining complex. The most effective one is seen outside Vanderberg's office window. Despite the use of rocks and pipes to add depth to the paintings, these are the least successful optical paintings to appear on "Star Trek," although one did resurface in "The Gamesters of Triskelion."

This episode was also the source of one of Dr. McCoy's most memorable profundities: "I'm a doctor, not a bricklayer."

In the procession of security men we see two familiar faces. Along with the ever-present Eddie Paskey there is Barry Russo (Lieutenant Commander Giotto), who later returned to "Trek" promoted to Commodore Robert Wesley in "The Ultimate Computer."

Ken Lynch (Vanderberg) was regularly seen as a police lieutenant in "The Plainclothesman (1950–54), and appeared as a coordinator of the U.S. space program in the series "Men into Space" (which was science fiction when it was produced).

"ERRAND OF MERCY"

#27

WRITER: Gene L. Coon
DIRECTOR: John Newland
PRINCIPALS: Kirk   Trefayne
Spock   Ayelborne
Sulu   Commander Kor
Uhura   Claymare

◄ *Stardate 3198.4:* As hostilities between the United Federation of Planets and the Klingon empire reach their peak, the *Enterprise* is dispatched to the strategically located planet Organia. The Organian Council, four smiling, elderly men, seem strangely unconcerned about the prospect of war centering about their planet. Klingon Commander Kor, with an occupation force, invades Organia. Kirk and Spock go undercover, disguised as two traders, but are betrayed by the council and condemned to death. The Organians rescue them very easily. As the moment of all-out war approaches, the Organians reveal themselves as omnipotent beings of pure energy. Using their mental abilities, they neutralize all weapons. Kirk realizes with horror that part of him had been anticipating the hostilities; he is also relieved to know that from now on the Organians will be watching to see that things do not get out of hand. ►

"Errand of Mercy" introduced two important extremes of the "Star Trek" universe: the Klingons and the Organians. In creating each, writer Gene L. Coon fulfilled the need for continuing villains in "Trek," and provided a control to keep the good guys and villains from each other's throats.

There's an old saying that "absolute power corrupts absolutely." This is apparently true only on a human level—the Organians, being more than human, elect to use their power to stop humans from corrupting the galaxy with war. These mysterious beings find humans "most distasteful" to be around. Having long ago evolved beyond their need for physical bodies and their related limiting qualities, the Organians do not like to be reminded of what they once were.

To produce this episode's villains, take every prejudice man has ever developed. Combine these with generous helpings of grease and grime, aggressive instincts, a tight tribal culture, and the opinion that the entire universe is worthless except for their little corner . . . and you have the Klingons.

Stuck in the midst of these two vastly different alien races are Kirk and Spock. Watched and secretly despised by the Organians, hounded by the Klingons, they manage to retain their best "Why me?" expressions throughout.

A large part of "Errand of Mercy's" underlying horror is brought out by talented director John Newland, no stranger to the macabre. He created the TV series "Alcoa Presents," better known by its syndication title "One Step Beyond." His talents as creator/host/director were as important to this series as Gene Roddenberry's to "Star Trek" and Rod Serling's to "The Twilight Zone." Newland even appeared in an episode of "One Step Beyond," "The Sacred Mushroom." "One Step Beyond" is still one of the most horrifying series on TV, largely due to Newland's use of documented supernatural experiences as the basis for the show's episodes.

Guest star John Colicos (Kor) really walks away with this episode: calculating his characterization to provide the direct opposite of William Shatner's Captain Kirk, Colicos's every twisted expression is a delight to behold.

Two travelers

"THE CITY ON THE EDGE OF FOREVER"

||||||||||||||||||||||||||||||||||||||||| #28

WRITER: Harlan Ellison
DIRECTOR: Joseph Pevney
PRINCIPALS: Kirk   Uhura
            Spock   Lieutenant Galloway
            McCoy   Edith Keeler
            Scott   Rodent
            Sulu   Chapel

The Guardian of Forever

◄ *Stardate 3134.0:* While treating Sulu after an accident on the bridge, Dr. McCoy accidentally injects himself with an overdose of cordrazine, an experimental drug. In a delirious state, he transports down to the planet below, to which the *Enterprise* has come to investigate strange ripples in time. Beaming down with a landing party, Kirk and Spock discover a living machine known as the Guardian of Forever. When McCoy leaps through the machine's portal, he vanishes into the Earth's past. Due to something he does there, history is changed and the *Enterprise* ceases to exist. The stranded landing-party personnel decide to try to undo what McCoy has done. Kirk and Spock leap through the device, into New York of the Depression era. There, Kirk meets and falls in love with Edith Keller, a progressive social worker. Spock manages to use vintage 1930 equipment to construct a tricorder monitoring device, and while replaying footage from the machine, he discovers that Edith has two possible futures. She will either begin a pacifist movement that will delay U.S. entry into World War II long enough for Germany to win—or she will die in a traffic accident. She is the focal point in time to which Kirk and Spock have been drawn. In order for history to resume its natural course, Edith Keeler must die. Kirk commits the most difficult act of his life when he prevents McCoy from saving her. Returning through space and time, Kirk, Spock, and McCoy discover they have been successful in their mission. ►

The differences between Harlan Ellison's original script (which won the Writers' Guild of America Award for the most outstanding dramatic episode teleplay for 1967–68) and the completed episode, which, as adapted by Gene Roddenberry, won the 1968 International Hugo Science Fiction Award, have long been the subject of intense debates in "Star Trek" fandom. Nonetheless, "The City on the Edge of Forever" is widely regarded as the best "Trek" episode produced.

Harlan Ellison's original story outline and first-draft script are very different from the filmed version: Edith Keeler is present in the New York of 1930, an *Enterprise* crewman does go back into the past and change history,

followed by Kirk and Spock, but from there the script bears no resemblance to the produced version.

Ellison's original script is television writing at its best. An intense tale filled with dynamic characters and memorable dialogue, it would be right at home beside his two acclaimed scripts for "The Outer Limits" ("Demon with a Glass Hand" and "Soldier"). It would have provided any anthology series with its best episode. Unfortunately, it could not have worked within the "Star Trek" format as it had developed.

The original version was written in May 1966, when the only "Star Trek" episodes that had been produced were "The Cage" and "Where No Man Has Gone Before." Ellison had no other examples to go by, and since it was known at the time that many changes in the format were being introduced, he devoted most of his attention to telling his story.

In Ellison's version the *Enterprise* crewman who went back through time and space was Beckwith, a drug addict. This meant that the episode revolved about a topic the network was reluctant to feature. It also meant that in "Star Trek's" time drug addiction was still a problem, and that it was also present among starship crews. There were other differences, too: the Guardians were depicted as an alien race who controlled the techniques of traveling through time, and in the New York sequences, Spock's alien appearance caused more significant problems for the travelers. There were also other characters, in particular a legless World War I veteran named Rodent who aided Kirk and Spock in finding Beckwith.

Edith Keeler is an innocent focal point, unaware of the forces at work around her. Kirk knows that if Edith knew all the facts, she would jump in front of the truck herself, to save all those who would otherwise have died. This probability does not make things any easier for Kirk. In Ellison's first-draft script, Kirk froze at the crucial moment; it was Spock who prevented Edith's rescue. (This ending, beautifully written by Ellison, would not have worked for "Star Trek." Although the audience would have sympathized with Captain Kirk, viewers would never again have been able to accept him as the prime mover of the series' events.) In the final version, Kirk *does* stop McCoy and thus fulfills his command responsibilities. In this moment he both sacrifices his world—and regains it.

In one respect it is easy to imagine Mr. Spock taking the initiative because the Vulcan could have communicated with nobody but his captain on Earth—and he would have ceased to think of Kirk in that role had Kirk failed to act out of loyalty to the universe. The episode emphasizes the ironic humor of Spock's situation. The Vulcan, with all his technical knowledge, is forced to find employment as a janitor and handyman, and in one of the most enjoyable comedy sequences in "Star Trek," savors a confrontation with a New York City patrolman who sees nothing but his ears and Kirk's stolen clothes.

This is one of the few "Star Trek" episodes that lent itself to the use of stock footage, including the footage of the Brooklyn Bridge. The historical "playbacks" of the Guardian's screen also include scenes from many old motion pictures.

Jerry Finnerman's cinematography is especially won-

Dr. McCoy, lost in time

derful in this episode. Specialized lighting and focal techniques give "City" an almost mystical visual quality.

As Kirk looks up into the sky at the end of the episode's teaser the camera follows his gaze in an optically achieved transition to a starry background that is very similar to a "Twilight Zone"—style fadeout.

Joan Collins (Edith Keeler) made her film debut in Britain in 1952. Upon her arrival in the United States, she appeared in such films as *Land of the Pharaohs* and *The Girl in the Red Velvet Swing*, in addition to a large number of other features for 20th Century-Fox. She was the female lead in *Quest for Love*, a romantic science fiction film involving a love affair spanning two parallel universes. On television she also appeared in episodes of "Mission: Impossible" (as a young spy who is killed after Jim Phelps falls in love with her), "The Man from U.N.C.L.E.," and "Batman," before achieving superstar status in "Dynasty."

Harlan Ellison is one of today's most prolific, honored, and controversial creators of speculative fiction—whose credits are too many to be covered adequately in the space available. His television contributions include an adaptation of his study of teenage gangs entitled "Memos from Purgatory" for "The Alfred Hitchcock Hour," featuring Walter Koenig.

Working with "stone knives and bearskins"

"OPERATION: ANNIHILATE!"

██ #29

WRITER: Stephen W. Carabatsos
DIRECTOR: Herschel Daugherty
PRINCIPALS: Kirk   Chapel
           Spock   Kartan
           McCoy   Peter Kirk
           Scott   Aurelan Kirk
           Sulu   Yeoman Zahra Jamal
           Uhura

◄ *Stardate 3287.2:* The planet Deneva, home of Captain Kirk's brother George and his family, is in the path of an interplanetary epidemic of mass insanity. Approaching the planet, the *Enterprise* intercepts a radio message from a Denevan pilot who deliberately steers his ship into the sun—destroying himself and an unknown danger. Beaming down with a landing party, Kirk discovers his brother dead, his sister-in-law Aurelan dying, and his nephew Peter unconscious. Deneva has been invaded by bat-size, amoeba-like aliens that intertwine with the human nervous system, manipulating their victims whom they cause excruciating pain. Spock is attacked and infected by one of the creatures. Kirk, remembering the Denevan who flew into the sun, theorizes that the creatures, who have proven resistant to everything Dr. McCoy has thrown at them, may be sensitive to intense light. Spock volunteers to be McCoy's guinea pig. The experiment works—but Spock has been blinded by exposure to the light. Too late, McCoy discovers that only ultraviolet light is needed to kill the creatures. A chain of trimagnesite satellites is orbited to free the Denevans from their nightmare—just as a fully sighted Spock returns to the bridge. Vulcans, it turns out, developed an extra eyelid to protect themselves from the harsh sunlight on their world. ►

The first-draft script, titled "Operation: Destroy," lacked any reference to Captain Kirk's brother. In that version, Aurelan was in love with Kartan, the young Denevan who flew his ship into the sun to escape the creatures' control. Aurelan and her father, who were not infected, were brought aboard the *Enterprise* and took part in the research that eventually destroyed the creatures. The final episode is much more meaningful, thanks to a consolidation of story elements and the addition of George Samuel Kirk.

James Kirk's brother is introduced to us in conversation in "What Are Little Girls Made Of?" There, it is established that George (only Jim calls him "Sam"), his wife, and three children saw the captain off on his five-year mission. We know virtually nothing about Kirk the family man, except that some of his relatives were killed on Tarsus IV years before he signed on the Enterprise.

Experiencing the loss of his brother with the captain makes us realize that Jim Kirk is as human as the rest of us, despite his carefully developed defense shields.

The demands upon James Kirk in this episode were brought beautifully to life by Shatner's performance, aided by what must be the most atypical bit of casting in "Star Trek." Despite the usual terrifying production deadlines, Shatner took time out to appear as the dead body of George Samuel Kirk, complete with grayed hair and mustache.

Kirk knows that if he cannot kill the creatures, he will be forced to destroy the planet Deneva and all its infected inhabitants to stop the spread of the "plague." Mr. Spock, also infected, is himself in danger. Add to this the loss of his brother, and Kirk's situation in this episode makes him a prime candidate for a vacation on Elba Two. Shatner's performance here is similar to the one he delivered in "The Enemy Within," although there he portrayed Kirk as an incomplete individual. During this episode, Kirk's strengths are still apparent, even though he is torn apart by the dual demands of his personal grief and the responsibilities of command.

"Operation: Annihilate!" was also a demanding episode for actor Leonard Nimoy. Throughout most of the story, Spock was fighting back intense agony. The actor's use of short, strangled movements, twitches, and special eye movements made the audience aware of what Spock was going through. Spock's apologetic and ironic approach to his predicament, along with the Vulcan's atypically wild and undisciplined attempt to take over the *Enterprise*, proved just as effective.

Spock—attacked by the flying creatures

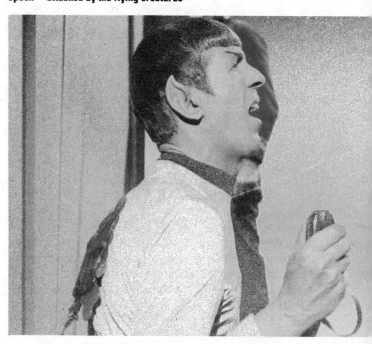

Exterior Deneva locations were photographed at the California headquarters of the T.R.W. Corporation. A series of symmetrical buildings, this modern complex provided the ideal surroundings for a colony of the future.

The parasitic aliens were marionettes constructed by Wah Chang, suspended from wires and swung back and forth across the set.

A surviving "blooper" features producer Roddenberry standing on a staircase used in this episode while dubbed voices (from the soundtrack of "Patterns of Force") shout "Hail the Führer."

FIRST SEASON PRODUCTION CREDITS

PRODUCERS Gene Roddenberry, Gene L. Coon
EXECUTIVE PRODUCER Gene Roddenberry
STAR TREK CREATED BY Gene Roddenberry
ASSOCIATE PRODUCERS Robert H. Justman, John D. F. Black
SCRIPT CONSULTANT Steven W. Carabatsos
THEME MUSIC COMPOSED BY Alexander Courage
MUSIC COMPOSED AND CONDUCTED BY Various
DIRECTOR OF PHOTOGRAPHY Jerry Finnerman
ART DIRECTORS Roland M. Brooks, Walter M. Jefferies
FILM EDITORS Robert L. Swanson, Fabian Tjordmann, Frank P. Keller, Bruch Schoengarth
ASSISTANT TO THE PRODUCER Edward K. Milkis
ASSISTANT DIRECTORS Gregg Peters, Michael S. Glick
SET DECORATORS Carl F. Biddiscombe, Marvin March
COSTUMES CREATED BY William Ware Theiss
POST PRODUCTION EXECUTIVE Bill Heath
MUSIC EDITORS Robert H. Raff, Jim Henrickson
SOUND EDITORS Joseph G. Sorokin, Douglas H. Grindstaff

SOUND MIXERS Jack F. Lilly, Cameron McCulloch
PHOTOGRAPHIC EFFECTS Various
SCRIPT SUPERVISOR George A. Rutter
MUSIC CONSULTANT Wilbur Hatch
MUSIC COORDINATOR Julian Davidson
SPECIAL EFFECTS Jim Rugg
PROPERTY MASTER Irving A. Feinberg
GAFFER George H. Merhoff
HEAD GRIP George Rader
PRODUCTION SUPERVISOR Bernard A. Widin
MAKEUP ARTIST Fred B. Phillips, SMA
HAIRSTYLES Virginia Darcy, CHS
WARDROBE MISTRESS Margaret Makau
CASTING Joseph D'Agosta
SOUND Glen Glenn Sound Co.
A Desilu Production in Association with Norway Corp.
Herbert F. Solow, executive in charge of production

7

SECOND SEASON

On March 14, 1967, NBC held its annual affiliates convention to inform all member television stations what the network's official schedule would be for the coming season. The schedule announced included 17 old series and 8 new ones. "Star Trek" was on the list of series that would be continued, but its old time slot of Thursday at 8:30 P.M. (Eastern Standard Time) was now occupied by another new NBC entry, "Ironside." "Star Trek," it was announced, had been moved to Friday evenings, 8:30–9:30 P.M. (E.S.T.).

NBC knew from the fan mail written to the series' stars and the network that most "Trek" viewers were teenagers, ranging from junior high school to university ages. Friday was a special night for students. There was no homework to do overnight and no tests the next day. Such things could be worried about on Sunday evenings. Given the choice between staying home to see a TV program or going out, most would choose the latter. This raises the question why NBC picked this time slot for "Star Trek." It was not that the network was disenchanted with the series—at least, not in print. NBC, in fact, seemed proud of the series, as shown by the network's promotional brochure for "Star Trek's" 1967–68 television season.

The brochure indicated that "Star Trek" had been nominated for five Emmy Awards during its first season on television: best dramatic series, outstanding supporting performance by a dramatic actor (Leonard Nimoy), special photographic effects, special mechanical effects, and film and sound editing.

Leonard Nimoy, NBC stated, had been honored with a tour of the Goddard Space Flight Center in Washington, D.C., by the National Space Club, and a dinner at which Vice-President Hubert Humphrey was the main speaker. Dr. Isaac Asimov was cited in the booklet as having called "Star Trek" "the first good television science fiction." The brochure also acknowledged that "Star Trek" was very popular in college dormitories and lounges.

Most important, the huge volume of fan mail received by the network was officially acknowledged by NBC. These letters indicated that most "Star Trek" viewers were regular watchers of the show and had their favorite performers. NBC was careful to stress that every cast member would be returning for the series' second season (no mention was made of Yeoman Janice Rand). The brochure assured network affiliates that Dr. McCoy, Mr. Sulu, Mr. Scott, and Lieutenant Uhura would each be the central character in an episode during the coming season. Mr. Scott became the central figure in "Wolf in the Fold," and McCoy was the hero of the third season's "For the World Is Hollow and I Have Touched the Sky," but for fans of Sulu and Uhura, this promise was never kept.

One of the most surprising network booklets devoted to "Star Trek" was prepared in August 1967 by the television network sales planning department of NBC. The booklet, called "Star Trek Mail Call," is exclusively concerned with the large amount of fan mail that had been sent on behalf of the show. The network, according to the brochure, was proud of the number of letters, their quality, and the cross section of people who were sending them. The cover of the booklet was blank except for two facsimile "postage stamps" of Captain Kirk and Mr. Spock. The "postmark" read "NBC Television Network, August 1967, N.Y., Star Trek Mail Call."

The first page acknowledged that the network had received 29,000 pieces of mail from "Trek" fans during the show's first year. The letters, said the network, had come from viewers who were deeply involved in "Star Trek." NBC was so impressed with this fan following that it honored "Trek" by comparing it to the only NBC series of that time to draw more fan response—"The Monkees."

The booklet, written largely for prospective sponsors, stated that much of "Star Trek's" fan mail was written by people who were associated in some way with the space program. Letters also came from students, housewives, and many others with scientific or intellectual backgrounds.

Television series and feature films aimed at intellectual audiences had failed in the past, the booklet stated. "Star Trek," however, had proven itself to be "one of America's best liked television programs. The "Trek" audience was specifically described as decision-makers—people who would be attractive to potential sponsors.

In addition to the categories of viewers mentioned earlier, the booklet also carried examples of letters received. Frequently used words included "logical" and "adult," "good adult escape," "believable conflict," "fascinating" (probably a Vulcan fan letter), and "thought provoking." In addition, letters poured in citing Shatner, Nimoy, and the series' other principals as convincing and skilled performers. The praise came from all parts of the country. Along with the letters, seven petitions were selected and printed in the booklet. One of these described how the entire city of Las Vegas came to a standstill whenever "Star Trek" was televised. School courses were changed to allow people to see "Trek." A local station had preempted "Star Trek" on a holiday to show a feature film instead, and because of numerous phone calls, the station was forced to change its schedule and show "Star Trek" later in the evening. People bought theater tickets only if they did not conflict with "Star Trek." It was almost a direct parallel to the days of old radio, when theaters closed so that everyone could listen to the popular "Amos 'n Andy" series.

Yet in December 1967, after all the fuss NBC had made about their high opinion of "Star Trek" and its ability to attract sponsors, "Trek" fans everywhere received a letter from John and Bjo Trimble warning that the series was again facing disaster. The letter announced that surveys taken in magazines indicated that while "Trek" was popular with the public, the Nielsen ratings were saying otherwise. The network, of course, was going by the Nielsens, and would continue to do so unless faced with another avalanche of fan mail pleading "Star Trek's" case.

Making sure that "Trek" remained on the air, the letter said, was a constant job that had to be accomplished by the fans. The threats of outright cancellation or conversion of the series into a "kiddie" format were both raised again. "Formula" TV shows were desirable to the networks and sponsors, the letter continued: "Star Trek's" fans had come to love the show as an eloquent experiment in creating a worthwhile future.

The Trimbles' letter was more ominous than the earlier letter from "the Committee," confirming that the second season ratings were not as high as they were expected to have been. The letter provided two suggestions for improving the situation.

First, the letter suggested that Gene Roddenberry should have a more direct hand in "Star Trek." If he could be encouraged to devote his complete attention to the series once more, as he had done during the first half of the first season, "Trek" would have its originator calling the shots again.

But the main problem was cited as "Star Trek's" Friday night time slot.

The puzzling thing about this letter is that it postdated NBC's "Star Trek Mail Call" pamphlet. The data discussed in that booklet indicated the same thing the Trimble letter was saying: that young, dynamic personalities tended to watch "Star Trek." Yet still, NBC had placed the show in a time slot where it was least likely to attract those viewers. The Trimble letter was not concerned with finding a reason for this. Its concern was to inform "Star Trek" fans of the unpleasant reality.

Once again, time was short. Television series are generally renewed in January or February, the letter revealed. The individual craftsmen who work in the television industry are likely to find other work if their current series seems to be in danger of cancellation. Even if these individuals can be replaced, the letter stated, their loss to the production would create morale problems for the remaining staffers.

The letter was a thorough and ambitious undertaking, a type of mail-order "midnight ride of Paul Revere." Fans had to rouse the populace and warn them that only *they* could help. To aid in this task, the Trimbles' letter was mailed along with a supplementary page entitled "How to Write Effective Letters to Save 'Star Trek,' " which outlined the fundamentals of what network and publicity people looked for in fan mail. On the other side of this sheet were bits of advice that assisted in making it clear that procrastination at that point could kill "Star Trek" as easily as the networks could.

Ensign Pavel Chekov (Walter Koenig)

Five addresses were recommended as main "targets" for the letters: (1) the president of NBC; (2) RCA (NBC's parent organization); (3) RCA's ad agency; and (4 and 5) two high-ranking people within NBC. In addition, fans were encouraged to appeal to local NBC affiliate stations, TV columnists, and *TV Guide* magazine. It was a well-conceived program that hurriedly educated the fans about what had to be done and how they should go about doing it.

The strategy worked better than expected. Rumors from New York and California referred to the many thousands of letters, cards, and phone calls that had been received, and how many hours were spent at NBC reading the mail, tabulating the letters, and writing related memos. All the fuss resulted in "Star Trek" being renewed once again.

Many changes in production personnel were made in the series' second season. Gene L. Coon, who had succeeded Roddenberry as "Trek's" producer during the first season, left and was in turn succeeded by John Meredyth Lucas. (Coon would continue to write for "Star Trek" during the series' second season, contributing to "Metamorphosis," "Who Mourns For Adonais?", "The Apple," "Bread and Circuses," and "A Piece of the Action.") John Meredyth Lucas's contributions to "Trek's" second season were three-fold. In addition to serving as producer, he also wrote ("The Changeling" and "Patterns of Force") and directed ("The Ultimate Computer"). He would also maintain his affiliation with "Star Trek" throughout the series' third season.

Steven W. Carabatsos, the series' script consultant during the first production season, was succeeded by D. C. Fontana. Desilu art director Rolland M. Brooks, who had also worked on "Mission: Impossible," left "Star Trek" during the first season. Walter M. Jefferies was the series' sole art director during the second production season. Music editor Robert H. Raff also ended his affiliation during the series' first season. He was succeeded by Jim Henrickson. At this point, Desilu also ceased to exist, and "Star Trek" became a Paramount production.

But the show's most visible change was the addition of Ensign Pavel Chekov, in the person of actor Walter Koenig.

Walter Koenig earned his B.A. degree in psychology before traveling to New York City and enrolling in the Neighborhood Playhouse, a famous school for actors. During his second year there, he was awarded a scholarship and worked as a hospital orderly to earn enough money for his living expenses. After appearing in off-Broadway productions for two years, Walter returned to Los Angeles, where he landed his initial television assignments.

Considering the degree of Mr. Chekov's popularity on "Star Trek," it is difficult to recall that an entire season of the series was done without him. The first official announcement of Chekov's arrival came in a press release issued by NBC on September 18, 1967.

According to NBC, a staff reporter for *Pravda*, the Russian newspaper, had reviewed a "Star Trek" episode he had seen televised in Germany. The critic was understandably upset at seeing an internationally (and interplanetarily) staffed spaceship without a Russian prominently in view. The *Pravda* reporter mentioned that since "Star Trek" is a show about space and space exploration, there should *certainly* be a Russian aboard since Russia was the first nation to begin man's ventures into outer space. The news report had far-reaching effects, and when Gene Roddenberry saw it, he could not help but agree.

When "Amok Time" was first screened over the Labor Day weekend in 1967 at the New York World Science Fiction Convention, one of the most significant surprises was the addition of Chekov to the *Enterprise* crew. Rumors had been circulating for a month before the convention that another crewman would be signing on for the purpose of attracting a larger number of younger, female viewers. At NYCON, everyone who saw "Amok Time" enjoyed Chekov's contributions to the episode and accurately anticipated that many future good moments would be provided by the ensign.

"CATSPAW"

WRITER: Robert Bloch
DIRECTOR: Joseph Pevney
PRINCIPALS: Kirk   Chekov
            Spock   Jackson
            McCoy   Lieutenant DeSalle
            Scott   Sylvia
            Sulu   Korob
            Uhura   Lieutenant Kyle

Spock and Kirk: all chained up with no place to go

◄ *Stardate 3018.2:* On planet Pyris VII, Kirk, Spock, and McCoy encounter a haunted castle and crewmen Sulu and Scott, who have been transformed into "zombies." Aliens Korob and Sylvia—disguised as a warlock and a witch—are responsible for the "trick or treat" trappings, using supernatural devices to terrify the men of the *Enterprise*. Only Spock is unaffected by their scare tactics. The aliens are on a mission of conquest, and have used a matter transmuter to assume human form. Sylvia, affected by her new body, attempts to ensnare Kirk into becoming her partner and lover. When Korob aids Kirk and company to escape, Sylvia changes into a gigantic black cat and crushes him. Kirk destroys the "magic wand" transmuter device, causing the castle to vanish and the aliens to resume their actual forms. In reality, they are fragile creatures and are destroyed by the planet's atmosphere. Sulu and Scotty are returned to normal, and "Halloween" is over. ►

This episode was conceived as "Star Trek's" Halloween segment for 1967. Everything the aliens devised within their custom-made haunted house is designed to chill the blood of Kirk and his people. The *Enterprise* crew, however, tend to think more in terms of science than superstition—and scaring Mr. Spock is a hopeless task. The Vulcan, who knows a good deal about Earth's history and customs, is completely in the dark when it comes to Terran superstitions. Perhaps he chooses to ignore the less scientific facets of his Terran education.

Ironically, the aliens must use shape-changing to survive in an Earth-type environment; this procedure is well known within Terran superstition, where it is referred to as "transvection" and generally applies to humans who change themselves into animals for evil purposes. The same device is used here and in "Assignment: Earth" to inform the audience of the shape-changing activities in the story. A piece of jewelry around the neck of the animal counterpart is later seen around the neck of the human after the transformation has been made.

Although the miniature corridor and cat look impressive in slow motion, the "giant cat" illusion is somewhat disappointing; no attempt is made to insert the actors into the same shot via mattes or split screen. The use of an offstage shadow, or an amplified "meow," proves inadequate in convincing us the cat is nearing the *Enterprise* crew.

The beautifully fashioned silver *Enterprise* charm is currently in the Smithsonian Institution's Air and Space Museum, still laminated into the transparent lucite block seen in the episode.

The alien forms of Korob and Sylvia are effective, though again ultimately disappointing. They are marionettes, composed of blue fluff, pipe cleaners, crab pincers, and other materials. The use of marionettes to depict aliens can be spectacular (as in *Close Encounters of the Third Kind*) or obviously accomplished to achieve an effect within a television budget (as in this episode, and in "The Outer Limits" segment "Cold Hands, Warm Heart"). Though convincingly alien, the creatures here were operated with thick, black threads that are painfully obvious even after the puppets have stopped moving.

An amusing moment occurs as Kirk is chained to a wall near McCoy and Spock. The captain begins to refer to McCoy as "Bones," until he notices a skeleton also chained to the wall. For the rest of the episode he refers to the doctor only as "McCoy" or "Doc."

Guest star Theo Marcuse (Korob) appeared in "Voyage to the Bottom of the Sea," "The Twilight Zone" ("To Serve Man" and "The Trade-Ins"), "The Time Tunnel" ("Devil's Island"), "The Invaders" ("The Leeches"), and several segments of "The Man from U.N.C.L.E." Antoinette Bower (Sylvia) appears in "Thriller" episodes "Waxworks" and "The Return of Andrew Bentley."

"METAMORPHOSIS"

████████████████████████████ **#31**

WRITER: Gene L. Coon
DIRECTOR: Ralph Senensky
PRINCIPALS: Kirk   Sulu
           Spock   Uhura
           McCoy   Nancy Hedford
           Scott   Zefram Cochrane

◄ *Stardate 3219.4:* The shuttlecraft *Galileo* is transporting ailing Assistant Federation Commissioner Nancy Hedford back to the *Enterprise* when it is suddenly drawn off course by a mysterious cloud creature. After depositing the shuttle on planet Gamma Canaris N, the entity vanishes. Kirk, Spock, McCoy, and Commissioner Hedford then meet another castaway—revealed as Zefram Cochrane, the famed scientist from Alpha Centauri who discovered space-warp drive over 100 years ago. At the age of 87, Cochrane decided that he wanted to die in outer space, so he boarded a ship and headed away from Alpha Centauri, only to be waylaid by the cloud creature, which Cochrane calls the Companion. Kirk communicates with the Companion by means of a universal translator and learns that the entity is in love with Cochrane. Cochrane is unable to accept this, especially since he is falling in love with Nancy Hedford. When Nancy's death is imminent, the Companion forsakes its immortal state to unite with the Earthwoman. Cochrane accepts the love of the Companion/Nancy and stays on the planet with her. ►

"Metamorphosis" is one of the most sensitive episodes of "Star Trek." As in his script for "The Devil in the Dark," writer Gene Coon here spoke out in a poetic editorial against mankind's talent of making enemies of creatures physically different from us. This is another application of the Vulcan principle of IDIC: Infinite Diversity in Infinite Combinations. In both adventures, Mr. Spock identifies closely with the entities targeted by prejudice: if his parents had given in to the same irrational attitudes, he never would have been born.

The "interracial romance" here is actually a complex triangle. Cochrane, though a native of Alpha Centauri, obviously comes from Terran stock: the Companion is more outwardly alien to us. Nancy Hedford *is* Terran, but her lack of familiarity with love makes her perhaps the most alien of the trio. She has never had time for romance, electing instead to devote herself to ending conflicts throughout the universe.

At first, Cochrane is overcome by prejudice regarding the Companion's attachment to him. The scientist's momentary lapse takes place despite his familiarity with other races. Part of his attitude may have been due to anger he felt at his own refusal to consider what the Companion actually thought about him. The first-draft script for this episode has one main difference from the final version: Scotty was included in the shuttle crew. The engineer would have enjoyed meeting Zefram Cochrane and talking shop with him. It was Scotty who got "zapped" by the companion and, together with Mr. Spock, constructed the device with which they hoped to short-circuit the entity.

Guest star Glenn Corbett (Cochrane) handles his role just right: at first he seems tired and bored, a man who has been weakened by such a long time away from his fellow creatures. Later his characterization becomes stronger, strengthened by human companionship and his growing love for Nancy Hedford.

Corbett is best remembered for his recurring role as Linc Chase in "Route 66" (1963–64). He was also a star of the series "The Road West" (1966–67), in which he played Chance Reynolds (his sister in the series was portrayed by Kathryn Hays). He also appeared in "Night Gallery" ("Brenda," with Barbara Babcock), "Land of the Giants" ("The Weird World," in which he also plays a space traveler trapped away from his native planet), and "The Man from U.N.C.L.E." ("The Hong Kong Shilling Affair"). Elinor Donahue (Nancy Hedford) is best remembered for her regular role as Betty Anderson in "Father Knows Best."

"Metamorphosis" was the first "Trek" segment to be scored by composer George Duning, whose other contributions to the series were just as sensitive. Duning is best known for his motion-picture scores, including *The Devil at Four O'Clock* (1961, Columbia), the supernatural comedy *Bell, Book and Candle* (1958, Columbia) and *Picnic* (1956, Columbia).

Spock and Kirk in front of Zefram Cochrane's house

"FRIDAY'S CHILD"

#32

WRITER: D. C. Fontana
DIRECTOR: Joseph Pevney
PRINCIPALS: Kirk   Eleen
            Spock   Kras
            McCoy   Maab
            Scott   Keel
            Sulu   Akaar
            Uhura   Duur
            Chekov   Grant

◄ *Stardate 3497.2:* The *Enterprise* visits planet Capella IV to prevent the Klingons from forming an alliance with the Capellans, a warlike but honorable people. When Captain Kirk prevents the slaughter of Eleen, the pregnant wife of deposed High Teer Akaar, he violates Capellan tradition. Kras, a visiting Klingon, is quick to capitalize on the situation, and as a result of his interference the landing party and Eleen become hunted criminals. After McCoy delivers Eleen's baby, she escapes and returns to the Capellans, telling them both the humans and her child are dead. The Klingon kills the current Teer—and then is himself killed. Eleen's newborn son, named "Leonard James Akaar," is named the new ruler. Kirk and his party leave Capella, having arranged diplomatic relations with the planet's government. ►

Devising a defense

"Friday's Child" deals realistically with the concept that, as we venture out into space, we are bound to experience cultures whose customs will seem at least a bit odd to Terrans. To illustrate this, the episode begins with a briefing at which Kirk and his people become acquainted with the proper way to stay respected (and alive) on Capella IV. Kirk's assignment in this adventure is similar to those of the first captains who came in contact with the natives of the South Sea Islands. After he thoroughly botches things, the landing party must face the added complications of a Klingon presence and Eleen's impending childbirth in this, the series' 1967 Christmas episode.

In the end everything works out smoothly, thanks to the Klingon urge for power. Kras the Klingon has misjudged the Capellans, who may like to fight but who also hate deceit. Everyone is left happy and content with the exception of Mr. Spock—forced to undergo the ordeal of holding a human baby.

The first draft of "Friday's Child" has Akaar's brother, "Maab," scheming with the Klingon "Keel" to kill Akaar on the planet "Ceres VII." Eleen hated her baby in this draft, and took it to Maab for him to kill in exchange for permitting her to live. McCoy, Kirk, and Spock were captured while attempting to rescue the child. The status-seeking Eleen outfoxed herself as Maab had her executed for committing adultery. The baby became the new Teer, while Eleen's father became the child's regent. Maab was executed by his people for attempting to plot with the Klingons. Kirk and company were pardoned and left as friends.

The Klingon battle cruiser did not make its debut until the third-season "Trek" episode "Elaan of Troyius": in this show a "fill-in" design was used, an animated flat-iron shape with a rear fin that resembles something out of the 1939 *Buck Rogers* serial. Glowing a bright orange on the *Enterprise* viewscreen, it is seen for several seconds and vanishes without ever becoming distinct.

Most of the outdoor sequences were again filmed at Vasquez Rocks, also seen in "Shore Leave," "Arena," and "The Alternative Factor."

Guest star Julie Newmar (Eleen) is a talented dancer and designer of clothes in addition to being a fine dramatic actress and comedienne. She has appeared in motion pictures since the early 1950s, including *Seven Brides for Seven Brothers* and *The Marriage-Go-Round,* and is best known to TV audiences for her portrayal of Catwoman on several episodes of "Batman."

Tige Andrews (Kras the Klingon) has been seen on television since he began his career as "Tiger" Andrews as a member of Sergeant Bilko's platoon on "The Phil Silvers Show." He later founded "The Mod Squad" (a series initially produced and written by Harve Bennett) as Captain Adam Greer.

"WHO MOURNS FOR ADONAIS?"

▮▮▮▮▮▮▮▮▮▮▮▮▮▮▮▮▮▮▮▮▮▮▮▮▮▮▮▮▮▮▮ **#33**

WRITERS: Gilbert A. Ralston, Gene L. Coon (story by Gilbert A. Ralston)
DIRECTOR: Marc Daniels
PRINCIPALS:

Kirk	Uhura
Spock	Chekov
McCoy	Apollo
Scott	Lieutenant Carolyn Palamas
Sulu	Lieutenant Kyle

Chekov, Kirk, & Scotty encounter a god

◄ *Stardate 3468.1:* In the vicinity of planet Pollux IV, the *Enterprise* encounters a huge, green hand that materializes in space and holds the starship motionless. The "hand" is not flesh and blood, but a form of energy belonging to a humanoid figure who identifies himself as the god Apollo, last survivor of the band of space travelers who visited old Earth and dwelt on Mount Olympus. He declares the *Enterprise* crew to be his "children," who will now stay on Pollux IV and worship him. When Mr. Scott objects to the attention Apollo shows to Lieutenant Carolyn Palamas, he is hurled through the air by a thunderbolt from Apollo's hand. The "god" also demonstrates other abilities, including the power to grow to giant size at will. Kirk orders Lieutenant Palamas, who has fallen in love with Apollo, to reject him. Then, using the *Enterprise*'s phasers, he destroys Apollo's temple, the source of the entity's abilities. Seeing that he has lost both his worshipers and his love, Apollo discontinues his physical existence to join his fellow gods. ►

The "ancient astronaut" theory postulates that space travelers visited Earth many centuries ago, and were accepted as gods by our ancestors. In the era of the United Federation of Planets, however, such an entity would be greeted and invited to join the organization as an equal member.

The United Federation of Planets governs itself with laws that owe much to the teachings that Apollo and his companions left on Earth. Mr. Spock would surely have realized this and tried his best to communicate peacefully with Apollo, had the alien not attacked the *Enterprise,* making instant enemies of Kirk and Spock and setting the stage for his own defeat. Apollo's destruction leaves Kirk stunned, and Carolyn in a state of shock; no one benefits from the *Enterprise*'s "victory" over the immortal. The Federation loses a powerful ally, to say nothing of his unfulfilled potential to become the greatest historian in the galaxy.

Montgomery Scott's attachment for Carolyn Palamas is the engineer's first entanglement with a woman in "Star Trek." His later involvement with Mira Romaine in "The Lights of Zetar" is one of the few other times we see Scotty devoting his attentions to ladies other than the *Enterprise.*

Fred Steiner's score for this episode is among the strongest in the entire series, and sections of it are present in many later "Star Trek" segments, including "Requiem for Methuselah."

"Who Mourns for Adonais?" has some well-executed photographic effects. Apollo's transformation into a giant is produced with a combination of clever camera angles and editing (we do not see him growing) and traveling mattes (standing in front of the landing party, looking down on them). Scotty's backflip after being hit by Apollo's (animated) energy bolt was actually executed by a stunt double wearing a special harness with which he was pulled backward on cue.

Apollo's temple was constructed on an indoor studio set. Swaying trees (courtesy of hidden stagehands) and dubbed-in bird sounds were combined with stock footage of an outdoor lake and adequately conveyed the illusion of being outdoors.

It is somewhat surprising that the scene in which Carolyn is ravaged by the wind, thunder, and lightning of Apollo was not snipped by network censors. One casualty of the episode, though, was the first-draft script's ending, in which Dr. McCoy proclaims that Carolyn is pregnant.

Guest star Michael Forest (Apollo) conveys moments of rage, resignation, and sensitivity with equal aptitude throughout the entire episode, thoroughly succeeding in his portrayal of a character who is more than human. Leslie Parrish (Lieutenant Carolyn Palamas) also runs the gamut of emotions, from cool professionalism to blatant hero worship.

"AMOK TIME"

||||||||||||||||||||||||||||||||||||||| **#34**

WRITER: Theodore Sturgeon
DIRECTOR: Joseph Pevney
PRINCIPALS: Kirk   Chapel
Spock   T'Pring
McCoy   T'Pau
Sulu   Stonn
Uhura   Admiral Komack
Chekov

◀ *Stardate 3372.7:* When Mr. Spock starts behaving oddly, Captain Kirk asks Dr. McCoy to examine the Vulcan. McCoy reports that Spock is undergoing internal processes that will be fatal if they continue. Spock explains that he has entered *pon farr,* the Vulcan mating cycle. If he does not return to Vulcan immediately to fulfill rituals and obligations that will culminate in his taking a wife, he will die. The captain disobeys direct orders from Starfleet, risking his career, and takes Spock to Vulcan instead of proceeding to inauguration ceremonies on Altair VI. Kirk and McCoy are invited to accompany Spock to Vulcan to witness the marriage *koon-ut-kal-if-fee.* T'Pau, an esteemed political figure in Federation circles, conducts the ceremony. It is not as placid or simple as Kirk expects it to be. T'Pring, Spock's betrothed since childhood, invokes her right to ritual combat, demanding that Spock fight a champion of her choosing to win her—and she surprises all by selecting Kirk as her champion. The captain agrees, only to discover the fight is to the death. Pleading that Vulcan's thin atmosphere places Kirk at a disadvantage, McCoy injects him with a tri-ox compound.

The combat begins—and Spock, deep in the *plak tow* (blood fever) kills his captain. The grief cancels his mating urge, and Spock returns to the *Enterprise*—to discover Kirk is really alive and well. The overjoyed Vulcan shows the first moment of emotion he has ever expressed on the *Enterprise* of his own accord. McCoy had injected Kirk with a knockout drug—not a tri-ox compound. Kirk's professional neck is saved as Starfleet Command approves T'Pau's request for the *Enterprise* to divert to Vulcan. ▶

As Mr. Spock evolved throughout the first season of "Star Trek," the series' fans began to develop an intense curiosity about his planet, Vulcan. If Spock, being only half-Vulcan, could do so many interesting things, what would full-blooded Vulcans be capable of? How would they live? What would their planet be like? While the first-season "Trek" episodes were being rerun on NBC, the first rumors of "Amok Time" leaked out to fandom. During the coming season there would be an episode that would actually take place on the planet Vulcan.

At the 1967 World Science Fiction Convention held in New York over the Labor Day weekend, "Amok Time" was shown for the first time, personally introduced by Gene Roddenberry. Some viewers reacted with surprise on seeing the episode begin aboard the *Enterprise,* rather than on Vulcan. After witnessing Spock's deterioration, most people stopped guessing what was going to happen until after the episode was over. Some expected to see Vulcans by the dozens, preferably in a city environment with new sets and optical paintings. Afterward there was speculation about the changes that might be introduced in Spock now that his heritage and physiology had been revealed in greater detail.

Working only with the fact that Spock came from Vulcan, a world of logical individuals who shun emotions, writer Theodore Sturgeon chose to think about the less-ordered facets of such an existence and produced a highly imaginative script, filled with wondrous details about the Vulcans. Sturgeon became so involved with the ethics and life-styles of Spock's people that he even suggested what fabrics should be used for their wardrobe.

In the original script, Kirk did not have to depend upon T'Pau's influence to justify his diverting the *Enterprise* to Vulcan: he knew the Federation officials on the other planet where the ceremonies were to take place and

Fight to the death

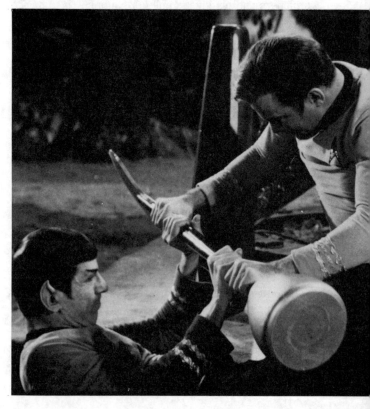

arranged to have the festivities postponed until after he got Spock back to Vulcan. As a tribute to "Star Trek" staffer D. C. Fontana, Sturgeon called this other planet "Fontana IV."

During the combat sequences, when the *ahn-woon* was announced, Kirk was puzzled when he did not receive a new weapon. He had no idea that *ahn-woon* meant "un-armed combat."

Visually, the finished episode suffers from the confined and all-too-obviously indoor sets depicting the planet Vulcan. Other means could have been used to achieve the look of another planet. In 1964, Paramount had released *Robinson Crusoe on Mars*, in which matte paintings of the planet's red sky were combined with footage shot in Death Valley and other locations. Exotic landscape footage could also have been tinted red and spliced into the episode to suggest the sky and higher temperature of Vulcan. The outdoor enclosure used in "Arena" could also have been redressed and utilized. Unfortunately, location shooting is very costly, and although there were other second-season "Star Trek" episodes partially shot outside of the studio, "Amok Time" was not.

Nonetheless, thanks to Jerry Finnerman's cinematography (especially his occasional hand-held camera that indicated Spock's frenzied point of view) the confined indoor sets of Vulcan are quite effective.

Composer Gerald Fried's wonderful score for this episode established him as *the* Vulcan musical expert on "Trek." His lonely bass guitar theme for Mr. Spock became the Vulcan's musical trademark and is heard in many other episodes.

William Theiss outdid himself in creating the wardrobe for "Amok Time," making good use of the helmets created for the Romulans in "Balance of Terror" and producing an all-new inventory of costumes that unfortunately were never reused. Considering the existence of these costumes, it is strange there was no other episode located on Vulcan.

This episode also contains one of the classic "Star Trek" bloopers. During the "koon-ut-kal-if-fee," when Kirk is attempting to convince T'Pau that he should be allowed to speak with his first officer, there are rapid cuts between close-ups of Spock (deep in the "plak tow"—the Vulcan blood fever) and longer shots of Kirk talking with the Vulcan matriarch. In the first of those longer shots, Leonard Nimoy can be seen leaning casually against the set wall, hands clasped behind his back—clearly unaware that the cameras were rolling! Subsequently, Nimoy can be seen realizing the takes were indeed live, and quickly rushing back into position.

In another embarrassing blooper, as the camera pans across the set on Vulcan, some traces of the overhead spotlights illuminating the location can be seen.

Guest star Celia Lovsky (T'Pau) was an excellent choice for the Vulcan matriarch. Her stage presence, exotic

Spock, deep in the *plak tow*

accent, and facial similarity to Leonard Nimoy carried her characterization across with great effectiveness. Her use of the word "human" as though the term were a curse was a good device. Ms. Lovsky was married to Peter Lorre and came with him to this country in 1935.

Arlene Martel (T'Pring) began her acting career billed as "Arlene Sax," and now works under the name "Tasha Martel." She can be seen in "The Outer Limits" episode "Demon with a Glass Hand" (written by Harlan Ellison), and in segments of "The Twilight Zone" and "The Man from U.N.C.L.E." Ms. Martel has appeared at many "Star Trek" conventions, including at least one memorable appearance as "T'Pring."

"THE DOOMSDAY MACHINE"

▮▮▮▮▮▮▮▮▮▮▮▮▮▮▮▮▮▮▮▮▮▮▮▮▮▮▮▮▮▮▮▮▮▮ #35

WRITER: Norman Spinrad
DIRECTOR: Marc Daniels
PRINCIPALS: Kirk   Washburn
           Spock   Russ
           McCoy   Commodore Matthew Decker
           Scott   Lieutenant Palmer
           Sulu   Lieutenant Kyle
           Elliot   Montgomery

Into the planet killer

◀ *Stardate 4202.9:* Investigating the destruction of several planetary systems, the *Enterprise* discovers the crippled starship U.S.S. *Constellation.* Commodore Matthew Decker, the *Constellation*'s captain, is in a state of shock, the only person left aboard the vessel. With his ship severely damaged, Decker had transported his entire crew down to a planet since destroyed by the gigantic destructive "berserker," a planet-killing weapon constructed by a long-dead alien race. While Kirk and party stay aboard to repair the *Constellation*'s engines and weapons system, Decker is beamed back to the *Enterprise* with McCoy. The guilt-ridden Decker takes command of the *Enterprise* and attempts to use the starship to confront and destroy the planet killer. Kirk contacts the *Enterprise* and enables Spock to take command away from Decker. The commodore steals a shuttlecraft and launches himself into the planet killer. Decker dies, but his strategy inspires Kirk to rig a self-destruct switch on the *Constellation* and send the damaged ship into the huge alien device. A transporter malfunction almost prevents Kirk from escaping the *Constellation* in time, just before the ship's exploding engines destroy the doomsday machine's destructive power forever. ▶

"The Doomsday Machine" combines elements of horror, obsession, guilt, and suspense to produce a well-executed episode that never slows down.

Commodore Matthew Decker is a man very similar to Captain Kirk—but he has made a terrible error. In choosing to beam his crew to safety, instead of keeping them aboard ship, Decker must live with the terrible knowledge that he caused their deaths. In holding himself responsible, Decker acquires a death wish so strong he doesn't even suspect he's trying to repeat the pattern with the *Enterprise* and Kirk's crew.

The Matt Decker we see during this episode is an approximation of what Kirk would become if he ever made a similar error. As Decker's starship log plays back we hear the calm and authoritative voice of a born leader, and can therefore appreciate the full horror felt by Kirk when he sees his old friend amid the ruins of the *Constellation.*

Decker's death wish culminates in his theft of a shuttlecraft, which he heads straight into the planet killer. With his death imminent, the commodore is simultaneously petrified and relieved that he is about to be reunited with his crew. Still, if Decker had heard Kirk's last plea, "We're stronger *with* you than *without* you," he might have tried to save himself.

Discovering Decker (and seeing in him his own captain) must have sent McCoy into a sympathetic stupor—for as the doctor searches for a valid reason to declare Decker unfit to assume command of the *Enterprise,* he forgets that he found Decker in a state of deep shock; hardly a starship captain's ideal condition.

William Windom's portrayal of Commodore Decker is one of the finest performances in the series. He ably conveys a sympathetic individual who has lost everything he ever deemed important. But Windom's Decker is also an antagonistic person: to degrade Spock, Decker permits the Vulcan to speak to Kirk at the command-chair intercom, beckoning Spock down to the lower portion of the bridge as though he were an unruly student. We share McCoy's urge to confine him to sick bay.

Kirk's escape from the *Constellation* is one of the classic "cliffhangers" in the series, well aided by the music of Sol Kaplan.

Writer Norman Spinrad's first science fiction novel, *The Solarians,* was published in 1966. His best-known novels are *Bug Jack Barron* and *Child of Fortune.*

A bit of artistic license was taken as the shuttlecraft entered the maw of the planet killer. If this sequence had been done true to proportion, the shuttle would have been too small to be clearly seen: instead, it was made to appear almost as large as a starship for that one scene.

The "auxiliary control room" on the *Constellation* is simply a redress of the *Enterprise* briefing room. Due to the large number of opticals necessary for this episode, there was no budget to create any new sets.

The black trim is missing from the "V" neck on Kirk's wraparound tunic. This is the only time the garment appears without it. Also lost, for one brief line of dialogue ("30 seconds later . . . poof!") is Scotty's Scottish brogue.

William Windom has starred in three television series, as Glen Morley in "The Farmer's Daughter" (1963–66), as John Monroe in "My World and Welcome to It" (1972), and as Stewart Klein in "The Girl with Something Extra" (1973–74). He can also be seen in segments of "The Twilight Zone" ("Miniature"), "Night Gallery" ("They're Tearing Down Tim Riley's Bar"), "The Invaders," and "Thriller."

Scotty in the *Constellation*'s engineering room

"WOLF IN THE FOLD"

▭▭▭▭▭▭▭▭▭▭▭▭▭▭▭▭▭▭▭▭▭▭▭▭▭▭▭ #36

WRITER: Robert Bloch
DIRECTOR: Joseph Pevney
PRINCIPALS: Kirk Sybo
Spock Tark
McCoy Morla
Scott Yeoman Tankris
Sulu Lieutenant Karen Tracey
Hengist Kara
Jaris

◄ *Stardate 3614.9:* Kirk and McCoy have taken Scotty to planet Argelius Two for therapeutic leave after an accidental head injury caused by a female crewmember. But a series of brutal murders of young women, murders apparently committed by Mr. Scott, suggest the engineer may have been more seriously injured than thought. Scotty can recall nothing, and Chief City Administrator Hengist wants him arrested immediately. Then a psychic reveals the real murderer—a previously unknown, ancient life form—Redjac—that first appeared on Earth as Jack the Ripper. The entity, in its current incarnation of Hengist, is trapped aboard the *Enterprise* and transported into outer space at maximum dispersion, scattering and effectively destroying the creature. ▶

Gene Roddenberry maintained "Star Trek's" high quality by never forgetting that science fiction is just the same as any other type of story in terms of its dramatic requirements. Any script must have a premise, a purpose, and believable characters; gadgetry and special effects are inserted to enhance the story. If these rules are followed, any good story can be transformed into science fiction, including tales of mystery and horror. Writer Robert Bloch combined generous helpings of both to make "Wolf in the Fold" one of the most interesting, terrifying, and unique "Star Trek" episodes.

In 1961, Bloch wrote an episode of Universal's TV series "Thriller" called "Yours Truly, Jack the Ripper." Adapted from the author's short story of the same title, the tale had "the Ripper" discovered terrorizing a 1960s American city. The story treated the Ripper as an unknown life form with an unusually long life span, something of a "demon" wandering at will throughout the world. The Scotland Yard inspector investigating the case was ultimately revealed to be the entity in human form.

"Wolf in the Fold" is more successful than its earlier cousin, due to the additional opportunities "Trek's" science fiction elements lend to the story. One of the most horrifying moments in any "Star Trek" episode occurs as Kirk casually observes that "when men moved out into the galaxy, that thing must have moved with them." Equally

Shore leave for Scotty

chilling is Scotty's description of the creature: "Cold, it was . . . like a stinking draft out of a slaughterhouse."

The suspense and horror we feel are increased by having Scotty suspected of being the murderer. Is Mr. Scott actually capable of committing murder, even after a serious head injury? The likelihood of his guilt would have been increased in a scene deleted from the final-draft script. When Lieutenant Tracy beamed down to administer the "psycho tricorder test," Scotty remarked "A woman!" Jaris then inquired about this remark; doesn't Mr. Scott like women, he wondered, leading Kirk to reply that Mr. Scott wasn't well due to a recent head injury.

Robert Bloch is best known as the author of *Psycho,* a 1959 novel filmed a year later by Alfred Hitchcock. For "Star Trek" Bloch also wrote "What Are Little Girls Made Of?" and "Catspaw."

The music for this episode was drawn from previously composed "Star Trek" scores, including Gerald Fried's "Catspaw," Alexander Courage's dance score from "The Cage" (used here as Kara dances), and Courage's dream music from the same episode (underscoring Sybo's empathic trance).

During the trance scene Jerry Finnerman positioned his camera high above the soundstage floor, and shot straight down onto the set. The angle, music, and editing make this a very effective sequence. The entity's possession of the *Enterprise* computer is shown with views of swirling, red-brown paints and double-exposed smoke.

Note the lack of resemblance between John Fiedler and his stunt double when Hengist tries to flee the *Enterprise* briefing room—perhaps the only negative feature of this episode.

John Fiedler (Hengist) is a skilled actor who forces his

presence to be as grating as his carefully controlled voice. Fiedler appeared regularly as Alfie Higgins, the fourth member of the cadet unit in "Tom Corbett, Space Cadet," (1950–56). He appeared in an unsold television pilot "Micky and the Contessa" (1966), in two episodes of "The Twilight Zone" ("Cavender Is Coming" and "The Night of the Meek"). In "The Night Stalker" he was mortician Gordon Spangler, affectionately dubbed "Gordy the Ghoul" by reporter Karl Kolchack.

"THE CHANGELING"

#37

WRITER: John Meredyth Lucas
DIRECTOR: Marc Daniels
PRINCIPALS: Kirk, Uhura
Spock, Chapel
McCoy, Mr. Singh
Scott, Lieutenant Carlisle
Sulu

◄ *Stardate 3451.9:* The *Enterprise* investigates the destruction of the Malurian System's four billion inhabitants and locates the unexpected source: a self-contained computer/space probe of great power called Nomad. The device threatens the *Enterprise,* but Kirk and company are temporarily saved when Nomad mistakes Captain James Kirk for its creator, Terran scientist Jackson Roykirk. Nomad, a space probe launched in 2020 to seek out alien life in the galaxy, had been damaged by a meteor that confused its programming and cut it off from Earth. It had then encountered an alien probe, Tan-Ru, which had been launched to secure sterilized soil samples. The resulting hybrid mechanism believes that its mission is to destroy imperfect life forms. Its altered programming and offensive/defensive weapons make "the changeling" capable of fulfilling its new mission. Kirk uses the machine's confused image of him as a basis for its destruction. He convinces Nomad that it is imperfect, and the device is transported out into space immediately before it self-destructs. ►

"The Changeling" is a good argument against humanity's egotistical assumptions of superiority. Nomad, created in an accident, is far more powerful than anything man has ever designed. How did all this power evolve? Neither of the two probes was equipped with anywhere near that much energy. How were the damaged machines able to synthesize the parts they needed to repair themselves and merge? Where did Nomad's enhanced capabilities come from? The story forces us to accept the presence of its superior science completely on faith. The episode is sufficiently intriguing so that we can take this point for granted and enjoy the episode as if the problem is not present—almost.

Part of the episode's attraction results from the sequence in which Nomad repairs "the unit Scott." The shock of seeing the engineer hurled (once again) through the air is surpassed as we learn he is dead. Nomad's casual offer to restore "the unit" to working order is completely unexpected, and Scotty's ignorance of what has happened to him makes the entire situation even stranger. One wonders if anyone ever bothered to sit Scotty down and explain what really occurred (it is fortunate that this adventure occurred after "Wolf in the Fold,"

or Scott's mental fitness in that segment would have been even more suspect) . . .

In tampering with Scotty and Lieutenant Uhura (whose memories Nomad wipes clean) Nomad cancels out any sympathy the audience may have had for it.

The most unusual sequence in this adventure is Mr. Spock's mind meld with Nomad. While in contact with the probe, the Vulcan seems simultaneously more human and more alien than usual.

The first-draft script of "The Changeling" began with the probe, called *Altair* in this version, absorbing the power of four photon torpedoes fired from the *Enterprise.* To contact *Altair,* Kirk jettisoned a huge cloud of ionized particles and beamed a huge "television" image of himself into space.

The probe did not board the *Enterprise* in this draft until the start of Act Two, at which point the starship personnel showed a great deal of curiosity about its capacities and mode of power. Scotty was "zapped" attempting to examine it, and was restored by the probe just as in the final version.

Mr. Spock seemed obsessed with the idea of salvaging the probe's knowledge banks before destroying it, and even pointed out that "killing" *Altair* would be an act of murder. In the end of the first-draft script Kirk used *Altair's* perfectly logical trend of thought to destroy the probe. The captain ordered all literary works in the starship's computer banks flash-fed into *Altair.* Unable to absorb this resulting torrential flow of illogic, *Altair* self-destructed.

Actor Vic Perrin, who supplied the voice of Nomad, was heard in other "Trek" episodes for shorter periods. His delivery of Nomad's dialogue, with just enough inflection to remain automated without being boring, adds much to the episode.

Nomad with Kirk

"THE APPLE"

||||||||||||||||||||||||||||||| **#38**

WRITERS: Max Ehrlich, Gene L. Coon (story by Max Ehrlich)
DIRECTOR: Joseph Pevney
PRINCIPALS:
Kirk	Sayana
Spock	Makora
McCoy	Hendorff
Scott	Yeoman Martha Landon
Chekov	Marple
Kyle	Ensign Mallory
Akuta	Kaplan

◄ *Stardate 3715.0:* Beaming down to Gamma Trianguli VI, an *Enterprise* landing party discovers a seeming paradise—until they encounter poisonous plants, exploding rocks, and extremely dangerous weather conditions. In contrast, the planet's inhabitants are a gentle, childlike people who call themselves the Feeders of Vaal. "Vaal" is a computer constructed many years before "in the dim time" by unknown entities, which survives by metabolizing the natives' offerings of food. The device is draining the energies of the *Enterprise* as well. The landing party must defeat Vaal and its people (led by the high priest Akuta) before the alien machine can destroy the starship. After a major battle with the villagers, and Mr. Spock's encounter with a lightning bolt, the starship's phasers destroy Vaal. ►

Of all the "Star Trek" episodes involving the destruction of a computer, this one is the weakest. For centuries, Vaal has been "baby-sitting," keeping its subjects in ignorance of social and technological progress (to say nothing of an ignorance of biology). Despite their cultural atrophy, the people are happy. There is no sickness and no jealousy, only complete harmony. Into this environment beam Kirk and company, bringing "the apple" into the planetwide "Garden of Eden." The analogy is complete: Vaal the computer appears to be a large serpent head carved in rock. Our people's "fruits of knowledge" are their phasers, communicators, and tricorders combined with their philosophy and experience. Vaal may look the part of the snake, but the serpent here is actually Kirk for wanting to introduce "the fruit of knowledge" to the Feeders of Vaal (if we continue the comparison to include Spock, the Vulcan emerges as the very devil . . .).

Captain Kirk is not likely to believe that "ignorance is bliss," especially when a machine is causing it. Kirk does not see himself as a destructive influence, but as an authority figure releasing the inhabitants to evolve their own culture and become their own providers.

Does Kirk have the right to assume this responsibility? He is probably in violation of the Prime Directive, for even if Vaal is a machine, we must assume that it was programmed by individuals who once ruled this planet, even if they were just "passing through" like the *Enterprise*.

Kirk takes it upon himself to give these people the right to run their own lives, *without* giving them the chance to decide what they actually want. He imprisons them when they try to feed Vaal, and the natives are helpless as the phaser banks of the *Enterprise* blast the computer in one of the most direct instances of "gunboat diplomacy" seen in "Star Trek."

As the Feeders of Vaal stand deprived of their deity and stripped of the immortality that Vaal had been providing for them, they laugh at their newfound freedom to enjoy sexual intercourse.

Most of the budget for this episode went to rent the large number of "greens" necessary to convert a studio sound stage into a jungle. Vaal himself did not cost too much to construct, having been made from heavy, crinkled paper, sprayed chemical foam, and other ingredients, helped along by chemically produced smoke. The computer's destruction was accomplished by animation effects similar to those seen in "Who Mourns for Adonais?"—although the disappearance of Apollo's temple is more spectacular than the end of Vaal.

Guest star Keith Andes (Akuta) became famous on television for starring as Police Lieutenant Frank Dawson in his syndicated series, "This Man Dawson" (1959). He costarred with James Doohan in "The Outer Limits" segment, "The Expanding Human." You will have to look closely at Vaal follower Makora to recognize actor David Soul. Soul appeared regularly as Joshua Bolt on "Here Come the Brides" (costarring with Mark Lenard) before achieving stardom as Ken "Hutch" Hutchinson on "Starsky and Hutch."

"Overfeeding" Vaal

"MIRROR, MIRROR"

#39

WRITER: Jerome Bixby
DIRECTOR: Marc Daniels
PRINCIPALS:
Kirk	Chekov
Spock	Tharn
McCoy	Lieutenant Marlena Moreau
Scott	Farrell
Sulu	Wilson
Uhura	Lieutenant Kyle

◄ *Stardate Unknown:* Kirk, McCoy, Scotty, and Uhura transport back to the *Enterprise* after initiating diplomatic relations with the peaceful Halkan Council. As a result of turbulent atmospheric conditions the transporter malfunctions, depositing them on an *Enterprise* in a parallel universe, where the Federation has developed along more barbaric principles. In return, the parallel universe's Kirk, McCoy, Scotty, and Uhura are deposited on our *Enterprise* where they are locked up by Mr. Spock. Transported into a hostile environment, the four struggle to remain alive until they return; if they *can* return. Kirk discovers his counterpart's secret weapon—the Tantalus Field, a stolen alien invention that instantly does away with parallel-Kirk's enemies. Foiling the parallel-Sulu's Gestapo-like security people, and an aborted assassination attempt by the parallel-Chekov, Kirk finds an ally in the parallel-Spock, who assists in their return trip. *Our* Mr. Spock returns the parallel crewmembers simultaneously, and everything is back to normal. ►

There's an old saying that "opposites attract," and this may be one reason why "Mirror, Mirror" is so popular. Coming face-to-face with your hidden, inner drives is something many people pay vast sums of money to arrange via psychoanalysis. For some of us the experiences endured by Kirk and company would be impossible to deal with. To the well-trained starship crew, however, it is just another difficult mission. Kirk has an edge on the others, already having confronted his "mirror image" in "The Enemy Within."

The differences between the two universes are expressed in obvious terms in the final version. The parallel-Federation becomes the equivalent of our Klingons, Romulans, and ancient brigands all rolled into one aggressive package.

A point of consistency is Mr. Spock (or rather, *both* of him). The parallel-Spock is a warrior advancing along with the conquests of the Galactic empire. Although careful to conduct his life along the lines of a logical game of chess, parallel-Spock still emerges as a man to be liked and trusted. In the final analysis Kirk realizes that the matrix holding both universes together is the inexorable flow of

The mirror-universe's Mr. Spock

logic. Things are evolving differently in the parallel environment, but the state of both universes will eventually be the same.

Kirk proves this to parallel-Spock with a logical demonstration. His premises read like a geometrical theorem ("Things equal to the same thing are equal to each other"). *Given:* the current waste of life and infliction of misery caused by the empire is not only undesirable, but will eventually lead to its destruction. *Conclusion:* any attempts by qualified personnel to hasten the end of the empire are not only in the best interests of the universe, but logical. Kirk indicates that parallel-Spock is the best-qualified person in this universe to begin that work. One can almost see the wheels turning in parallel-Spock's head. With the Tantalus Field placed at his disposal, parallel-Spock is left with the knowledge that change is needed, the conviction to carry those changes through, and the power to safeguard himself from the illogical empire.

To reinforce the alien background of the parallel development, many changes were created in the *Enterprise* sets and personnel. The most evident is parallel-Spock's beard, which makes the Vulcan appear even more impressive than usual. The crew's costumes were also altered to accomplish a warlike garishness similar to Klingon uniforms: insignia were attached to the opposite locations they usually occupy on the shirts. Because of their specialized nature, these costumes were never again used in "Star Trek."

A significant alien impression is conveyed by the parallel-Sulu. The capable, exuberant, and likable Sulu of our world is transformed into a furtive, lustful figure. Dr. McCoy's benevolence is strongly conveyed here, and DeForest Kelley's ever-sensitive portrayal makes it painfully clear that McCoy, the only one who is almost left behind, is also the only man who could never have survived within the hostile dimension.

Nichelle Nichols' portrayal of Uhura makes the communications lieutenant seem even more forceful, adaptable, and gorgeous than usual.

Jerome Bixby's story outline for "Mirror, Mirror" had Kirk beaming into the parallel universe alone, finding a parallel-Federation where phasers were as yet still unknown. The parallel-Federation was *not* evil, just a bit backward, and had just lost a war to the Tharn empire (the name was retained for the Halkan leader in the final draft). Kirk used electronic parts from the ship's systems to build a phaser weapon and conquer the Tharn.

In the outline, Kirk was subject to fainting spells. The entire parallel universe was also undergoing physical changes and was treating Kirk like an invading germ, gradually poisoning him. The parallel-Kirk was *married.*

The parallel-*Enterprise* crew worked closely with Kirk to defeat the Tharn.

The outline's parallel-Spock was more Vulcan than human, and more savage in temperament. McCoy was the one with the beard, a fact that initially made Kirk recoil from him in shock. The parallel-McCoy was injured in the final confrontation with the Tharn, while our McCoy had also been injured back home. Upon returning, Kirk met the nurse who had treated McCoy in our universe: our counterpart of the parallel-Kirk's wife.

In addition to the more blatant physical changes in the *Enterprise* sets, such as the empire's symbol of a planet bisected with a sword, there are other differences. Kirk's command chair is given a higher back (later seen on Commodore Wesley's chair in "The Ultimate Computer"). Objects commonly seen in other episodes are inverted. Knives are a standard part of starship dress. The engineering set is shown from a different angle by means of an elevated control room, also seen in "I, Mudd."

"Mirror, Mirror" was written by science fiction and fantasy author Jerome Bixby: he also wrote "Requiem for Methuselah" and "The Day of the Dove." "The Twilight Zone" adapted his story *It's a Wonderful Life,* concerning a young boy who could work miracles not unlike those performed by "Charlie X." He also wrote the science fiction film *IT! The Terror from Beyond Space* (1958, United Artists).

"Mirror, Mirror" was nominated for science fiction's Hugo Award.

Uhura takes chances with parallel-Sulu

"THE DEADLY YEARS"

⦚⦚⦚⦚⦚⦚⦚⦚⦚⦚⦚⦚⦚⦚⦚⦚⦚⦚⦚⦚⦚⦚⦚⦚⦚⦚⦚⦚⦚ #40

WRITER: David P. Harmon
DIRECTOR: Joseph Pevney
PRINCIPALS:
Kirk	Chapel
Spock	Robert Johnson
McCoy	Elaine Johnson
Scott	Commodore George Stocker
Sulu	Dr. Janet Wallace
Uhura	Lieutenant Arlene Galway
Chekov	Yeoman Doris Atkins

An aged Captain Kirk

◄ *Stardate 3478.2:* While visiting planet Gamma Hydra IV on a routine mission, an *Enterprise* landing party consisting of Kirk, Spock, Dr. McCoy, Scotty, Chekov, and Lieutenant Arlene Galway are exposed to a strange disease. The illness, radiation poisoning caused by exposure to a comet, causes greatly accelerated aging. Robert Johnson (age 29) and his wife Elaine (age 27) have been transformed almost overnight into aged individuals whom McCoy is powerless to save. The entire landing party, with the exception of Chekov, begin to age rapidly as McCoy desperately seeks an antidote. Kirk becomes forgetful, McCoy irritable—and Lieutenant Galway, possessed of an extraordinarily high metabolic rate, dies. Dr. Janet Wallace, an old "friend" of Kirk's, aids the researchers. Commodore George Stocker, aboard the *Enterprise* en route to his new command at Starbase 10, orders Spock to convene an extraordinary competency hearing. The Vulcan does so reluctantly—and after Kirk's weaknesses are exposed, Stocker assumes command. He heads the starship toward Starbase 10—straight into the Romulan Neutral Zone. With the *Enterprise* surrounded, McCoy discovers the antidote—adrenaline—in time to enable the restored Kirk to save the day with the tried-and-proven "corbomite" bluff. ►

Science has already enabled us to extend our lifetimes, and by the time of "Star Trek's" future the age of retirement will probably be closer to 100 than to 65. No matter in what era we live, we grow old gradually while enjoying our lives. Unfortunately this is not so in "The Deadly Years."

Kirk and company had faced identity crises before in "The Naked Time," "Mirror, Mirror," and other adventures, but the threat of old age and the deprivation of the strength necessary for the performance of their starship duties is an especially unpleasant prospect.

Captain Kirk, to whom virility is especially important, does not age as quickly as the others because of his intense determination to retain his youth. Mr. Spock, due to his Vulcan heritage and life span, also ages comparatively slowly. Dr. McCoy, shouldering the responsibility of dis-

covering a cure for the ailment, ages quickly, and Scotty quickest of all, due to his metabolism. As Dr. McCoy observes, different people age at different rates.

People adopt certain mannerisms as they grow older. These are augmented by various bodily changes. The posture becomes stooped, the voice quavers, and the eyes squint. To convey these mannerisms, actors William Shatner, DeForest Kelley, Leonard Nimoy, and James Doohan made very effective use of their stage training. To supplement their talents, makeup artist Fred B. Phillips and his staff created their earliest transformations with the use of wigs and penciled makeup. Later changes were accomplished with rubber appliances, special padding, and oversized costumes, used to convince viewers that muscles were atrophied. DeForest Kelley manipulated his rubberized lips to make it appear that he had no teeth. William Shatner spoke with a slight slur and manipulated his hands as though every action was painful. Leonard Nimoy, wearing gray sideburns and heavy eye makeup, squinted his eyes and rasped his voice. James Doohan, decked out in completely gray hair and eyebrows, sat in the briefing room sad-faced and all but motionless.

The repeated views of young Uhura and Sulu reinforced the images of Kirk and company becoming old before our eyes. The aging has another effect on Dr. McCoy. It restores his Southern accent and "old country doctor" mannerisms to the fullest we ever see them on "Star Trek."

Commodore Stocker manages to catch Mr. Spock off guard on the matter of the Vulcan's being more qualified for command than the aged Captain Kirk. Had Spock been his normal self, Stocker could never have tricked him into admitting the truth using logic. Spock is not spared by Dr. McCoy, either. Having established that taking the antidote is anything but pleasant, McCoy gleefully informs the Vulcan that he has removed all the breakables from sick bay in preparation for his visit.

Kirk's return to normal was originally filmed differently from the version seen in the aired episode. It was originally planned to have Kirk take the antidote and, accompanied by the still-aged Spock, return to normal slowly while en route from sick bay to the bridge. For unknown reasons, this sequence was eliminated and replaced with another showing Kirk returning to normal on the sick-bay bed.

In a marvelous bit of respect to the series' continuity, Mr. Chekov turns and smiles at Mr. Sulu as Kirk mentions "corbomite." Though not part of the *Enterprise* bridge crew during "The Corbomite Maneuver," this suggests that (1) Sulu had filled him in on what happened during that adventure, or (2) Chekov had been on the *Enterprise* in some other department. The second alternative seems more likely, since Khan remembers Chekov in *ST II: TWOK* although "Space Seed" was another segment that took place before we were introduced to the ensign.

Sarah Marshall (Dr. Janet Wallace) has costarred with William Shatner in an episode of "The Nurses" (ironically entitled "A Difference of Years"). She can also be seen in "Thriller" ("The Poisoner" and "God Grant That She Lye Still") and "The Twilight Zone" ("Little Girl Lost"). In the "Daniel Boone" episode "Hero's Welcome," she costarred with Charles Drake.

Charles Drake (Commodore Stocker) created a sympathetic character (even if Kirk did describe him as "a chairbound paper pusher"). He appeared in many feature films, including *Now, Voyager* and *A Night in Casablanca*, and the science fiction films *It Came from Outer Space* (1953, Universal) and *Tobor the Great* (1954, Republic). He hosted a syndicated series ("Rendezvous") in 1958.

"I, MUDD"

#41

WRITERS:	Stephen Kandel, David Gerrold	
DIRECTOR:	Marc Daniels	
PRINCIPALS:	Kirk	Stella Mudd
	Spock	Norman
	McCoy	"Alice" Series
	Scott	"Herman" Series
	Sulu	"Barbara" Series
	Uhura	"Maisie" Series
	Chekov	Lieutenant Rowe
	Harry Mudd	Ensign Jordan

◀ *Stardate 4513.3:* An extraordinary *Enterprise* crewman, Norman, locks the starship on course for an unknown planet—and then reveals himself as an android. Arriving at their destination, Kirk and company discover an entire race of extremely sophisticated androids, and their apparent leader—Harry Mudd, who crash-landed on their world after escaping from the scene of his most recent crime. The androids desire to protect mankind from its own destructive impulses by occupying and controlling the galaxy. The seizure of the *Enterprise* is their first step toward this goal. Mudd plans to be their emperor, but the androids, recognizing him as a severely flawed example of humanity, decide to strand Harry with the *Enterprise* crew after they leave in the starship. Mudd aids Kirk, Spock, McCoy, Uhura, Scotty, and Chekov in defeating the androids, using illogical behavior to give their controller—Norman—an electronic nervous breakdown. ▶

In "I, Mudd" the most likable arch-villain in the universe stages his nontriumphal return, this time attempting to hoodwink a planet of androids. Fortunately, the androids are perceptive and make poor pigeons for the con man. After permitting Harry to run rampant, the machines come to understand that Harcourt Fenton Mudd is an extremely misguided entity. From him, they learn about greed, lust, gluttony, deceit, and other unpleasant human characteristics. It is no wonder the androids conclude that mankind needs their specialized assistance to survive. Mudd and the misguided androids provide the materials for the funniest "pull out the plug" story seen on "Star Trek."

Even Mr. Spock seems to enjoy himself, behaving in a very non-Vulcan manner. He lies, indulges in pantomime, and takes great delight in behaving foolishly. He is the expert in logic, and what he does to the poor androids is enough to drive *anybody* to a state of complete collapse.

Harry Mudd, who is certainly enjoying himself at the start of this adventure, is definitely not having a good time at the end. Unfortunately for Harry, he has elected to gloat about having deserted his wife Stella. Mudd remembers her as quite a monster, and so his visualization of her resembles the bride of Frankenstein. Combining the vocal deliveries of Ethel Merman and the Wicked Witch of the West, Stella gave the cowardly Mudd the impetus to begin his wanderings through space. Harry has created the duplicate of his wife solely for the pleasure of being able to order it to "shut up." Kirk, with a sense of humor every bit as perverse as Mudd's, induces the androids to mass-produce the Stella model to serve as Harry's "probation officers" during his long stay on the planet.

The first draft script for "I, Mudd" devoted more attention to Norman's act of diverting the *Enterprise* to Mudd's planet. After an examination revealed Norman as an android, Scotty expressed an urge to take Norman apart—quickly adding that it was "nothing personal." Norman understood.

Richard Tatro (Norman) deserves a special award for never cracking a smile throughout the entire episode. There are some funny outtakes from this segment, which feature *many* people not being able to keep their composure.

This was composer Samuel Matlovsky's only "Star Trek" assignment. His pleasant string-and-brass melodies capture the humor of the situation without losing sight of the serious intent of Captain Kirk's program of calculated mayhem.

Using identical twins for each android "series" aided the photographic-effects budget for the episode. Through the imaginative use of split screens, as many as six of one model were shown at once, while two of the same model required nothing but an additional costume.

Harry helps out

"THE TROUBLE WITH TRIBBLES"

#42

WRITER:	David Gerrold	
DIRECTOR:	Joseph Pevney	
PRINCIPALS:	Kirk	Captain Koloth
	Spock	Cyrano Jones
	McCoy	Mr. Lurry
	Scott	Korax
	Uhura	Arne Darvin
	Chekov	Admiral Fitzpatrick
	Nilz Barris	Ensign Freeman

◄ *Stardate 4523.3:* The *Enterprise* is diverted to Space Station K-7 to protect an important shipment of quadro-triticale, a specialized grain; there, Captain Kirk finds his patience severely taxed by Federation Undersecretary of Agricultural Affairs Nilz Barris and his pesty assistant, Arne Darvin. The arrival of a Klingon ship, commanded by the arrogant Captain Koloth, complicates matters still further. Station Commander Lurry must grant the Klingons permission for rest and recreation on K-7 under the terms of the Organian Peace Treaty, while protecting the glorified wheat. Kirk's most serious problem turns out to be space trader Cyrano Jones, a dealer in rare commodities including "tribbles." Tribbles, living fluffballs that do nothing but coo, eat, and multiply, soon threaten to overwhelm the *Enterprise*—and the space station. The tribbles find their way into the grain bin and devour the grain. Widespread tribble casualties reveal that the grain was poisoned. The Klingon-hating tribbles expose Arne Darvin as a Klingon spy. Scotty beams the *Enterprise*'s crop of tribbles to the Klingon ship as a parting gift. ►

"Tribbles" is loaded with dangerous situations for Kirk and company: Klingons are present in force, a veritable "swarm" of them including a spy planted within Federation space station ranks; the entire population of a planet comes close to being poisoned; and a life form that could conceivably overrun the galaxy—or at least, the *Enterprise*—is introduced.

Despite these serious occurrences, "Tribbles" usually prompts "Trek" fans to giggle, laugh, or at least smile at the thought of Kirk's treatment of Nilz Barris, Scotty's fight with the Klingons, the antics of Cyrano Jones, and Kirk's close encounter with a grain bin filled with tribbles.

The secret of this episode's appeal lies in the contributions of writer David Gerrold and director Joseph Pevney. Pevney, who directed serious episodes of "Star Trek" including "The City on the Edge of Forever," began his career in vaudeville. His other television directing credits include episodes of "The Munsters," so his comedy expertise is no surprise. A strong script, expert performances (especially those of Shatner and Nimoy), and

Uhura and Chekov begin a tribble-packed adventure

the music of the late Jerry Fielding account for the rest of this segment's success.

Kirk juggles all his problems—the Klingon Captain Koloth, Cyrano Jones, Barris, Darvin, and thousands of tribbles—without dropping any of them before the solution presents itself. McCoy attempts to tackle the tribble-overpopulation problem; Mr. Scott has a knock-down-drag-out fight with the Klingons *not* because they insult his captain, but because his beloved *Enterprise* is ridiculed; Uhura shows her charms; and Chekov has a brief taste of Scotch. Even Mr. Spock gets into the spirit of the episode with his pun: "He heard you: he simply could not believe his ears" (partially inspired by Mad Magazine's "Star Trek" satire in which this gag also appeared).

Chief Engineer Montgomery Scott, sometimes neglected in the midst of "Star Trek" adventures, figures prominently in this episode's action. We learn of his passion for studying technical journals, and see that Scotty's academic side sometimes outweighs his urge for shore leave. He also has the segment's final punch line: when Kirk asks what became of the tribbles, Scott says he gave them to the Klingons: "I transported the whole kit and kaboodle into their engine room—where they'll be no 'tribble' at all."

Tribbles were an instant success, and many individuals (including writer David Gerrold) began to create them to sell through the mail and at conventions, where they are still available. A major toy company once advertised a line

of tribbles, and more limited quantities of the colorful furballs materialized on keychains, stickpins, bracelets, and shirts.

The cast of "Tribbles" includes some veteran character actors: Whit Bissell (Mr. Lurry) has long been associated with the Screen Actors Guild, and can be seen in many feature films including the original *The Invasion of the Body Snatchers, I Was a Teenage Frankenstein, The Time Machine,* and *The Creature from the Black Lagoon.* On television, he appeared regularly as General Heywood Kirk in "The Time Tunnel" and in episodes of "One Step Beyond," "The Invaders," "Voyage to the Bottom of the Sea," and other science fiction and fantasy series. William Schallert (Nilz Barris) appeared in the films *The Man from Planet X* and *The Incredible Shrinking Man,* and on television in "The Patty Duke Show." The late Stanley Adams (Cyrano Jones) cowrote the "Star Trek" episode "The Mark of Gideon." He costarred in episodes of "The Twilight Zone" and "Lost in Space," and in a 1966 episode of "The John Forsythe Show" ("Funny, You Don't Look Like a Spy") he appeared along with a character named "Miss Tribble."

William Campbell (Captain Koloth) also appears as "The Squire of Gothos." Koloth was intended as a recurring character, but the next time a Klingon was needed, Campbell was not available and a different actor (and character) was used.

"BREAD AND CIRCUSES"

#43

WRITERS: Gene L. Coon, Gene Roddenberry (story by John Kneubuhl)
DIRECTOR: Ralph Senensky
PRINCIPALS:
Kirk	Septimus
Spock	Flavius
McCoy	Captain R. M. Merik/Merikus
Scott	Claudius Marcus
Uhura	Drusilla
Chekov	Maximus

◄ *Stardate 4040.7:* Captain Kirk, Mr. Spock, and Dr. McCoy visit planet 892 IV, after they discover the wreckage of the S.S. *Beagle,* a Federation vessel. On the surface they meet a band of primitively dressed people—"sun" worshipers—before their capture by a group of well-armed individuals. Kirk and company learn that the planet is technologically on a par with 20th-century Earth. The world's civilization, though, closely resembles that of ancient Rome as it would have been if the Roman empire had lasted into our time. Kirk meets Captain Merik, the former commander of the *Beagle,* and discovers that Merik betrayed his crew, instructing them to beam down so that they could die in the arena. The *Beagle*'s captain is now known as First Citizen Merikus, and the empire's proconsul, Claudius Marcus, is using him to convince Kirk to beam down the *Enterprise* crew. McCoy and Spock are sentenced to die in the arena, and Kirk's execution seems imminent. Sensing that something is wrong, Scotty cuts off the planet's electrical power, enabling Kirk to free Spock and McCoy. Merik saves the trio, giving Kirk a stolen communicator before the proconsul stabs him. Back on the *Enterprise,* Kirk realizes that the persecuted Children of the "Son"—what the "sun" worshipers were actually calling themselves—were that planet's counterpart of the early Christians. ►

This episode is a prime example of Gene Roddenberry's parallel-worlds theory being put into practice. Paramount Pictures had contemporary studio settings that are seen here, as well as in "Miri," "A Piece of the Action," and other segments of "Trek." The studio was also the point of origin for the historical epics produced by Cecil B. DeMille, including *The Sign of the Cross, Cleopatra,* and *The Crusades.* Bits of all these wardrobes are seen in "Bread and Circuses." A few location shots completed the settings for this adventure.

The story features a group of people whom Kirk and company initially think are "sun" worshipers. In actuality, as Uhura dramatically points out at the close of the episode, they are "Son" worshipers. The powerful but inherently peaceful Flavius is very suggestive of earlier

counterparts in religious cinematic epics, especially Dimitrius in *The Robe,* though the script does not push this to the point that it interferes with the story.

This is one of the few times we are treated to a serious discussion between Spock and McCoy. The two are locked together in a cell, and considering their imminent death, they dwell upon the motivations behind their traditional feud. Mr. Spock proudly states that he is not afraid to die and is in fact prepared for it. Dr. McCoy counters by theorizing that Spock is not afraid to die because he has always been more fearful of living. The short conversation ends with both uniting in their worry over what has become of Captain Kirk, the bond that holds them together. The sequence is sometimes entirely edited out of syndicated prints of the episode.

In the hands of "Star Trek's" dominant Genes (Roddenberry and Coon), this episode also becomes a marvelous satire of survival within the television industry. Proconsul Maximus assumes that because Kirk and company are so technologically advanced, they have long forgotten about the entertainment medium called "television." When Kirk is told that television entails constant (literal) battles to remain in public favor, Kirk seems to be familiar with the problem. One of the guards also taunts a gladiator with a threat that says it all: "You bring this station's ratings down, and we'll do a *special* on you!"

This episode's script went through several drafts, most of which were very different from the final concept. In one version, Spock was in need of treatment for the Vulcan equivalent of appendicitis. In a later draft, Kirk

Escape Ploy

violated the Prime Directive by revealing his mission to Septimus, the leader of the Children of the Son. Spock and McCoy then argued over whether or not the Directive had actually been disobeyed. In an interesting touch, the empire's doctors studied anatomy by examining the losers of arena events, and were anxious to learn the "inside story" of Mr. Spock.

Guest star Rhodes Reason (Flavius) is the brother of actor Rex Reason, seen in many science fiction and horror films. Rhodes is featured in segments of "The Time Tunnel" and "Thriller." Ian Wolfe (Septimus) has an acting career that dates back to 1935, when he appeared in *The Raven*. He also appears as Mr. Atoz in "All Our Yesterdays." The announcer during the games is Bartell LaRue, whose voice is heard in several "Star Trek" segments, notably as the Guardian in "The City on the Edge of Forever".

John Kneubuhl, who wrote this episode's story, also scripted some of the most popular episodes of "Thriller," including "Pigeons from Hell" and "Para Benjamin."

"JOURNEY TO BABEL"

#44

WRITER:	D. C. Fontana	
DIRECTOR:	Joseph Pevney	
PRINCIPALS:	Kirk	Sarek
	Spock	Amanda
	McCoy	Thelev
	Uhura	Shras
	Chekov	Gav
	Chapel	Lieutenant Josephs

◀ *Stardate 3842.3:* The *Enterprise* is en route to an important Federation conference on a planet code-named Babel. Traveling aboard are delegates from many worlds, including Vulcan's Ambassador Sarek and his Terran wife Amanda—revealed as Mr. Spock's parents. Spock and his father have not spoken for 20 years, a fact that causes embarrassment for Kirk, but not for his first officer. The journey is also complicated by an unidentified vessel following the *Enterprise* and tension between various delegates, especially Sarek and Tellarite Ambassador Gav. When Gav is murdered, Sarek is the prime suspect. The stress reveals Sarek is suffering from a heart condition and needs an immediate operation to save his life. Only his son can serve as the blood donor, but when Captain Kirk is attacked and stabbed by Thelev, a member of the Andorian party, Spock assumes command. Despite the danger to his father's life, he refuses to step down until the unidentified ship following the *Enterprise* is stopped. Spock's mother is unsuccessful in her appeals to her son to permit the operation to be performed. Kirk fakes a return to the bridge to trick Spock into reporting to sick bay. The vessel, an Orion ship, attacks and is destroyed. Thelev is exposed as a surgically altered Orion posing as an Andorian and commits suicide on the bridge. The operation on Sarek is successful and the ambassador resumes diplomatic relations with his son. ▶

"Journey to Babel" is one of the most popular "Star Trek" episodes, due to its introduction of Spock's parents, the profusion of aliens, and the segment's constant flow of action.

"Trek" fans learned about this segment at the same science fiction convention at which "Amok Time" was first seen. At that gathering, no details of the script were known, and most fans guessed that the story would unfold at Spock's family residence on Vulcan. However, as Sarek would say, "no matter": the finished result is interesting and welcome despite its lack of more glimpses of Vulcan. D. C. Fontana, utilizing her customary attention to characterization, sensitivity, and continuity, created a "Trek" masterpiece in "Journey to Babel."

Throughout the story, Mr. Spock appears to feel very

Meeting the ambassador's party: Kirk, Amanda, Spock, Sarek and McCoy

uncomfortable as his childhood (in the person of his mother) follows him about the *Enterprise*. To conceal his anxiety from the starship crew, and Dr. McCoy in particular, Spock attempts to act more unemotional than usual.

In the midst of all the episode's serious occurrences, there are also some very humorous moments, including Spock's revelation that his pet "teddy bear" was actually a Sehlat with six-inch fangs.

D. C. Fontana's first-draft script for "Journey to Babel" tells the same story seen in the final version of the episode, with minor differences. It also contains some touches not found in the final version. Sarek, Amanda, and their party were transported aboard the *Enterprise*. By using the shuttlecraft (stock footage and the existing set) in the final version, the cost of a "transporter" sequence was eliminated from the budget. Amanda engaged in a short debate with her son, unsuccessfully attempting to restore conversation between Sarek and Spock.

The most important ambassadors (including Sarek, Shras the Andorian, and Gav the Tellarite) were shown at a formal dinner. When this sequence was edited from the script, its dialogue was added to the final version's buffet scene. In supplementary dialogue that did not survive into the final version, we learned that Sarek and Amanda had been married for 38 (Vulcan?) years, that Sarek had been an astrophysicist before assuming his political career, and that Sarek's father was Ambassador Shariel, a famous Vulcan.

The relationship between Sarek and Amanda is enig-

matic: they love each other, yet he is a Vulcan, able to indulge in only an occasional smile and other expressions of his love, including the ritual finger-touching gesture.

Mark Lenard (Sarek) won the hearts of "Star Trek" fans everywhere with his characterization of the elder Vulcan, a role that permitted the performer to emote only minimally. When Lenard reappeared as Sarek in *Star Trek III*, fans rejoiced. By that time he had become a frequent guest at "Trek" conventions. He also appeared in the "Star Trek" episode "Balance of Terror."

Jane Wyatt (Amanda) is one of the most famous performers to appear in a role on "Star Trek." A graduate of New York's Barnard College, her stage career began in the 1930s. In 1935 she appeared in a Broadway production of *Lost Horizon,* and two years later she costarred in the film of the same title. Ms. Wyatt is best remembered by TV watchers as Margaret Anderson, another famous mother, in "Father Knows Best."

Composer Gerald Fried's score for "Amok Time" supplies most of the music heard in this episode.

The only distinctive special effect in this segment is the Orion starship, a star-shaped animation that is never clearly seen.

Two interesting items appear in Dr. McCoy's office: the couch from Kirk's starbase quarters in "Court-Martial" and the Tantalus Field device from "Mirror, Mirror."

Spock and Chapel in sick bay

"A PRIVATE LITTLE WAR"

#45

WRITER: Gene Roddenberry (story by Jud Crucis)
DIRECTOR: Marc Daniels
PRINCIPALS: Kirk   Chapel
            Spock   Nona
            McCoy   Dr. M'Benga
            Scott   Apella
            Uhura   Krell
            Chekov   Yutan
            Tyree

◄ *Stardate 4211.4:* The *Enterprise* journeys to the planet Neural, which Kirk had visited 13 years before. The Klingons are attempting to take over the planet by arming one segment of the population (the Hill People) while remaining in the background. Spock, wounded in an ambush, returns to the *Enterprise* while Kirk and McCoy search for Tyree, the tribal leader Kirk had befriended in his youth. Kirk, bitten by a deadly Mugatu, is cured by Tyree's mystic witch-wife, Nona. While Kirk tries to persuade Tyree to fight with the weapons the Federation will provide for his men, Nona indulges in intrigues of her own. She steals Kirk's phaser, but the Hill People murder her before she can demonstrate its power. Her death turns Tyree into a fighting man. Kirk and McCoy leave the planet, saddened that they could do nothing to end the hostilities, having instead compounded the conflict by providing a balance of power. ►

The Mugatu

The story told in "A Private Little War" was patterned after the Vietnam conflict, still raging when this episode was produced. Kirk himself cites the parallel in the situation, and mentions that a balance of power must be employed on Neural exactly as it was implemented in 20th-century conflicts on "Old Earth."

Kirk is operating at a disadvantage here as a result of several factors. Mr. Spock, who usually advises him on delicate matters such as these, is fighting for his life on the *Enterprise* (adding even more tension to Kirk's burden during this assignment). Dr. McCoy, who is with Kirk on Neural, is opposed to his captain's strategy. Kirk is also saddened by his part in ending a "paradise" type of existence, something he has done on other occasions. He is also affected by the calculating charms of Nona, the wife of his old friend Tyree.

Tyree understands very little about what is happening to his way of life. He sees Jim as his friend "from another place," a very special person he hopes can find the means to end the nightmare initiated by the Klingon-backed Hill People. The story's conflicts are made even more dramatic by intercutting from the planet back to the *Enterprise,* to check on Mr. Spock's condition. Spock is being tended to by Dr. M'Benga, an able young physician (who interned in a Vulcan ward) later seen in "That Which Survives."

In contrast to the medical treatment administered by Dr. M'Benga and Nurse Chapel is the mystical cure that takes the Mugatu poison out of Kirk. Nona, a Kanutu (a Neuralese witch doctor, uses her own brand of medicine combined with local folklore and plants.

Don Ingalls wrote the first-draft script of "A Private Little War." This earliest version contains more specific references to the Vietnam conflict. The Neuralese tribesmen dressed in Mongolian-type clothes, and Apella (the puppet of the Klingons) was described as a "Ho Chi Minh" type. A security man was shot during the initial attack, and Spock stayed with the landing party in that initial draft.

Kirk's first visit to the planet had taken place shortly before this encounter. The friendship between Kirk and Tyree developed completely during this second visit. When the beast (called a "Gumato") attacked Kirk, Spock killed it with a spear rather than use a phaser near the tribesmen.
· In this draft the Klingon ship was smuggling ready-made rifles to the Hill People. There was also a personal conflict between Kirk and "Krell" the Klingon: he had met the captain during the Organian Peace Conference and had disliked him on sight.

The Mugatu was designed, fabricated, and performed by makeup-effects artist Janos Prohaska (also the Horta in "Devil in the Dark" and Yarnek in "The Savage Curtain").

"THE GAMESTERS OF TRISKELION"

▮▮▮▮▮▮▮▮▮▮▮▮▮▮▮▮▮▮▮▮▮▮▮▮▮ #46

WRITER: Margaret Armen
DIRECTOR: Gene Nelson
PRINCIPALS: Kirk   Galt
           Spock   Shahna
           McCoy   Lars
           Scott   Kloog
           Uhura   Ensign Jana Haines
           Chekov   Tamoon

Kirk reasons with the providers of Triskelion

◄ *Stardate 3211.7:* As Captain Kirk, Lieutenant Uhura, and Ensign Chekov are about to beam down on a routine survey mission, they are abducted by a powerful transporter beam. They arrive on the planet Triskelion in the trinary star system M-24 Alpha. Kirk and company learn that they are to be used as gladiators, to fight in games staged for the amusement of "the Providers," the rulers of the planet. While Mr. Spock attempts to locate his captain, Kirk and his companions experience various ordeals including excruciating pain inflicted by Galt, the master thrall. When the *Enterprise* arrives and orbits Triskelion, the Providers capture the starship. To save all aboard, Kirk proposes a wager with the Providers, who are actually aged and bored beings reduced to disembodied brains. Kirk is pitted against three thralls including Shahna, whom he has attempted to teach about love and loyalty. He wins the contest, the Providers free the thralls, and the *Enterprise* proceeds on its way. ►

Most of the technologically developed aliens who outclass the Federation in "Star Trek" appear to be interested in other people's good. In this episode we meet the Providers, who do not seem interested in anything but their games.

In convincing the creatures that they should free their thralls, Kirk creates a challenge for the bored superbrains, handling them as he would handle computers in other "Trek" episodes. Perhaps we are being asked to believe that the disembodied aliens, who have spent many centuries dependent upon their life-support machines, have acquired the attributes of machines themselves, and are therefore easy prey to Kirk's usual strategies of bluff and combat coupled with compassion.

Fate plays into Kirk's hands in other ways during this tale. Whereas Mr. Chekov is paired with Tamoon, unattractive to say the least from the ensign's viewpoint, Kirk gets Shahna, who resembles a "spacemate of the month" foldout in some 23rd-century magazine. He knows exactly how to handle the situation, and proceeds to enlighten her regarding such Terran customs as hugging, kissing, and discussing freedom. Kirk is so wrapped up with Shahna that after an initial dramatic outburst he seems to forget about Lieutenant Uhura, who has a thrall of her own to worry about.

While all this is going on, there are some pretty heavy things happening in this episode (aside from the advances made on Chekov by Tamoon). After being kidnapped the members of the landing party are continually mistreated, hurt, and forced to live as slaves. Lieutenant Uhura is left in the hands of someone whose designs on her are not aesthetic. Is it worth all this unpleasantness to get the point of the episode across? The answer is debatable.

The first-draft script, entitled "The Gamesters of Pentathlan," featured Mr. Sulu instead of Mr. Chekov. Actor George Takei was away on location in his feature-film role for *The Green Berets* at the start of "Star Trek's" second production season, and was unable to appear in several episodes, including this one. The script was changed to feature actor Walter Koenig, with Chekov and the large thrall Tamoon appearing as the oddest couple seen in "Star Trek."

Angelique Pettyjohn (Shahna) appeared in the feature film *The Mad Doctor of Blood Island* and has appeared at recent "Star Trek" conventions both in character as Shahna and as herself. Jane Ross (Tamoon) steals the show: her size, solid yellow complexion, and bright green lipstick drive Chekov crazy with desire . . . to get away from her. Although her scenes are brief, Ms. Ross shows a flair for comedy that make her scenes among the pleasanter features of this episode. Dick Crockett (Andorian thrall) coordinated the stunts for this episode and appeared in many "Trek" segments, including the fight sequence in "The Trouble with Tribbles."

The glass bubble in which the Providers brains are shown is the top of Lazarus' ship from "The Alternative Factor".

"OBSESSION"

#47

WRITER: Art Wallace
DIRECTOR: Ralph Senensky
PRINCIPALS: Kirk   Chekov
            Spock   Chapel
            McCoy   Ensign Garrovick
            Scott   Ensign Rizzo
            Uhura

◀ *Stardate 3619.2:* While Kirk was a young lieutenant serving on the U.S.S. *Farragut,* half the crew, including Captain Garrovick, were killed by a cloudlike creature Kirk felt he could have destroyed—had he not hesitated before firing. Eleven years later Ensign Garrovick, the son of the late captain, is stationed on the *Enterprise.* On the surface of Argus X a landing party, including the ensign, encounters the same gaseous creature. Several are killed but the cloudlike entity escapes and this time Kirk blames Garrovick, who also waited before firing. The creature leaves Argus X and Kirk chases it through space—when it suddenly turns to fight. It enters the *Enterprise* and begins to emerge from the ventilation shaft in Garrovick's quarters. Spock is with the ensign, and the Vulcan is the first person encountered by the creature. Tasting Spock's copper-based blood, it flees back toward its native planet, Tycho IV. Kirk and Garrovick prepare a trap, baited with a large jar of human blood attached to a matter/antimatter bomb. The creature is destroyed, and both Kirk and young Garrovick, realizing phaser fire was inadequate to hurt the creature, are freed from their earlier guilt. ▶

Perhaps the most well-known study in obsession is Herman Melville's novel *Moby Dick.* Fortunately for the *Enterprise,* Captain Kirk's motivation in this instance is *not* obsession. If it were, Kirk would have been just as unbalanced as Commodore Decker was in "The Doomsday Machine." Spock would have been correct in worrying about his captain's mental health, and Kirk might very well have destroyed his career, if not the *Enterprise.*

Kirk's declaration of war against the creature is based upon facts. An entity that feeds upon human blood, can be either solid or immaterial at will, propels itself through space at enormous speeds, and has *intelligence,* would be dangerous to any settlement within the galaxy. Add to these the fact that the entity in question plans to reproduce, and it becomes even more necessary to destroy it as quickly as possible.

Mr. Spock is somewhat out of character at several points in this episode. He betrays an emotional concern for the well-being of Ensign Garrovick, though he is useless as a psychiatrist because he cannot admit to having feelings. When the creature makes an unscheduled appearance through the vent of Garrovick's quarters, which the ensign has accidentally left open, Spock stays behind to perform one of the most illogical acts of his career. In the privacy of the closed cabin, the Vulcan technological wizard deliberately places his hands against the grid through which the creature is coming, and attempts to stop the gaseous entity while being fully aware that this useless act may cause his death.

Fortunately, the luck of the Vulcans is still with Spock. Just as his "forgotten" inner eyelids kept him from going blind in "Operation: Annihilate!" his copper-based blood saves him from the creature. In all fairness to the Vulcan, Spock may have recalled that the salt vampire (in "The Man Trap") rejected the taste of his bodily chemistry and could have been gambling that this creature would do the same.

Stephen Brooks (Garrovick) costarred in recurring roles in three television series: "Mr. Novack," "The Doctors and the Nurses," and "The F.B.I."

One of the landing party killed by the creature is Mr. Leslie, a crewmember who makes many appearances in "Star Trek." We see him lying dead on the ground, despite the fact that he makes other appearances in later "Trek" adventures. Actor Eddie Paskey, who played this role, also appeared as other crewmembers in previous "Trek" segments including Mr. Connors in the sick-bay sequence of "Mudd's Women."

Captain Kirk—bait for the vampire cloud

"THE IMMUNITY SYNDROME"

▭▭▭▭▭▭▭▭▭▭▭▭▭▭▭▭▭▭▭▭▭▭▭▭▭▭▭▭▭▭ **#48**

WRITER: Robert Sabaroff
DIRECTOR: Joseph Pevney
PRINCIPALS: Kirk Sulu
Spock Chekov
McCoy Chapel
Scott Lieutenant Kyle
Uhura

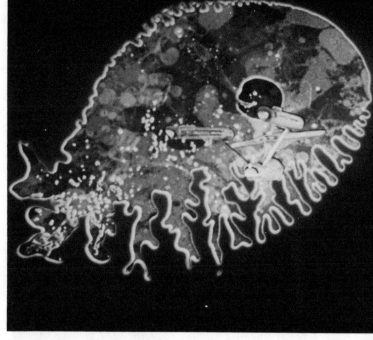

The Enterprise becomes an antibody

◀ *Stardate 4307.1:* The *Enterprise* is en route to investigate the mysterious loss of contact with solar system Gamma 7A, when Spock suddenly receives a stunning psychic bolt. The U.S.S. *Intrepid,* a starship manned entirely by Vulcans, has just been completely destroyed. In deep space, the *Enterprise* then encounters a huge living creature, a gigantic one-celled life form resembling nothing so much as a giant amoeba. The entity is cutting a destructive swath through the entire universe, and is responsible not only for the destruction of the *Intrepid,* but system Gamma 7A as well. Kirk realizes that his starship may be the only means of stopping the creature before it can end all life in our galaxy—for it is about to reproduce. The *Enterprise* assumes the role of "antibody" and presses forward to attack. The crew feels the effects of invading the giant intruder as fatigue and depression, and Spock pilots the shuttlecraft into the "heart" of the creature to determine its weakest spot. Just before the creature can replicate, an antimatter charge is fired into the creature's nucleus, killing it. The Vulcan succeeds in returning to the *Enterprise* as his life-support systems are about to expire. ▶

Due to the expensive opticals required for this episode, costs for other aspects of "The Immunity Syndrome" were held to a minimum. The only "guest" is the one-celled creature, created especially by the Vanderveer Photo Effects artists. No new *Enterprise* sets are seen, and even the views of the shuttlecraft were created for other episodes and combined with backgrounds produced by the Vanderveer people.

In "The Immunity Syndrome" we see more of the continuing feud between Mr. Spock and Dr. McCoy. Both are science specialists, and each thinks of himself as Kirk's closest friend. Despite being on opposite sides of the scale when it comes to emotion, they both manage to do their jobs. When Spock and McCoy both volunteer for this mission, the nature of their relationship becomes clearer to the "Star Trek" audience, but not to Kirk (who is too busy worrying about which of his friends he will have to "condemn" by assigning him the mission).

Despite their jealousy, Spock and McCoy actually think of each other as very close friends. The mission must be fulfilled by *someone,* and McCoy feels intense guilt that he

will not be the one going out to die. Of course, it does not occur to McCoy to be honest with Spock and tell him this. He instead expresses his guilt in more sarcasm directed at the Vulcan. This good-natured ribbing of the Vulcan may have been for Spock's own good, for he knows that "Bones" would only admit his liking for him if the death of one (or both) of them was certain.

Dr. McCoy does not even wish Spock success for this reason, although he almost silently mouths a prayerful plea for his friend to come back safe and sound. Later, to keep up the pretense of their mutual "feud," Spock comments: "Tell McCoy he should have wished me luck."

Robert Sabaroff's outline for "The Immunity Syndrome" described the creature as a gigantic virus living within a "black hole" that surrounded it. Three unmanned probes were dispatched to study the phenomenon. The weakness, depression, and fear suffered by the starship crew were emphasized more than they were in the completed script. At one point during the outline's action, McCoy nearly died.

McCoy and Spock were united in their enthusiasm over the chance to study the creature.

The *Enterprise*'s polarity, and that of everything aboard, was reversed due to the ship's proximity to the entity. This accounted for the crew's illnesses. Spock left the ship in a shuttle along with two crewmen. Their reports were radioed back to the *Enterprise* while the organism tried to digest the shuttle.

The theory of a universe within a universe within a universe, etc., was discussed, and the conclusion reached that man's purpose in this universe might be to serve as antibodies against the onslaught of the giant virus.

"A PIECE OF THE ACTION"

||||||||||||||||||||||||||||||||||||||||||| #49

WRITERS: David P. Harmon, Gene L. Coon (story by David P. Harmon)
DIRECTOR: James Komack
PRINCIPALS: Kirk   Bela Oxmyx
           Spock   Jojo Krako
           McCoy   Kalo
           Scott   Zabo
           Uhura   Tepo
           Chekov   Mirt
           Lieutenant Hadley

◄ *Stardate 4598.0:* One hundred years before the start of the *Enterprise*'s five-year mission, the Federation vessel U.S.S. *Horizon* visited the isolated planet Iotia. The Iotians, a highly imitative people, modeled their planet's culture after a book left behind on their world by one of the crew of the *Horizon*. The book, *Chicago Mobs of the Twenties,* inspired the Iotians to duplicate the gangs of old Chicago. At first the *Enterprise* landing party, consisting of Kirk, Spock, and McCoy, have difficulty. Bela Oxmyx, a key gang leader who first makes contact with the starship crew, wants to use the *Enterprise*'s weapons to take over Iotia. Rival gangster Jojo Krako has the same idea. By playing according to Iotia's unique "rules," Kirk finally succeeds in uniting the planet's most influential gangsters, setting up a world government headed by Oxmyx. Kirk leaves behind the fiction that the Federation will expect an annual "piece of the action" from Iotia's new government. McCoy accidentally leaves behind his communicator, which Kirk worries may lead the Iotians to become a super-technical giant by the time of the Federation's next visit. ►

Although "Star Trek" has its share of comedies, it is essentially a serious television series concerned with the welfare of the universe. "A Piece of the Action" is therefore a very strange episode, the only humorous segment structured around the contamination of a planetary culture by the crew of a starship.

Kirk accepts the bizarre state of affairs on Iotia and proceeds to play along with it. Perhaps this strategy came from his experiences in "Bread and Circuses," where he learned (literally), "when in Rome, do as the Romans do." Thanks to Kirk's acceptance of the situation, we are treated to a delightful exercise in burlesque: the adventure could easily have been called "The Untouchables Syndrome."

There are some priceless moments in this episode, such as the card game "fizzbin" Kirk uses to escape from one gang's clutches and his attempt to drive a vintage car (the only time in "Star Trek" in which any *Enterprise* crewmember used a surface vehicle for transportation).

Space-age gangsters

Even Mr. Spock plays along with the situation, showing off a "heater" (machine gun) and zoot suit. Additional precious moments include Mr. Scott's attempt to master 20th-century slang, and Krako's abbreviated visit to the *Enterprise*.

The first-draft script for this episode was entitled "Mission into Chaos," and contained some complications not found in the final version. In that draft, the mission was to negotiate a friendship and alliance treaty with planet Dana Iotia 2, on the border of the Romulan Neutral Zone. Romulans had approached Boss Oxmyx to make a similar deal, leading Oxmyx to defy both the Romulans and the Federation.

When the Romulans learned that Kirk was talking to Oxmyx, they sent two emissaries (Rorek and Ramo) to the headquarters of Boss Krako, and provided two Romulan weapons (called "morkons") so that Krako could hit Bela Oxmyx. Meanwhile, Kirk and company had escaped using the card game "farfel" (in which the losing hand was known as "drek"), and they regained possession of the morkon weapons. This infuriated the Romulans, who beamed down a squad that was in turn surrounded by an *Enterprise* security squad. Boss Oxmyx then negotiated a treaty with Kirk due to his fear of the Romulans.

The bosses, in trying to elect an ambassador to the Federation, each voted for themselves. This resulted in all 12 of them beaming up to the *Enterprise* to appear before the Federation Council. The earliest draft ended with Kirk gleefully anticipating what would happen when the Council met the Iotians.

Anthony Caruso (Bela Oxmyx) has appeared as a gangster on many television series, including "The Adventures of Superman" ("Czar of the Underworld"). Vic Tayback (Jojo Krako) had recurring roles in three television series: Officer Haseejian in "The Streets of San Francisco," Pizuti in "The Super," and police captain Barney Marcus in "Griff" before his most famous part as Mel, the diner owner in "Alice."

"BY ANY OTHER NAME"

■■■■■■■■■■■■■■■■■■■■■■■■■■■■■■■■■■■ **#50**

WRITERS: D. C. Fontana, Jerome Bixby (story by Jerome Bixby)
DIRECTOR: Marc Daniels
PRINCIPALS:
Kirk	Rojan
Spock	Kelinda
McCoy	Hanar
Scott	Tomar
Uhura	Lieutenant Shea
Chekov	Drea
Chapel	Yeoman Leslie Thompson

◄ *Stardate 4657.5:* Rojan and his fellow Kelvans have journeyed from their native Kelva in the Andromeda Galaxy, assuming human form to determine if our galaxy is suitable for colonization by the Kelvan empire. Now ready to return home with their report, Rojan lures the *Enterprise* with a fake distress call and succeeds in taking over the starship. The Kelvans intend to use it for transportation back to their home in Andromeda. Preparing for the 300-year journey, Rojan, Kelinda, and the other Kelvans transform the *Enterprise* crew into small, tetrahedral blocks—save for Kirk, Spock, McCoy, and Scotty. Spared from the conversion process, the four plot to regain control of their starship. To do this, they take advantage of the aliens' newly acquired human emotions. With the aid of carefully cultivated jealousy, a little food, alcohol, and drugs, the Kelvans soon find themselves at each other's throats, enabling Kirk and company to retake the *Enterprise* and restore the crew to normal. The Kelvans realize that they cannot return to Andromeda: now too human to survive there, they agree to permit the Federation to locate a habitable world for them to settle on. ▶

The situation in this episode is very serious, entailing the murder of an *Enterprise* crewman, the theft of the starship, and the prospect of Kirk and his crew reduced to inanimate forms and forced to embark on a journey over three centuries in duration. Despite these crises, "By Any Other Name" is an enjoyable adventure.

One of the most charming points about "Star Trek" is its ability to fill us with confidence about the future of mankind, without ignoring human weaknesses. This segment is filled with reminders that humans are not perfect creatures, and that sometimes our "imperfections" can also serve as our greatest strengths.

Beginning with the discovery that Kelvans are unfamiliar with their new human state, Captain Kirk and his companions launch an attack in which the "superior" aliens are hopelessly outclassed.

In one unforgettable sequence, Mr. Scott goes to work on the alien Tomar, determined to put him out of action by getting him thoroughly drunk. Scotty's entire stock of drinkables is exhausted during this valiant attempt, including a bottle of alien liquor that even Mr. Scott knows nothing about except that "it's green!" Scotty almost walks away from the successful attempt, leaving the alien unconscious. At the last instant, just before Scotty is about to leave his cabin to report to Kirk, the engineer joins his alien drinking companion in a state of total oblivion.

As usual, in the midst of the crisis, Captain Kirk finds a reason to romance a woman: in this case, the attractive Kelinda. Her seduction by the captain fires up Rojan's romantic instincts and points out just how human the Kelvans are becoming.

The purple galactic barrier created for "Where No Man Has Gone Before" is also seen here. No attempt is made to hide the fact that it's stock footage—in fact, when Kirk is told about the barrier by Rojan, he comments: "Yes, I know. We've been there before."

Guest star Warren Stevens (Rojan) is no stranger to fans of science fiction films, having served early in his acting career as Dr. Ostrow in *Forbidden Planet*. He had recurring roles in three television series, "The 77th Bengal Lancers," "The Richard Boone Show," and "Return to Peyton Place." He was also the voice of film tycoon John Bracken in the first season of "Bracken's World." (During the series' second year the voice of Bracken was supplied by Leslie Neilsen, who portrayed Stevens's Commander Adams in *Forbidden Planet*.) Stevens also appeared in "The Outer Limits" ("Keeper of the Purple Twilight"), "The Twilight Zone" ("Dead Man's Shoes"), and "One Step Beyond" ("The Riddle"). In one of the best episodes of "Science Fiction Theatre" ("Time is Just a Place") he portrayed a fugitive in time.

Robert Fortier (Tomar) gave a great straight-faced performance as Scotty's drinking partner. He had previously worked with William Shatner in the M-G-M television pilot "Alexander the Great."

Scotty gives his all for the ship

"RETURN TO TOMORROW"

▮▮▮▮▮▮▮▮▮▮▮▮▮▮▮▮▮▮▮▮▮▮▮▮▮▮▮▮▮▮▮▮▮▮ **#51**

WRITER: Gene Roddenberry (story by John T. Dugan)
DIRECTOR: Ralph Senensky
PRINCIPALS: Kirk   Chapel
Spock   Dr. Anne Mulhall
McCoy   Sargon
Scott   Thalassa
Uhura   Henoch
Sulu

◄ *Stardate 4768.3:* Answering a mysterious S.O.S. from Arret—a planet presumed long dead—Kirk, McCoy, and Dr. Anne Mulhall are transported underground to confront the last three survivors of that world's civilization. Sargon, Thalassa, and Henoch have preserved their conscious minds within containers and have remained in this state for centuries. They now wish to "borrow" the bodies of Kirk, Spock, and Dr. Mulhall so that they can construct android bodies to house their minds on a permanent basis. Sargon assures Kirk that his people will be safe, their minds encased for a short time within the same containers his people now occupy. McCoy is concerned about the high metabolic rate necessary for "possession." The real danger, however, is Henoch, who appropriates Spock's body without any intention of returning it. Henoch telepathically forces Nurse Chapel to poison Sargon (in Kirk's body) and then destroys the globe that houses Spock's mind. Fortunately, Spock's consciousness had already left the globe, hidden within the mind of Nurse Chapel. Henoch is tricked into leaving Spock's body—and destroyed. Sargon and Thalassa vacate the bodies of Kirk and Dr. Mulhall voluntarily, announcing (after one last kiss) that they will be happy to roam throughout the universe together in their noncorporeal state. ►

"Return to Tomorrow" explores the plight of highly advanced aliens—who miss their human condition. Their predicament, and the individuals themselves, are treated with dignity in a fine script that is well directed, contains more than the usual amount of suspense, and is supplemented with a sensitive musical score.

Kirk is immediately responsive to Sargon's request to borrow his body and two others of his crew. Dr. McCoy is against the project due to the physical dangers involved. When Kirk sees that McCoy is not thinking beyond the issue of personal risk, the captain indulges in another of his "pep talks" in favor of exploration, education, and the establishment of relations with alien life forms regardless of personal risk.

What Kirk has not taken into account is that, although Sargon appears to be just as idealistic as the captain, the others in the exchange (Henoch and Thalassa) are not quite as selfless in their desires. Henoch has been trying to become a participant in the universe's oldest romantic duet and has been repeatedly spurned. Now that he has a body once again, Henoch renews his romantic campaign with the greatest of vigor. This makes the situation extremely awkward. Sargon, in Kirk's body, is completely absorbed in his newfound host and is supposedly off somewhere flexing Kirk's muscles. Fortunately, Sargon is not as gullible as he seems to be. He is really off assuring the safety of Spock's mind by spiriting the Vulcan's consciousness into the body of Nurse Christine Chapel.

This episode marks yet another challenge for the considerable acting talents of Leonard Nimoy. In "Return to Tomorrow" he portrays not only the stoic Vulcan, but the evil and calculating Henoch as well. The actor completely changed his facial expressions and physical bearing to make this transition. In earlier episodes Nimoy had proven his ability to handle humor as Spock. In this episode he proved what an effective "heavy" he could be as well, with a personality other than that of the Vulcan.

William Shatner's trancelike mannerisms in the underground cavern where he is first "possessed" by Sargon are also very effective. Shatner amplified the mystical nature of this exchange by imitating the behavior of a medium being manipulated by his "control." The impression of shifting consciousness was reinforced by the use of an echo effect on the voices of the "possessed" Kirk, Dr. Mulhall, and Mr. Spock.

George Duning once again proved himself the best choice to compose the most sensitive scores for "Star Trek"; his melodies for Sargon and Thalassa suggest ancient power coupled with love and desperation.

The android body was portrayed by an unidentified actor whose upper body and head were completely encased with sprayed-on latex (except for the holes through which he breathed). In the famous " 'Star Trek' Blooper Reel" we see him removing his makeup while someone tells him, "You *wanted* show business, son? Well, goddamn it, you *got* it." In the same blooper reel we also see William Shatner clowning around by grasping Sargon's globe and announcing, "Have no fear: Sargon is here."

"Return to Tomorrow" marked the first "Star Trek" appearance of actress Diana Muldaur (Dr. Anne Mulhall/ Thalassa), who returned as Dr. Miranda Jones in "Is There in Truth No Beauty?" She is also featured in the film *The Other* and in Gene Roddenberry's TV pilot, "Planet Earth."

Sargon takes possession of Kirk's body

"PATTERNS OF FORCE"

▮▮▮▮▮▮▮▮▮▮▮▮▮▮▮▮▮▮▮▮▮▮▮▮▮ #52

WRITER: John Meredyth Lucas
DIRECTOR: Vincent McEveety
PRINCIPALS: Kirk   Melakon
           Spock   Isak
           McCoy   Daras
           Scott   Abrom
           Uhura   Eneg
           Chekov   Davod
           John Gill

Spock engineers a jailbreak

◄ *Stardate 2534.0:* Arriving at the planet Ekos, the U.S.S. *Enterprise* is fired upon by atomic missiles, although records indicate that the planet does not possess such technology. Kirk and Spock beam down to investigate. In an effort to centralize Ekos's political structure, Federation cultural observer John Gill (a teacher of Kirk's at Starfleet Academy) has recreated a frightening imitation of Nazi Germany. Intending only to imitate the efficient Nazi bureaucracy, Gill has been subjugated by his aide, Melakon, who runs Ekos as a police state, using the drugged Terran as a figurehead. Kirk works with the underground of Zeon, a nearby planet whose inhabitants have become targets of Melakon's persecution. Infiltrating Melakon's headquarters as Gill is about to deliver a rigged speech on television, Kirk and McCoy revive the historian. Gill is able to denounce the regime before Melakon kills him. The Ekotians turn on Melakon, and Gill's misguided experiment comes to an end. ►

Whenever we meet people from Kirk's Academy days, or someone respected within the United Federation of Planets, they seem to be tragedies waiting to happen. Some, like Dr. Roger Korby, do not have any control over their impending doom; others, such as Dr. Tristan Adams, appear to court disaster for reasons of their own. John Gill appears to be the only one of the crowd to achieve his own downfall out of sheer idiocy. Gill was apparently foolish enough to forget how the original Nazi regime became so efficient, and the ambitious and deranged Melakon was there to capitalize on his mistakes.

"Patterns of Force" reminds us just how easily Nazi Germany could all happen again unless we are careful to remember the historical reality. The names featured in the episode resemble their historical counterparts. The victimized planet is "Zeon" (for "Zion"), and principal Zeon character names include "Isak" (for "Isaac"), Davod (for "David"), and "Abrom" (for "Abraham") (if this seems to be pushing things, try taking the name of the episode's party chairman, "Eneg," and spelling it backward . . .).

In the midst of the savage happenings, the episode provides some funny moments. Kirk, who has recently been soundly flogged, bends over to furnish Spock with a human platform so that the Vulcan can engineer their escape. As Kirk suffers in silence, Spock steps all over his highly sensitive back. The prisoner in the next cell wonders if the two are committing suicide in some unusual manner. Kirk wonders if their neighbor is correct after Spock has been on his back for a while.

More humor is provided by Dr. McCoy, who beams down with uniform boots that are too tight. Spock next takes an excursion into black comedy, informing Kirk that he makes a convincing Nazi.

It can be argued that the humor is necessary to break up the tension of the story—but a case can also be made that the episode should not have been produced at all. As in "The Gamesters of Triskelion," does the violence help provide the foundation for the adventure—or is the story just an excuse for the violence? This episode is more disturbing than "Gamesters of Triskelion" because the latter is sheer fantasy, whereas "Patterns of Force" concerns a horrible (and relatively recent) chapter in history. It should not be forgotten, but does it really work as an episode of "Star Trek"?

Guest star David Brian (John Gill) is a respected actor who should have been seen for more than the second he is on screen during this episode. He is best remembered by television fans as the star of his own series, "Mr. District Attorney."

Skip Homeier (Melakon) would later appear as Dr. Sevrin in "The Way to Eden." A former child actor, he starred in his own television series, "Dan Raven," and also appears in episodes of "Science Fiction Theatre," "The Outer Limits" ("The Expanding Human," with James Doohan and Keith Andes), and "One Step Beyond."

Visitors to Paramount studios may recognize the Ekosian's Nazi headquarters as the Producers' Building—and the site of Gill's broadcast as the Director's Building.

"THE ULTIMATE COMPUTER"

▮▮▮▮▮▮▮▮▮▮▮▮▮▮▮▮▮▮▮▮▮▮▮▮▮▮▮▮▮▮▮▮▮▮▮ #53

WRITER: D. C. Fontana (story by Laurence N. Wolfe)
DIRECTOR: John Meredyth Lucas
PRINCIPALS: Kirk   Uhura
              Spock   Chekov
              McCoy   Dr. Richard Daystrom
              Scott   Commodore Robert Wesley
              Sulu   Ensign Harper

◄ *Stardate 4729.4:* Dr. Richard Daystrom, who developed the Duotronic Breakthrough in computer technology 25 years ago, fears he is now regarded as a prodigy who has lost his touch. Obsessed with proving himself, Daystrom uses his own mental patterns to program his new M-5 computer and convinces Starfleet Command that it should test the machine by installing it on the U.S.S. *Enterprise.* Although Captain Kirk expresses reservations about the machine's presence, the first tests appear successful. When Commodore Robert Wesley leads a squad of four starships in practice maneuvers against the M-5-run *Enterprise,* the computer takes complete control of the starship and responds as though the attack is real. The crew of the starship *Excalibur* is killed. Kirk, treating the M-5 like an errant child, forces the machine to realize it has committed murder. The machine sentences itself to death by lowering the *Enterprise*'s shields—just as the rest of the wargames fleet moves in to attack. Scotty and Spock "pull out the plug" on M-5, restoring the *Enterprise* to Captain Kirk's control. Kirk then calls off the fleet. ▶

"The Ultimate Computer" serves as a powerful reminder that if man patterns his machines after himself, they reflect his weaknesses as well as his strengths. And as man's machines become more advanced, the relationship between human beings and their manufactured servants also grows more involved. In the era of "Star Trek," mankind has reached a point at which his machines are extremely complex by our century's standards. Captain Kirk regards the *Enterprise,* one of the most complex machines of that era, as his base of operations. He does not enjoy the idea of machines that think for themselves.

Kirk has been known to destroy machines that dominate humans, as the populations of Beta III ("The Return of the Archons"), Eminiar VII ("A Taste of Armageddon"), and Gamma Triaguli VI ("The Apple") could testify. He cares deeply about the rights of man versus the power of the machine, especially since Samuel T. Cogley prevented his career from being destroyed by a computer's "testimony" in "Court-Martial."

In "The Ultimate Computer," Kirk finds his command of the *Enterprise* threatened by a machine. He is jealous of M-5 and its efficient operation of his ship. Despite this, he is honestly concerned with the question of whether the M-5 is more qualified than he is to run the starship.

Dr. McCoy finds it difficult to diagnose the situation, for the physician, in addition to being greatly concerned about his friend's future, shares his captain's suspicion of machines. But he must reach his conclusions using facts, not emotions. In this instance McCoy trades places with Spock, who is more sympathetic to Kirk than to the machine. Spock's devotion to the captain is expressed eloquently in this episode.

Fortunately for Kirk and company, the situation is completely and finally resolved as the M-5 (and Dr. Daystrom as well) prove unfit to command the *Enterprise.* Unfortunately, command cannot be wrested from the M-5 by convening a competency hearing: before control of the *Enterprise* is regained, an engineering officer is dead, an ore freighter is destroyed, the crew of a starship has been murdered, and the *Enterprise* is almost decimated as well.

Actor William Marshall (Dr. Daystrom) provides one of the most impressive performances seen in "Star Trek," as the only man besides Kirk who is completely committed to a mechanical device. Marshall's imposing physical stature combines with his intense vocal and emotional delivery to present a dramatic presence which matches Kirk's. In feature films, Marshall was the genie in *Sabu and the Magic Ring* and is probably best known to fans of fantasy and horror films as *Blacula.*

The voice of the M-5 computer was provided by James Doohan.

Kirk shares the command chair with the M-5 unit

"THE OMEGA GLORY"

▮▮▮▮▮▮▮▮▮▮▮▮▮▮▮▮▮▮▮▮▮▮▮▮▮▮▮▮▮ #54

WRITER: Gene Roddenberry
DIRECTOR: Vincent McEveety
PRINCIPALS: Kirk   Sirah
            Spock   Wu
            McCoy   Captain Ronald Tracey
            Sulu   Lieutenant Galloway
            Uhura   Lieutenant Leslie
            Cloud William Dr. Carter

◄ *Stardate unknown:* The *Enterprise* discovers the starship *Exeter* in orbit around planet Omega IV, its crew reduced to crystallized powder by a deadly virus. Kirk, Spock, and McCoy, exposed to the disease, beam down to the planet in search of a cure—and meet *Exeter* Captain Ronald Tracey. Tracey believes that something in Omega's atmosphere can induce immortality in humans, as it apparently has in the planet's Asian rulers, the Kohms. To assure a place for himself on this planet, Tracey has violated the Prime Directive by using phasers against the Kohms' enemies, the Yangs. When the Yangs capture Tracey's village, Kirk discovers the planet Omega is the scene of a parallel evolution resembling war-ravaged counterparts of the Yankees (Yangs) and Communists (Kohms). Tracey denounces Kirk and Spock, implying that the Vulcan is a representative of Satan. Kirk, however, gains the trust of the Yangs by reciting their "worship words," actually a distorted version of the preamble to the United States Constitution. Prolonged exposure to the atmosphere of Omega cures our people of the virus, and with Tracey under arrest, they return to the *Enterprise*. ►

"The Omega Glory" is an exciting action episode, similar to "A Private Little War." Both involve frontier cultures, though this episode adds a misguided starship captain who has broken the Prime Directive.

A good deal of the drama is provided by Captain Tracey (Morgan Woodward), a strong figure even in the throes of his obsession with immortality. And this episode also contains an anachronism to the series continuity: the Kohms claim to be 1,000 years old, though interstellar travel has only been possible for 200 years at this time.

For the scenes involving the American flag, composer Fred Steiner provided the only original music written for this episode.

The first-draft script of "The Omega Glory" was written as a possible second pilot episode script, and is considerably different from the episode that was ultimately produced; instrumentation and terminology was closer to that of "The Cage."

The ship's computer with the female personality seen in "Tomorrow Is Yesterday" was also present in that draft. Kirk and Spock coped with that problem with the same degree of amusement and irritation seen in the later episode.

The script contained one shocking touch: the chief medical officer of the S.S. *"Argentina"* was slated to be shown dissolving on camera.

On Omega, Kirk discovered a captain Tracey who looked younger than he did when Kirk had previously seen him. Tracey's transformation was due to psychosomatic facial and emotional improvement caused by his respite from starship command responsibilities.

The most interesting differences between the first and final drafts of the script concern Mr. Spock. In the earliest draft, he used his power over women to obtain information from a young Omegan female. Later in the script the Vulcan touched the top of another woman's head and she became docile, sinking to the floor where she sat in a dazed condition. Spock brought the girl out of her trance by closing her eyes and slapping her face. This "hypnosis," witnessed by another Omegan, led to Spock's being declared a servant of the devil. The closeups of Mr. Spock's eyes as he wills the Yang woman to bring the communicator are the only feature that was carried over from the original first-draft script, regarding Spock's "powers."

The first draft climaxed in a western-style gunfight between Kirk and Tracey, during which Tracey shot Spock twice, once at point-blank range with an old-fashioned rifle. Spock survived because his heart was located in his abdominal area rather than his chest in this earliest allusion to the Vulcan's physical peculiarities.

Exiled on Omega

"ASSIGNMENT: EARTH"

▭▭▭▭▭▭▭▭▭▭▭▭▭▭▭▭▭▭▭▭▭▭▭▭▭▭▭▭ #55

WRITERS: Art Wallace (story by Art Wallace and Gene Roddenberry)
DIRECTOR: Marc Daniels
PRINCIPALS: Kirk   Gary Seven
Spock   Roberta Lincoln
McCoy   Cromwell
Scott   Colonel Nesvig
Sulu   Sergeant Lipton
Uhura   Security Chief
Chekov   Isis

◄ *Stardate unknown:* The *Enterprise* travels backward in time to the Earth of 1968 to discover how our planet managed to avoid destroying itself. The ship intercepts an incredibly powerful transporter beam and a humanoid named Gary Seven, both en route to Earth. After a battle in which he proves immune to a Vulcan nerve pinch, Mr. Seven escapes. Kirk and Spock follow to learn the truth about him, and to make sure that he does nothing to jeopardize the planet. Seven has been dispatched to our world to prevent the launching of an orbital atomic bomb by America. With the unwitting aid of his young secretary Roberta Lincoln, Seven eludes Kirk and transports himself to Cape Kennedy to sabotage the rocket's controls. Scotty attempts to beam Gary aboard before his mission is completed, but Roberta accidentally activates controls that divert Seven to his New York City headquarters. Kirk and Spock arrive and take control of the situation. Seven has diverted the rocket off-course, and it is now heading back to Earth where it will explode on impact. After Spock proves unable to work Seven's computer, Kirk permits Seven to take the controls again. He detonates the rocket, saving history from being altered. As the *Enterprise* returns to its own time, Gary Seven and Roberta ready themselves for other missions. ►

In "Tomorrow Is Yesterday" it was established that with proper safeguards, the U.S.S. *Enterprise* could navigate back and forth across time as well as space. With a variety of story possibilities that were not dependent upon time travel having already been bought for the series, "Trek" producers Roddenberry and Coon did not utilize this ability until they tackled "Assignment: Earth."

Throughout the episode, much remains unknown about Gary Seven. We know that he first lies to Roberta, telling her that he's from the CIA: is he telling Captain Kirk the truth when he says he is an Earthman raised on another world? During a fight, Seven exhibits an immunity to Spock's nerve pinch: is this immunity the result of some form of martial-arts training or physical modification—or is Gary Seven not human at all? He is familiar with the Vulcans. He knows that the *Enterprise* is from the future

because the ship's human crew is working side by side with a Vulcan. Kirk and his crew have their hands full attempting to determine the truth about the visitor, whose people could have influenced the history of Vulcan as well as that of the Earth.

Gary Seven may have been telling the truth regarding his human roots. His coworker, Isis, is established as being a shape-changer. The audience has no idea whether Isis is a cat who can appear as a woman, a woman who can appear as a cat, or a third variety of creature who can assume both (and other) appearances at will. The same possibilities can apply to Gary, unless Isis is simply a member of another race recruited by the people who trained Gary for his mission.

"Assignment: Earth" first appeared as a half-hour series pilot script, dated November 14, 1966 (written while "Star Trek's" first season was still in production). In the original concept, Gary Seven was an Earthman from the future who had been sent back to our era to combat the Omegans, an evil alien race that had mastered time travel. Working as a private investigator in a large, unnamed city, Mr. Seven was aided by the bewildered young Roberta Hornblower in his fight against the shape-changing Omegan agents, Harth and Isis. The Omegans, who could mentally enslave Earthmen, strove to change history to their advantage by corrupting various Terran individuals. Gary Seven's amazing scientific devices included a computer that could alter the recent past, canceling out damage that had been done by the Omegans. No one from the *Enterprise* appeared in this pilot version of the script, and there was no mention of the "Star Trek" universe.

When "Assignment: Earth" apparently did not sell as a separate television series, the concept was rewritten into the "Star Trek" format. This first-draft script, dated December 20, 1967, established the presence of the *Enterprise* in our era by having the bridge crew watch an episode of NBC's television series "Bonanza" on the starship's main viewscreen.

Gary Seven's transporter beam came from even farther across space than it did in the final concept.

After Seven was confined in the *Enterprise* brig, he revealed his mission to Dr. McCoy, turning the tables on "Bones" by asking him to think like "a doctor, not a mechanic."

Young Roberta *London*, recruited by Mr. Seven, was beamed up to the *Enterprise* for interrogation. The frightened Roberta was soothed by Uhura, who reassured her that she was still among Earth people.

When Kirk prophesied that Gary and Roberta would have "many interesting adventures together" he was referring to the "Assignment: Earth" series that never materialized.

"Assignment: Earth" makes good use of NASA footage of Cape Kennedy. The "Star Trek" cameras never actually visited Florida for this episode. All scenes at the

Cape were accomplished with a combination of stock footage and Paramount studio locations. One imaginative optical composite is a split screen, consisting of a Paramount sound stage topped by a rocket on its launching pad. For close-ups of Gary Seven crawling along the rocket's gantry crane, rear-projected views of Cape Kennedy were integrated with footage of actor Lansing on a small mock-up set constructed in the studio.

Music editor Jim Henrickson did his usual good job of taking musical cues written for previous "Star Trek" episodes and combining them to further heighten the tense and pleasant aspects of this segment.

Guest star Robert Lansing (Gary Seven) has starred in many motion pictures, including *The 4-D Man* (with Lee Meriwether) and *Empire of the Ants* (with Joan Collins). His starring roles in television series include "The Man Who Never Was", "87th Precinct," and "Twelve O'Clock High." He has also guest-starred in episodes of "Thriller" ("The Fatal Impulse," with Elisha Cook, Jr.), "One Step Beyond" ("The Voice"), and "The Twilight Zone" ("The Long Morrow," with Mariette Hartley).

Teri Garr (Roberta Lincoln) was first seen on "The Sonny and Cher Show." Her feature-film appearances include *Young Frankenstein, Close Encounters of the Third Kind, Tootsie,* and *After Hours.*

Other performers in this episode include Bruce Mars ("Finnegan" in "Shore Leave") as a policeman, Bartell LaRue (the voice of "The Guardian of Forever") as the voice of Mission Control, Paul Baxley (stuntman and actor in other "Trek" segments) as the Cape Kennedy security chief, and James Doohan as a Cape Kennedy radio voice.

SECOND SEASON PRODUCTION CREDITS

PRODUCERS   Gene L. Coon, John Meredyth Lucas
EXECUTIVE PRODUCER   Gene Roddenberry
ASSOCIATE PRODUCER   Robert H. Justman
SCRIPT CONSULTANT   D. C. Fontana
ASSISTANT TO THE PRODUCER   Edward K. Milkis
THEME MUSIC BY   Alexander Courage
MUSIC COMPOSED AND CONDUCTED BY   Various
DIRECTOR OF PHOTOGRAPHY   Jerry Finnerman
ART DIRECTOR   Walter M. Jeffries
FILM EDITORS   Bruce Schoengarth, Donald R. Rode, Fabian Tjordmann, John W. Hanley
UNIT PRODUCTION MANAGER   Gregg Peters
ASSISTANT DIRECTORS   Elliot Schick, Rusty Meek, Phil Rawlins
SET DECORATORS   Joseph J. Stone, John M. Dwyer
COSTUMES CREATED BY   William Ware Theiss
PHOTOGRAPHIC EFFECTS   Various
SOUND EFFECTS EDITOR   Douglas H. Grindstaff
MUSIC EDITOR   Jim Henrickson
RE-RECORDING MIXERS   Elden E. Ruberg, CAS, Gordon L. Day, CKS
PRODUCTION MIXER   Carl W. Daniels
SCRIPT SUPERVISOR   George A. Rutter
CASTING   Joseph D'Agosta
SOUND   Glen Glenn Sound Co.
MAKEUP ARTIST   Fred B. Phillips, SMA
HAIRSTYLES   Pat Westmore
GAFFER   George H. Merhoff
HEAD GRIP   George Rader
PROPERTY MASTER   Irving A. Feinberg
SPECIAL EFFECTS   Jim Rugg
KEY COSTUMER   Ken Harvey
A Desilu (Paramount) Production in association with Norway Corp.

Space travellers at Cape Kennedy

8

THIRD SEASON

The letter-writing campaign to save "Star Trek," initiated by Bjo and John Trimble's December 11, 1967 mail appeal, was so successful that it eventually received the praise of the NBC television network. In 1968 NBC published an updated version of their August 1967 network booklet "Star Trek Mail Call," which acknowledged the receipt of 115,893 letters, all the result of the Trimbles' campaign. Of those, 52,358 letters, NBC stated, were received during the month of February 1968. "Star Trek" fans were referred to as "loyal and articulate," and the booklet closed by saying "Trek" fans were present "in ever-increasing numbers."

NBC seemed proud of "Star Trek" and its growing number of fans, and many media surveys reported that "Trek" was very popular with the public. But the Nielsen ratings were still saying otherwise. Despite their protestation of faith in the series, the Nielsens are what NBC felt it had to go by.

The network first announced that for the series' third season "Star Trek" would be aired on Mondays at 7:30 P.M., E.S.T.: had the network kept to this decision, "Star Trek" would have been opposite "Gunsmoke" and "The Avengers."

It came as a shock to many people, especially Gene Roddenberry, when NBC changed "Star Trek's" slot to Fridays at 10:00 P.M., E.S.T. The series' opposition would be "Judd for the Defense" and the second half of the "CBS Friday Night Movie." On March 15, 1968, when NBC made its programming plans for "Star Trek" public, Roddenberry stated:

We do not feel that 10:00 P.M. is the best time at all. NBC had told us previously that they saw this as a 7:30 or 8:00 P.M. show because of its appeal to the younger adults in the audience.

Roddenberry, currently serving as "Star Trek's" exec-

utive producer, offered to resume his original position of line producer if NBC would change the series time slot. This would have meant his playing a larger role in determining the actual content and appearance of the series. Roddenberry had served as line producer for the first half of the first season, and his resumption of that role would have meant a return to the values present in the series at that time.

The New York Daily News reported that though Roddenberry was attempting to convince NBC that it should change its mind about the late-night Friday slot, it was not likely that the network would alter its schedule again. The *News* was correct. NBC set their final fall schedule with "Star Trek" firmly in place on Fridays at 10:00 P.M. Gene Roddenberry remained in his executive position.

Fred Freiberger became the new line producer. Freiberger had cowritten the screenplays for *The Beast from 20,000 Fathoms* and *The Beginning of the End*. and had been associated with "The Wild, Wild West" during its last season. After "Star Trek" he would go on to produce the last season of "Space: 1999." Another important personnel change was the replacement of cinematographer Gerald P. "Jerry" Finnerman (who had photographed "Star Trek" since "The Corbomite Maneuver") by Al Francis.

These switches resulted in a significant change in "Star Trek's" literary and visual format. Though there are fans who like the third season shows, the majority agree that most of the "Trek" episodes produced in the final season were ultimately lacking (exceptions include "The Paradise Syndrome," "Is There in Truth No Beauty?", "The Tholian Web," "For the World Is Hollow and I Have Touched the Sky," and "The Day of the Dove").

Indicative of the drop in quality to come was the third season opener "Spock's Brain." Other episodes had begun production before this tale (five of them were scored before music for "Spock's Brain" was recorded on August 26, 1968), including "The Paradise Syndrome" and "The Enterprise Incident," two excellent adventures. But

"Spock's Brain" was chosen to open the broadcast season, and on the night it was telecast, "Star Trek" fans must have wondered if it had been worth all those cards and letters to save the series just to see Mr. Spock lobotomized without the loss of a hair.

Mr. Spock was certainly the character who had the most exposure during "Trek's" third season. The evidence would indicate, however, that Dr. McCoy's operation to restore the Vulcan's brain in the season opener was not entirely successful. During these last segments Spock joined a band of space hippies in a "jam session," sang ballads, laughed and recited poetry, reacted emotionally toward an illusion, voluntarily discussed Vulcan sexual matters with a woman he had just met for the first time, came close to strangling Dr. McCoy, tasted meat, and conspired to mutiny. The actual responsibility for these activities and attitudes, however, does not lie with Mr. Spock but with those who chose to exploit his "box office" potential—at the expense of "Star Trek's" continuity and credibility.

These changes were not lost on the fans or the press: in its September 25, 1968, issue, *Variety* reported that "Star Trek" "retains its vigor and spatial spookiness, although its chief characters are largely caricaturres and the dialogue tends to turgidity." The male crewmembers, *Variety* added, were kept occupied looking at "women in tight spacesuits," and the paper concluded that the best thing about "Star Trek" was its special effects.

In addition, NBC frequently preempted "Star Trek." There were no "Trek" episodes telecast on December 13 and 27, 1968, and February 7, 1969. No first-run episodes were aired from March 21 to June 3, 1969—when the last first-run show, "Turnabout Intruder," was televised. The five-year mission of the U.S.S. *Enterprise* had apparently come to a premature end.

"SPECTRE OF THE GUN"

#56

WRITER:	Lee Cronin (Gene Coon)
DIRECTOR:	Vincent McEveety
PRINCIPALS:	Kirk Doc Holliday
	Spock Morgan Earp
	McCoy Wyatt Earp
	Scott Virgil Earp
	Uhura Johnny Behan
	Chekov Ed
	Sylvia

◄ *Stardate 4385.3:* The *Enterprise* encounters a "warning buoy" marking the territorial boundary of Melkotian space. Kirk ignores their message to turn back—whereupon the Melkots transport Kirk, Spock, McCoy, Scotty, and Chekov to a surrealistic recreation of a Wild West town drawn from Kirk's memory. The landing party will reenact the famous gunfight at the O.K. Corral—in the losing roles of the Clanton gang. But when Chekov, cast as Billy Clanton (who survived the gunfight), is "killed" before the showdown, Spock realizes all they are experiencing is unreal. Using a trio of Vulcan mind melds, Spock enables his friends to reject the illusion, so that when their enemies, the Earps, shoot, the bullets pass harmlessly through the landing party. Kirk refuses to return fire on the Earps and Doc Holliday, because he knows that they are simply phantoms created by the Melkots. The aliens are convinced of Kirk's peaceful intentions—and invite the *Enterprise* to open diplomatic relations. ►

The story outline for this episode, entitled "The Last Gunfight," omitted Ensign Chekov. A security officer appeared in his place and was killed—but did not return. The sequence with the warning buoy was not included, and the aliens were called "the Shawnians."

Throughout the outline, Kirk and company experienced frustrations. The "townspeople" could come and go as they pleased, but the *Enterprise* people were stopped by force fields geared to their individual body readings. When Kirk visited the Earps' office to convince them that he was not who they thought he was, he indicated Spock's pointed ears. Wyatt responded that Frank McClowery always looked that way.

The outline had additional chores for Dr. McCoy. Aware of Doc Holliday's tuberculosis symptoms, he offered to cure the gunfighter, but the illusion declined treatment.

The outline climaxed when Kirk and company ambushed the pseudo-Earps. The Earps commented on the "code of the West" having been violated, and promptly vanished. The Shawnians decided that Kirk was insane because the "code" was in his memories but he did not adhere to it. The aliens did not believe in punishing irrational creatures, and the starship was freed.

The final episode is more effective than the outline because it allows Kirk and company to escape from the threat without resorting to tactics that would not win the aliens as allies of the Federation. Somewhere along the line someone (probably Gene Coon) decided to duplicate the conclusion of "Arena," in which the Metrons learn that the men of the Federation are not barbarians after all.

Having every *Enterprise* crewman hear the voice of the warning buoy in his own language enabled this episode to draw on several previous "Trek" adventures. Spock, undoubtedly remembering what happened in "Catspaw," "The Squire of Gothos," and "The Cage," points out the need to ignore what must be illusion and concentrate on what is known to be real. Kirk, in deciding to continue onward in the face of danger, surely recalled the outcomes of "The Corbomite Maneuver" and "Arena." "Spectre of the Gun" combines these two bits of philosophy for the first time in the series.

The combination of spotlights and odd camera angles on the Earps in the climactic sequences made them appear as soulless phantoms. To emphasize the town's artificial appearance, no attempt was made to hide the shadows of windblown trees on the red sky backdrop (the settings are incomplete because they are based upon Kirk's fragmented and idealized memories of the Wild West). The final execution of the mind melds and the gunfight is flawless. The landing party stands fearlessly as the Earps' bullets rip harmlessly through them into the fence—an eerie, altogether effective scene.

James Doohan is heard once again as the voice of the Melkot warning buoy. The Melkot is voiced by character actor Abraham Sofaer, who also appeared as the Thasian in "Charlie X."

The Melkotian buoy resembles an hourglass, a symbol of suspense and danger ever since *The Wizard of Oz*. The Melkot itself, a small, rubber creation, was designed and built by artist Mike Minor, who would later contribute to "Star Trek" feature films.

Guest star Ed McCready, playing the town barber, also appeared in "Dagger of the Mind" and "Miri."

McCoy and Kirk—ready for the showdown

"ELAAN OF TROYIUS"

#57

WRITER: John Meredyth Lucas
DIRECTOR: John Meredyth Lucas
PRINCIPALS: Kirk   Chapel
Spock   Elaan
McCoy   Lord Petri
Scott   Kryton
Sulu   Technician Watson
Uhura   Evans
Chekov

◄ *Stardate 4372.5:* Though the Tellun star system's two planets, Elas and Troyius, are both Federation members, they have been at war with each other for centuries. Due to recent Klingon interest in the area, it is imperative that the two worlds now make peace. The *Enterprise* is assigned to transport Elaan, the Dohlman of Elas, to Troyius for her marriage to that planet's leader. Elaan is arrogant and seems to be ignorant of the marriage's importance. Petri, the Troyian ambassador attempting to teach Elaan Troyian social graces, is stabbed by the Dohlman. The future of the marriage, the alliance, and the ultimate fate of the Tellun system are all at stake as Kirk attempts to educate Elaan. The captain's task is complicated not only by her reluctance, but also her body chemistry. When she cries, her tears, containing a chemical intoxicant, cause Kirk to fall in love with her. Meanwhile a Klingon vessel threatening the *Enterprise* is aided by Kryton, a member of the Dohlman's party. He sabotages the ship's power by fusing the dilithium crystals—and then commits suicide. Kirk discovers Elaan's jewelry is composed of dilithium crystals—a fact that both explains the Klingons' interest in her planet and enables the *Enterprise* to defeat the Klingon ship. Charmed by Kirk, Elaan determines to succeed in her mission to unite Elas and Troyius—and the captain frees himself from Elaan's spell by remembering that his first love is the starship *Enterprise.* ▶

With a name derived from Helen of Troy and a plot borrowed from *The Taming of the Shrew,* "Elaan of Troyius" is nevertheless an enjoyable "Star Trek" episode that includes action, suspense, intrigue, and humor.

Elaan is quartered in Lieutenant Uhura's cabin (also viewed in "The Tholian Web"), which enables us to learn more about the communications officer. A zebra-skin bedspread; African sculptures, masks, and decorated wall panels reveal Uhura's individuality and artistic tastes.

Kirk's attempt to "tame" Elaan, and the Dohlman's attempts to avoid the captain's teachings, are balanced by the diplomatic (although cynical) efforts of Petri, the Troyian ambassador assigned the difficult mission.

This episode marks the first appearance of the Klingon battle cruiser, which had been spoken about in previous episodes but was seen only as a "blip" on the *Enterprise* screen or (in "Friday's Child") as a vague shape that looked nothing like the design introduced in this episode.

William Ware Theiss created an impressive assortment

The Klingon ship makes its first appearance

of costumes for this episode. All Elaan's dresses reveal the Theiss trademark—exposed portions of the feminine anatomy.

A scene in the *Enterprise* recreation room, showing Kirk, McCoy, and Uhura listening as Spock played his Vulcan lyre, was filmed but edited from the final print. The concert was Uhura's idea, suggested during a briefing of what could be done to calm Elaan down before anyone else was injured. The briefing-room dialogue, also left on the cutting room floor, went as follows:

UHURA
Music!

KIRK
What?

UHURA
It's supposed to soothe the savage breast.

SPOCK
Very true. In ancient times the Vulcan lyre was used to lull the fury of the mating time.

KIRK
You have a Vulcan lyre in your quarters, Mr. Spock.

SPOCK
I have not played it in some time.

KIRK
But you still know how? Play well?

SPOCK
I took second prize in the all Vulcan music competition.

SCOTT
Who got first prize?

SPOCK
My father.

The music was piped through the *Enterprise* audio system into Uhura's cabin, where it was heard by Elaan and led to the first romantic confrontation between the Dohlman and Kirk.

France Nuyen (Elaan) had previously worked with William Shatner during the Broadway run of *The World of Suzie Wong* in 1958–59. Her most famous motion picture role was as the young daughter of "Bloody Mary" in *South Pacific*. Ms. Nuyen also appeared opposite Jeffrey Hunter in the 1966 science fiction/espionage film *Dimension Five*. Jay Robinson (Petri) is best known as the mad emperor Caligula in the feature-film epics *The Robe* and *Demetrius and the Gladiators.*

"THE PARADISE SYNDROME"

#58

WRITER: Margaret Armen
DIRECTOR: Jud Taylor
PRINCIPALS: Kirk   Chapel
            Spock   Miramanee
            McCoy   Salish
            Scott   Goro
            Sulu   Lumo
            Chekov

◄ *Stardate 4842.6:* Beaming down to a beautiful Earthlike planet threatened by collision with a huge asteroid, Kirk, Spock, and McCoy discover a village of peaceful tribesmen, akin to American Indians. Near their village is a huge obelisk, covered with incomprehensible writing. As Kirk explores this structure he falls through a trapdoor and is exposed to a strange ray that renders him unconscious. McCoy and Spock fail to find him, and are forced to return to the *Enterprise* to destroy the asteroid. Kirk revives, suffering from partial amnesia, and is discovered by the Indians, who revere him as a god. The *Enterprise* fails to fracture the asteroid with high-power phaser beams and damages its engines: the ship is forced to precede the asteroid back to the planet at sublight speed, a journey of several months. During this time Kirk has fallen in love with, and married, the beautiful priestess Miramanee. Meanwhile, Spock deciphers the writings on the obelisk, which his tricorder had recorded, and learns that an ancient race called the Preservers had "seeded" the planet and provided an asteroid deflector, housed within the obelisk. Kirk, now Medicine Chief Kirok, has no idea how to activate the obelisk. Spock and McCoy beam down just as Kirk and Miramanee are being stoned by the frightened tribesmen. The asteroid is deflected and Kirk's memory is restored, but the pregnant Miramanee dies along with Kirk's unborn child. ►

"The Paradise Syndrome" is an atypical "Star Trek" episode in several respects. Although the story centers around Kirk, we see the captain functioning not in his traditional capacities but as the leader of a tribe of primitives on a planet far from the location and life-style of the *Enterprise.*

Still, Kirok is a leader of men, whose abilities are very special and whose experience is necessary for his village to survive. Kirk's memories of Federation technology enable the Indians to enjoy the benefits of irrigation, food preservation, and the use of lamps for the first time. Yet even in this situation, when Kirk has escaped from the *Enterprise*, he is haunted by visions of her and dreams of "the strange lodge that moves through the sky."

This episode's exotic flavor was aided greatly by location photography throughout: the initial view of the lake and the Indian village far away evokes an extremely peaceful image, a return to a simpler past that McCoy refers to as "the Tahiti syndrome."

The obelisk's size and shape make an effective contrast to the Indian culture, producing an impact similar to that of *2001: A Space Odyssey*'s monolith.

The story outline of this episode, called "The Paleface," indicated that this planet was located in a meteor and asteroid belt and was the only world in the region that contained life. The asteroid deflector was originally represented as a totem pole covered with hieroglyphics. Kirk's amnesia was brought about by a head wound, which led to the captain's confused mental state. Spock, unable to destroy the asteroid, beamed down to evacuate the Indians. Kirk (Kirok) perceived the landing party as enemies; Spock stunned his captain and returned him to the *Enterprise*, transporting him up along with the Indian population. The Indians had to be sedated aboard the ship; it was the first time they were ever in such confined areas. Kirk's memory was restored when he realized that he was fighting his friend Spock. The deflector mechanism was hidden in a vast, underground area in a cavern the Indians said was inhabited by a spirit. The Indians, including Miramanee, who *survived* pregnant with Kirk's child, were returned to their planet.

Director Jud Taylor began his Hollywood career as an actor, appearing in "The Fugitive" and "Dr. Kildare" (a series he also produced). His television directorial credits include horror, fantasy, and TV movies, such as *Weekend of Terror, Search for the Gods, The Disappearance of Flight 412, Future Cop,* and *Return to Earth.*

Composer Gerald Fried contributed much beautiful music to "Star Trek," and in "The Paradise Syndrome," sensitive melodies suggest the alien yet familiar nature of the extraterrestrial Indian community, and the love affair between Kirk (Kirok) and Miramanee. Fried's battle-sequence melodies are reminiscent of his score for "Amok Time."

The views of the *Enterprise* traveling backward in front of the asteroid are extremely effective, as are the phaser-beam and deflector-beam sequences involving the purple heavenly body (which would later be featured in "For the World Is Hollow and I Have Touched the Sky").

The purple memory beam that gives Kirk his amnesia and the orange-yellow deflector beam both add to the visual quality of this episode.

Sabrina Scharf (Miramanee) had portrayed a native American before, in the "Daniel Boone" episode "Requiem for Craw Green," which featured Jeffrey Hunter. Ms. Scharf also appeared in "The Man from U.N.C.L.E." Rudy Solari (Salish) had recurring roles in four television series; as Frank in "Redigo" (1963), Nagurski in "The Wackiest Ship in the Army" (1965–66), Casino in "Garrison's Gorillas" (1967–68), and as the attorney in "Return to Peyton Place" (1972–74). He is also seen in segments of "The Outer Limits" and "Voyage to the Bottom of the Sea." Richard Hale (Goro) appeared in the "Thriller" episode "Remarkable Dr. Markesan."

Kirok

"THE ENTERPRISE INCIDENT"

▭▭▭▭▭▭▭▭▭▭▭▭▭▭▭▭▭▭▭▭▭▭▭▭▭▭▭▭▭ #59

WRITER: D. C. Fontana
DIRECTOR: John Meredyth Lucas
PRINCIPALS: Kirk   Uhura
            Spock   Chekov
            McCoy   Chapel
            Scott   Romulan Commander
            Sulu   Romulan Subcommander Tal

◄ *Stardate 5031.3:* Captain Kirk, in an overworked and confused state, takes the *Enterprise* into Romulan space, where the starship is immediately surrounded by Romulan ships which demand her surrender. Kirk and Spock beam aboard the Romulan flagship, and Kirk attempts to explain his ship's trespass as equipment failure. But Spock denounces his captain, stating he deliberately acted without orders in entering Romulan territory. Dr. McCoy is then beamed aboard the Romulan vessel to examine the increasingly erratic Kirk—who, infuriated beyond reason, suddenly turns and attacks Spock. Spock, acting in self-defense, unthinkingly uses the Vulcan death grip, killing Kirk. McCoy returns with the captain's body to the *Enterprise.* The female Romulan commander is highly interested in Mr. Spock and attempts to induce him to defect to the Romulans. Spock seems to be interested in her offer.

But the entire affair has been a hoax, to gain possession of the Romulan cloaking device (there is, of course, no such thing as the Vulcan death-grip). Kirk, surgically altered to resemble a Romulan, is beamed back aboard the flagship and steals the device. After the theft is discovered, Spock is declared a spy. As he awaits execution, Chekov locates the Vulcan using the *Enterprise*'s sensors. Spock is beamed back to the *Enterprise* along with the Romulan commander. The *Enterprise* escapes by using the cloaking device, hurriedly put into operation by Scotty. Kirk is left with an unexpected bonus—the Romulan commander—while Spock must contemplate the deceit he has practiced on the woman. ►

In "Balance of Terror" we first met the Romulans, and discovered them to be a mysterious but honorable people. In "The Enterprise Incident" we learn they have formed an alliance with the Klingons, presumably due to both parties' wish to defeat the United Federation of Planets.

Like "Balance of Terror," this episode is a study in comparative values. Vulcans do not lie, so the Romulan commander believes Spock's statements regarding his captain. Spock justifies his actions as a charade to preserve the system to which he has pledged his loyalty.

A Romulan named Kirk

Neither the Romulan Commander nor Spock bears the other any grudge, and although there can be no further relationship between them, it is understood that each was merely seeking to fulfill his duty.

Kirk's "nervous breakdown" is expertly portrayed by William Shatner. He appears unsure of his priorities and distrustful of everyone: his apparent attempt to kill Spock is disturbingly convincing. Shatner used a very effective repertoire of mannerisms during his scenes as a madman, letting his arms hang loosely at his side and permitting his mouth to hang open at times.

The first draft of "The Enterprise Incident" stressed the attraction between Spock and the Romulan commander based upon their common heritage.

The cloaking device of the first draft was a prismatic type of mechanism. It was stored in a laboratory waiting to be installed in another Romulan ship, rather than being a mechanism that was already operational when Kirk obtained it. The Vulcan death grip was applied at the back of the neck, rather than directly over the face.

Both Kirk and McCoy were surgically altered to appear Romulan, and they accompanied Spock to the Romulan vessel to steal the cloaking device. When Spock was discovered in the forbidden corridor, McCoy had to talk Kirk out of attempting to rescue the Vulcan. Spock, in turn, lied and gave the impression that he had been alone and had destroyed the device (the device was simply the top of Nomad attached to Sargon's sphere).

Photographic effects abound in this episode. Special mattes were produced of the Klingon battle-cruiser miniature, and when these were combined, they enabled the alien vessels to surround the *Enterprise*.

Joanne Linville (Romulan commander) also appeared in episodes of "The Invaders," "The Twilight Zone," "One Step Beyond," and "Great Ghost Stories."

The ear tips on the Romulans are not as graceful as those used for the Vulcans and are similar to the ears seen in the "Star Trek" feature films. The diminished size of their ears may also have affected the logical development of the Romulans. Why else would they indulge in such bizarre activities as making agreements with Klingons and drinking from square glasses?

"AND THE CHILDREN SHALL LEAD"

#60

WRITER:	Edward J. Lakso	
DIRECTOR:	Marvin Chomsky	
PRINCIPALS:	Kirk	Gorgan
	Spock	Tommy Starnes
	McCoy	Professor Starnes
	Scott	Mary Janowski
	Sulu	Ray Tsingtao
	Uhura	Steve O'Connel
	Chekov	Don Linden
	Chapel	

◄ *Stardate 5027.3:* Arriving at the planet Triacus, the *Enterprise* finds that the scientists in the Starnes scientific expedition have all committed suicide to escape an evil presence—"the enemy within." The colony's children are unharmed and strangely oblivious to their parents' deaths. Beamed aboard the starship, the children are cared for while Kirk attempts to discover the truth. Meanwhile, an evil entity named "Gorgan," a "friendly angel" summoned by the children and made powerful by their belief in him, has stolen aboard the *Enterprise* with the intention of using the starship to take him to other planets and other innocents. To prevent the *Enterprise* crew from fighting him, Gorgan renders Kirk incapable of giving orders, frightens the ship's officers with illusions, and convinces Spock that nothing is wrong. Kirk's distress shocks Spock back to normal. Fighting Gorgan, they show the children tricorder tapes of their parents—and their graves. Suddenly the youngsters see Gorgan not as a "friendly angel" but for what he actually is: an ugly, evil force. Rendered harmless by the loss of his followers, the entity fades into nothingness. ►

Seeing innocent children in the grip of evil forces is usually horrifying, as in films such as *The Space Children* and *Invaders from Mars*. This episode examines not only the effects of evil on the children but the nature of the evil as well. Gorgan is first cousin to "Redjac" of "Wolf in the Fold," a living embodiment of hate and evil that attacks everything in its path.

Captain Kirk treats Gorgan much as he would treat any entity (man or machine) that stood in the way of happiness, fulfillment, and freedom of choice. After initially encountering Gorgan in a cave on Triacus, Kirk proceeds to drag the evil out of the darkness and into the open. On the bridge of the *Enterprise*, Kirk exorcises the evil Gorgan from his starship.

Noted attorney Melvin Belli's portrayal of Gorgan appears stilted. This is partially due to the static positions his character had to maintain due to the photographic effects involved. Belli's delivery is unemotional, not the

A worried Kirk with the U.F.P. flag

sort of impassioned presentation one would expect from either an alien entity or a defense attorney.

Craig Hundley (Tommy Starnes) also appeared as the captain's nephew, Peter Kirk, in "Operation: Annihilate!" More recently, as a musician, he contributed exotic sounds to *Star Trek II: The Wrath of Khan.* Melvin Belli's son Caesar appeared as Steve O'Connel.

"SPOCK'S BRAIN"

61

WRITER: Lee Cronin (Gene L. Coon)
DIRECTOR: Marc Daniels
PRINCIPALS: Kirk   Uhura
            Spock   Chekov
            McCoy   Kara
            Scott   Luma
            Sulu

◄ *Stardate 5431.4:* While the starship *Enterprise* is on a routine mission in deep space, a young woman materializes on the bridge and renders everyone on board unconscious. The bridge crew awakens to find Spock missing. McCoy summons Kirk to sick bay, where he has discovered Spock lying motionless on a diagnostic bed. The young woman has stolen Spock's brain! They have only 24 hours to find it before his body dies. Kirk follows the alien's trail to the sixth planet in the Sigma Draconis system. McCoy fabricates a device to control Spock's brainless body, and they, Kirk and Scotty beam down. On the planet's surface they discover a primitive all-male tribe—the Morgs—who are provided for by an underground race of beautiful women—the Eymorgs—who live in a scientifically advanced environment they do not understand. Led by Kara, the brain thief, the women are using Spock's brain to administer their planet's power. After some difficulty Kirk locates Spock's brain and, using a wondrous device called "the Teacher," McCoy gains enough temporary knowledge to reverse Kara's damage and restore the Vulcan to normal. Kirk encourages the Eymorgs to share their scientific knowledge with the Morgs to rebuild civilization on their planet. ►

While *Abbott and Costello Meet Frankenstein* was in production at Universal Pictures in 1948, its title was *The Brain of Frankenstein.* When viewed in context with the remainder of "Star Trek," "Spock's Brain" is almost as funny even without the presence of Abbott and Costello.

The concept behind this episode is an interesting one. It has long been known that the human brain is "the controller" of the body's functions, and it is not inconceivable that another planet's scientific developments would center on coordinating the machinery of its world with a humanoid brain. Provided, of course, that sufficient technology was available and that the proper brain could be found.

The problems of this episode lie in the manner in which the delicate operation is treated. Add this oversimplified delivery to the casual manner in which Mr. Spock's disembodied brain communicates with Kirk and company and the spectacle of the brainless Spock being led around like a marionette, and the segment emerges as something quite beyond belief.

In "The Menagerie," Dr. McCoy confirms that medical science in "Star Trek's" era has learned to tie into all bodily organs *except* the brain. It therefore seems highly unlikely that, while McCoy *could* sustain life within Spock's brainless body in sick bay, he could animate it and still keep it alive *outside* the confines of the ship. All that is used to accomplish this is a small, hatlike device and a wristlet.

When Spock's voice is heard over Kirk's communicator, it is not explained how the Vulcan's brain manages to synthesize Spock's voice although body and mind have been separated.

The sequence involving the Teacher machine and its transformation of Dr. McCoy is very well done. DeForest Kelley's performance, the machine's design, the cinematography, and McCoy's observation that "a *child* could do it" almost manage to make the act of restoring Spock's brain a believable feat.

But the operation is ultimately impossible to accept, as Spock advises the doctor how to proceed when the knowledge gained from the Teacher begins to fade.

Lee Cronin's story outline for "Spock's Brain" featured the Vulcan's disembodied mind employing Vulcan techniques of discipline to avoid going insane.

When Kirk discovered Mr. Spock's voice coming over his communicator, Spock asked that his brain be disconnected from the machines that were keeping it alive, a reaction caused by the Vulcan's belief that his new existence was nonproductive. Later, when Spock became aware that his brain was coordinating the vital functions of an entire planet, Spock had to be ordered to stop his control over the machines so that his brain could be restored to his body.

There was no mention of a Teacher in this draft, and Dr. McCoy received no transfusion of any special knowledge except for a study of that planet's advanced surgical techniques. Combining these with his own medical experience, he was able to restore Spock's brain. Working with alien doctors, McCoy did most of the actual work.

As Spock began to recover, he announced that the doctor had not done enough studying. Some of the Vulcan's ganglia had been jangled, but with the aid of his special mental disciplines he was already beginning to regain physical control over himself.

Spock—in search of his brain

"IS THERE IN TRUTH NO BEAUTY?"

#62

WRITER: Jean Lisette Aroeste
DIRECTOR: Ralph Senensky
PRINCIPALS: Kirk   Uhura
Spock   Chekov
McCoy   Dr. Miranda Jones
Scott   Lawrence Marvick
Sulu   Kolos

Spock wearing the Vulcan I.D.I.C. medallion

◄ *Stardate 5630.7:* The Medusans are a race with wonderful mental abilities, including navigational capabilities exceeding those of humanoids. Physically, the Medusans appear as energy patterns arranged in frequencies and colors that are too dazzling for humanoid eyes to behold. In a pioneering experiment, the lovely Dr. Miranda Jones beams aboard the *Enterprise* with Kolos, a Medusan encased within a protective container. Traveling with them is Lawrence Marvick, one of the men who designed the engines of the starship *Enterprise.* Marvick, rendered irrational by his love for Miranda, is to aid in an exchange of technical information with the Medusan, "translated" by the telepathic Dr. Jones. Jealous of the attention Dr. Jones lavishes on the alien and infuriated by her refusal to marry him, Marvick attempts to kill the Medusan. The sight of the alien renders Marvick insane. In the throes of his madness he takes control of the *Enterprise,* plunging the starship into another dimension. Mr. Spock dons a protective visor and melds minds with the Medusan to guide the *Enterprise* back home. While separating from Kolos, Spock forgets his visor. The Vulcan's life and sanity are in danger until Dr. Jones puts aside her jealousy of Spock's superior telepathic abilities and cures the Vulcan by entering his temporarily disordered mind. Finally, Miranda's ability to look upon the Medusan without harm is explained. She is revealed to be completely blind, her dress being a complex sensor web that gives her the ability to "see" obstacles and judge distances. ►

"Is There In Truth No Beauty?" is one of the most successful "Star Trek" episodes. The story has sensitivity, mystery, action, is faithful to the series' regular characters, and successfully explores the "IDIC" theme while providing constant surprises.

The focal point of this tale is Dr. Miranda Jones, who inspires love in Marvick, envy in Mr. Spock, and the interest of Captain Kirk. Miranda wants nothing to do with these men: her sole concern is developing her mental rapport with Kolos, the Medusan.

We have previously witnessed a humanoid in love with an alien. The Companion was ultimately united with Zephram Cochrane in "Metamorphosis" after she merged with Terran Nancy Hedford; the romances between Sarek

of Vulcan and Amanda of Earth, and Carolyn Palamas with the alien Apollo provide additional examples that in "Star Trek's" era, as man travels through the universe, anything is bound to happen, and often does. In this unusual relationship, two minds are attracted to each other despite their physical differences (Kolos may lack *any* physical form at all).

The scene at dinner, as Miranda perceives someone contemplating murder, is well staged, and just as dramatic as the "seance" in "Wolf in the Fold," although nothing supernatural is at work here. What is baffling is that Mr. Spock does not feel the same "vibrations" that Miranda does regarding the unhappy and unstable Mr. Marvick.

Scotty almost signs the death warrant of the *Enterprise.* Knowing that Marvick is one of the designers of the starship's engines, he cannot resist inviting the engineer to visit and try to operate the controls of the vessel. This results in disaster for the ship and permits the creation of some of the most beautiful photographic effects in the entire series. The animated, purplish effects are similar to those seen in "Where No Man Has Gone Before."

Mr. Spock's mind meld with Kolos is well handled; the Vulcan had joined minds with some extraordinary entities before, particularly the Horta in "The Devil in the Dark," but this episode gives Leonard Nimoy a rare chance to emote. Spock, while a Vulcan/Medusan, smiles and even recites poetry to Lieutenant Uhura.

The story outline of "Is There In Truth No Beauty?" featured Miranda taking part in the first collaboration between humans and Medusans, a project code-named "Ariel." Larry Marvick was honest in expressing his dislike of the Medusan: he conveyed his sentiments directly to Miranda. After Marvick's exposure to the Medusan, he invaded the bridge, killed two crewmen, wrecked the *Enterprise* communications console, and accelerated the starship out of our universe and into the void.

Dr. Jones, in the outline, had previously discussed the theory of navigation in interdimensional voids, which led Mr. Spock to mind-meld with the Medusan. The meld took hours to complete. Spock's complex entanglement with the alien was canceled out by Miranda's guiding the Vulcan through a mental recreation of his fight with Captain Kirk as seen in "Amok Time."

Diana Muldaur (Dr. Miranda Jones) also appears in "Return to Tomorrow," as Dr. Ann Mulhall.

"THE EMPATH"

#63

WRITER: Joyce Muskat
DIRECTOR: John Erman
PRINCIPALS: Kirk Thann
Spock Lal
McCoy Dr. Ozaba
Scott Dr. Linke
Gem

◄ *Stardate 5121.0:* The *Enterprise* journeys to the Minarvan system to rescue Federation researchers Dr. Linke and Dr. Ozaba before the Minarvan sun goes nova. Kirk, Spock, and McCoy discover record tapes that show the missing doctors literally disappearing into thin air. While trying to discover what happened, the three are also seized and materialize in the presence of the "kidnappers," aliens Lal and Thann. Kirk and company discover that Linke and Ozaba are dead, their bodies preserved in huge specimen jars. The only other living being present is Gem, a beautiful young woman who cannot speak. Kirk and McCoy are taken one at a time and experimented on by Lal and Thann, resulting in terrible injuries to the captain and the doctor. They discover Gem is an empath who can absorb their injuries and pain into her own body.

When McCoy is gravely injured, Kirk is prevented from aiding him or inducing Gem to cure him. Although she knows that his injuries and pain may kill her, Gem begins to cure Dr. McCoy. The entire, apparently senseless series of brutalities has been a test to determine whether or not Gem's race is worthy of being saved from a disaster that will soon engulf her planet's solar system, which unfortunately also contains another inhabited planet. This is the only means that Lal and Thann could devise to determine which population can be saved, as they lack the means of rescuing both populations in time. Kirk and his friends are safely returned to the *Enterprise*. ►

"The Empath" teaser, which shows the two Federation researchers disappearing, promises an interesting mystery, but the remainder of the segment develops into something completely different.

Aliens Lal and Thann are faced with a problem: there are two planets of humanoids that are about to be destroyed, and they possess only enough time and technology to save one civilization. They seem to care a great deal about making the right choice in the matter. This evidently means they have compassion, but if this is so, why do they go to such lengths to hurt innocent people, indulging in the cruelest behavior possible? Of course, these are aliens who may have different moral standards and customs, but these differences (if any) do not answer the questions viewers must ask regarding the aliens' motives. For instance, why didn't the aliens ask the United Federation of Planets for assistance instead of making mincemeat out of two doctors and attempting to do the same to Kirk and company?

The most interesting facet of this episode is Gem, the empath. Kathryn Hays (Gem) deserves a great deal of credit for the success of her scenes. She is an excellent mime, and although Gem never utters a single word throughout the story, Ms. Hays's gestures and facial expressions create as sensitive a character as could be created through the use of dialogue.

Ms. Hays, who appears regularly on the soap opera "The Guiding Light," had a recurring role as Elizabeth Reynolds in "The Road West." She can also be seen in segments of "The Man from U.N.C.L.E." and "Night Gallery" ("She'll Be Company For You," with Leonard Nimoy).

Composer George Duning scored some of "Trek's" most sensitive music, including "Metamorphosis" and this episode's theme for Gem.

"Nightmare," an episode of "The Outer Limits," also featured a series of ordeals inflicted on Earthmen by humanoid aliens. In that 1963 segment, the outrages were also a test (a wargame being carried out with the participation of friendly aliens called "Ebonites"). As in "The Empath," the sets in "Nightmare" were sparse, with some of the action taking place surrounded by total darkness—and both were directed by John Erman.

Dr. McCoy in a pensive mood

"THE THOLIAN WEB"

□□□□□□□□□□□□□□□□□□□□□□□□□□□□□□ #64

WRITERS: Judy Burns, Chet Richards
DIRECTOR: Ralph Senensky
PRINCIPALS: Kirk   Uhura
            Spock   Chekov
            McCoy   Lieutenant O'Neil
            Scott

◄ *Stardate 5693.4:* The *Enterprise* discovers another Federation starship, the U.S.S. *Defiant*, adrift in an unexplored quadrant of space. Beaming aboard in spacesuits, Kirk, Spock, McCoy, and Chekov find the *Defiant*'s entire crew victims of violent deaths. The ship is rapidly drifting into a parallel dimension and becoming "nonexistent" in this one. The landing party returns to the *Enterprise*—except for Kirk, who is stranded aboard the *Defiant* when it vanishes. Mr. Spock is able to calculate when and where the ghost ship will rematerialize, and at that time, the *Enterprise* will be able to rescue Captain Kirk, if his oxygen supply lasts.

The wait proves hazardous. This segment of space, because of its peculiar physical properties, renders the starship's crew members hostile to each other. Then the Tholians, an alien race unknown to the Federation, enter the scene and accuse the *Enterprise* of trespassing in their sector of space. They weave an energized "web" around the starship. The expected "interphase" between universes occurs—but the *Defiant* fails to rematerialize, and Kirk is presumed dead. The crew's morale begins to deteriorate even further. Then several crewmembers, and finally the entire bridge crew, see the captain's ghostly figure floating before them. Kirk is alive, Spock realizes, and there is still a chance to save him. He manages to flee the Tholian web, taking Kirk's ghostly form along with the *Enterprise*. The captain is finally beamed aboard, his suit's oxygen supply almost exhausted. ►

"The Tholian Web" provides Kirk with his greatest adventure, during which he literally journeys "where no man has gone before" and returns to tell about it. Because of Kirk's absence from the *Enterprise* throughout most of the story, we see how much the starship crew depends upon him.

In "The Paradise Syndrome," Kirk was also isolated from the *Enterprise*—but presumed missing, not dead. In this episode the captain is *completely* out of the picture, and things aboard the starship begin to fall apart. The symptoms generated by the "hostile" segment of space have something to do with the problem, but the conflict between Dr. McCoy and Mr. Spock comes from within themselves.

The viewing of Kirk's last will and testament clarifies

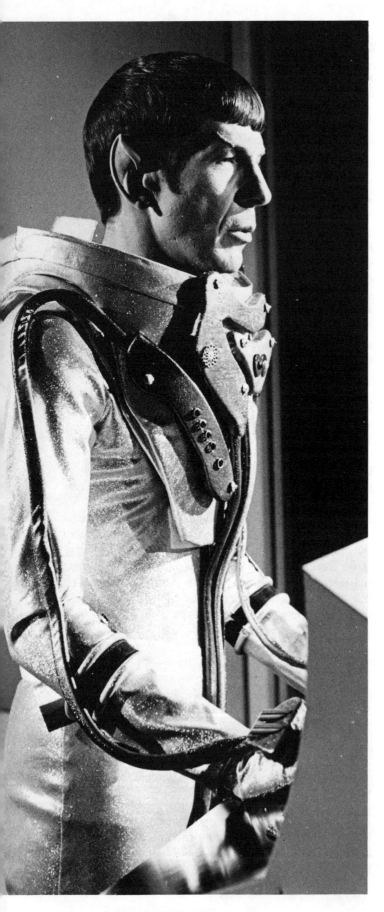

much about the relationship between the three and aids in resolving the conflicts generated in this adventure. When Spock actually calls McCoy "Bones," it is both moving and a pleasant surprise.

The story outline for this episode, entitled "In Essence Nothing," began as the *Enterprise* found the lost starship *Scimitar* and beamed a landing party aboard to investigate. They were protected by life-support shields (personal force fields), not space suits.

Kirk was immediately presumed dead in this draft. Uhura left the memorial service for Kirk early, profoundly affected, and saw the captain's spectral body. At first McCoy did not believe her; after a physical examination, however, he changed his mind but failed to convince Spock. He berated the Vulcan for being too logical and refusing to allow any hope that Kirk was still alive. At Chekov's suggestion, Spock decided to take the *Enterprise* into the dimension into which the *Scimitar* had vanished. This action caused the Tholians' web to shatter.

In the other dimensional plane, the starship had the upper hand, leading the Tholians to accept the overtures of peace initiated by the retrieved Captain Kirk.

Director Ralph Senensky ably balances all the elements present in this episode, a task he also accomplishes in his direction of "Is There In Truth No Beauty?" His work on the series conforms with Gene Roddenberry's conception of "Star Trek" as a period piece. Senensky had considerable experience within the western genre, directing episodes of "The Big Valley," "The High Chaparral," and "The Wild, Wild West." His other science fiction and fantasy work includes "The Twilight Zone" ("Printer's Devil") and "Night Gallery" ("The Ghost of Sorworth Place").

Visually, this episode is a dream come true for special-effects fans, with miniature photography, animation effects, and a manufactured alien being. "Star Trek" won a well-deserved Emmy Award for this episode. Some of the effects were contributed by artist Mike Minor, who went on to work in the "Star Trek" feature films.

Spock trying to retrieve the lost Captain Kirk

"FOR THE WORLD IS HOLLOW AND I HAVE TOUCHED THE SKY"

#65

WRITER: Rick Vollaerts
DIRECTOR: Tony Leader
PRINCIPALS: Kirk   Scott
           Spock   Natira
           McCoy   Admiral Westervliet

◄ *Stardate 5476.3:* The *Enterprise* encounters the asteroid Yonada—unknown to its inhabitants actually a large, spherical spaceship, now on a collision course with a Federation planet. Dr. McCoy, who has just discovered he is terminally ill, insists on joining the landing party to Yonada. They discover the population within is governed by a sophisticated computer called "the Oracle," programmed to conceal the true nature of Yonada from its people until the unique ship reaches its journey's end. But something has gone wrong with the Oracle's programming—and Kirk and Spock must find some way to alter it.

Meanwhile, McCoy falls in love with Natira, high priestess to the Oracle. She wishes to marry him, but only if he will stay on Yonada with her and obey the will of the Oracle. Captain Kirk and Spock penetrate the Oracle's defenses and reprogram it to bypass the asteroid. Yonada, built centuries before by the Fabrini civilization, includes a computer bank with the advanced medical knowledge of that society. Contained in its memory is the cure for McCoy's ailment. Natira realizes that Dr. McCoy's place is with his own people, although she will always love him. Kirk promises McCoy that when Yonada reaches its destination the *Enterprise* will be there to greet Natira and her people. ►

"For the World Is Hollow and I Have Touched the Sky" is another of "Star Trek's" successful love stories, and one of the most memorable segments of the entire series.

The Star Trek Writers' Guide mentioned that Dr. McCoy had been married before he joined Starfleet. This marriage ended in divorce, and probably because of the painful breakup of the relationship, McCoy left behind his daughter, Joanna, who was studying to become a nurse on Earth. We never learn anything about McCoy's marriage in the series, and we never meet his daughter. From time to time, McCoy's Southern-gentleman charm was directed toward various guests aboard the *Enterprise*, and in "The Man Trap" we actually meet a representation of Nancy Crater, a former female friend of Leonard's.

In this sensitive story, Dr. McCoy's love-at-first-sight affair with the beautiful and dedicated Natira is well handled. Natira senses McCoy's warm personality despite

his gruff exterior, and DeForest Kelley again makes the audience aware that McCoy is much more complex than he is usually depicted as being.

In the story outline for this episode, *Mr. Scott* was ill with an irreversible blood condition: his red blood cells were crystallizing as a result of a rare condition brought about by exposure to radiation. Scotty had three years to live.

When the asteroid was discovered, only Kirk and Scotty beamed down into the "ship." They were well received by the people there, whose religion praised visitors who came from outside Yonada. Space regulations permitted Scotty to retire to any place of his choice. Kirk attempted to talk his friend out of staying. Yonada was on a collision course with a *highly populated planet.* Scotty was so anxious to stay that he struck Kirk and challenged him to a fight.

When the walls of the room began to close in on them, Kirk phasered through the wall into the engine room. The Oracle finally apologized and exchanged its knowledge banks with the starship's computer, making Scotty's cure possible.

Director Tony Leader has extensive credits in TV westerns including episodes of "Rawhide," "Sugarfoot," and "Lawman." He won the 1965 Western Heritage Award for his direction of "The Virginian" episode, "The Horse Fighter." In the science fiction department he directed

McCoy and Kirk on Yonada

one of the eeriest segments of "The Twilight Zone," "Long Live Walter Jameson," and the premiere episode of "Lost in Space."

This episode is a feast for the eyes, featuring new footage of the asteroid effect created for "The Paradise Syndrome," and William Ware Theiss's colorful costumes (especially that created for Katherine Woodville).

Guest star Katherine Woodville (Natira) also appears in episodes of "The Night Stalker" ("Primal Scream") and "Secret Agent" ("Colony Three"). Woodville is married to actor Patrick Macnee. John Lormer (Old Man) also appears in the "Star Trek" segments "The Cage" and "The Return of the Archons."

"THE DAY OF THE DOVE"

#66

WRITER: Jerome Bixby
DIRECTOR: Marvin Chomsky
PRINCIPALS: Kirk   Uhura
           Spock   Chekov
           McCoy   Kang
           Scott   Mara
           Sulu   Lieutenant Johnson

◄ *Stardate unknown:* The *Enterprise* and a Klingon battle cruiser commanded by Kang cross paths orbiting planet Beta XII-A. Kirk is convinced that the Klingons have murdered the Federation colonists on the planet: Kang thinks the *Enterprise*'s captain is responsible for damaging the Klingons' ship (and killing most of his crew). He takes the Federation personnel prisoner on the planet's surface. Kirk and the landing party beam aboard under guard— but a signal arranged with Spock enables him to turn the tables on Kang by beaming up before the Klingons. Kang and his crew are detained—but in reality, all the trouble has been caused by a malevolent energy being that feeds off aggressive instincts. The entity is now aboard the *Enterprise*—and turns the starship into a battleground. Phasers are transformed into swords, fatal wounds heal, injured individuals recover to fight again and again. Chekov goes completely berserk and assaults Kang's wife, science officer Mara. Kirk stops the ensign, then tells Mara that Federation crewmen and Klingons have a common enemy aboard the *Enterprise*. With her assistance, he is able to convince Kang they are all being manipulated by a hostile entity. The two commanders call a truce and join in a backslapping session of mutual laughter. The creature, having no taste for all these good feelings, is driven off the *Enterprise*. The Klingons are dropped off at the nearest Federation outpost. ►

"The Day of the Dove" is a well-conceived tale, similar to "Wolf in the Fold." Redjac, in that episode, also survived by absorbing negative emanations. But this entity is more powerful and furthers hostilities by manufacturing false recollections of atrocities, including Mr. Chekov's rage at the death of his brother, Piotr. Mr. Sulu sets this record straight, recalling that Chekov *never had* a brother.

The balance of hatred between the Klingons and the Federation in "Errand of Mercy" is back in full force here. Kirk's recognition and hatred of this hostility enables him to determine that an unknown factor is responsible for the *Enterprise*'s predicament. The final scene in which Kirk and Kang stand together and laugh to get the entity to leave is an indication that the Organians are correct. One day it will be possible for humans and Klingons to work together in friendship (the fact that

Kang almost breaks Kirk's back with one good-natured slap is incidental).

Hostilities were accented in this episode with the use of "hot" red and brown lights focused on the Klingons, both planetside and in the *Enterprise*'s engineering section. Typically, the optical effect designed for the Klingon transporter is harsher than the Federation transporter effect.

This is the only 'Trek' segment to feature a female Klingon. William Theiss designed an effective variation of the standard Klingon uniform, and Fred Phillips' makeup aided Susan Howard's exotic, credible, and attractive portrayal of Mara.

Guest star Michael Ansara (Kang) plays his part with all the expertise acquired from years of portraying exotic heroes and villains in feature films and television. Among his other TV guest roles are appearances in "The Outer Limits" ("Soldier," written by Harlan Ellison), "Voyage to the Bottom of the Sea," "The Time Tunnel," "Lost in Space," "Land of the Giants," and "The Man from U.N.C.L.E."

Scotty in the ship's transformed armory

"PLATO'S STEPCHILDREN"

▭▭▭▭▭▭▭▭▭▭▭▭▭▭▭▭▭▭▭▭▭▭▭▭▭ **#67**

WRITER: Meyer Dolinsky
DIRECTOR: David Alexander
PRINCIPALS: Kirk   Alexander
           Spock   Parmen
           McCoy   Philana
           Uhura   Eraclitus
           Chapel   Dionyd

◀ *Stardate 5784.0:* Answering a distress call from the planet Platonius, Dr. McCoy beams down with Kirk and Spock to aid the stricken Platonian leader, Parmen. Although Parmen and his people have no resistance to physical disease, they are powerful telekinetics. After McCoy cures their leader, the Platonians attempt to persuade him to stay—and when he refuses, they enslave the landing party. The Platonians' dwarf jester, Alexander, befriends Kirk and attempts to help, but is powerless to interfere because of his lack of telekinetic powers. Parmen forces Kirk, Spock, and McCoy to undergo humiliating experiences, some of which drive the Vulcan to his psychological breaking point. Crewmembers Uhura and Chapel are also beamed down and forced to enact bizarre charades with Kirk and Spock to amuse the Platonians.

Dr. McCoy determines that the chemical substance kironide is responsible for the powers of Parmen and his followers. McCoy mixes a concentrated batch of the substance, but Alexander does not accept the injection. The jester does not wish to possess the same type of powers as his masters. Kirk and Spock take the dosage and develop the Power, canceling out the effectiveness of Parmen's deadly pranks. Our people leave Platonius, taking Alexander, who will be dropped off at a nearby Federation outpost to begin a new life. ▶

"Plato's Stepchildren" is similar to "The Gamesters of Triskelion" and "The Empath," involving Kirk and company in bizarre, demeaning, and dangerous activities. And just as "The Empath" has Gem, this episode features Alexander, the one humane member of the Platonian population.

In other episodes the *Enterprise* crew find themselves pitted against telepaths (the Talosians in "The Cage" and the Melkots in "Spectre of the Gun"), but the telekinetic Parmen and his Platonians are the most irrational. Their cruel antics are offset by the presence of Alexander, who lacks the Power and therefore has never lost sight of his humanity. Throughout the episode, Alexander provides our people with encouragement and attempts to minimize the damage caused by Parmen.

In the performances induced by Parmen, both Kirk and

Spock endure highly unpleasant experiences. Spock performs his song, "Maiden Wine." Kirk is forced to slap his own face repeatedly. But the episode is best remembered for the kiss between Captain Kirk and Lieutenant Uhura—the first interracial kiss on network television.

The story outline for this segment, entitled "The Sons of Socrates," had the *Enterprise* being tossed about in space by Parmen's power. In the scenes involving the degradation of the *Enterprise* crew, Kirk was paired with a young yeoman who admired him greatly, and Uhura was paired with Dr. McCoy. Uhura sang the song. Spock was forced to hit McCoy, and the doctor was compelled to butt the Vulcan in the stomach as Christine and the female yeoman were forced to fight. At the end of the outline, no mention was made of Kirk and company's losing their powers after they had left the planet.

Liam Sullivan (Parmen) was regularly featured as Ma-

jor Mapoy in the television series "The Monroes" (in which Ron Soble also had a recurring role), and is also visible in segments of "The Twilight Zone" ("The Silence"), "Lost in Space" ("His Majesty Smith"), and in episodes of the soap opera "The Secret Storm" (in the recurring role of Dr. Alan Dunbar).

Michael Dunn (Alexander) is best remembered by television viewers for his charmingly villainous recurring characterization, Dr. Miguelito Lovelace in "The Wild, Wild West" (1965–69). He can also be seen in episodes of "Night Gallery" ("The Sins of the Fathers") and "Voyage to the Bottom of the Sea" ("The Wax Men"). His most famous feature film appearance was in the 1965 film, *Ship of Fools*.

Writer Meyer Dolinsky also scripted episodes of "The Outer Limits" ("Zzzzz," "O.B.I.T.," and "Architects of Fear").

Another friendly confrontation between McCoy and Spock

"WINK OF AN EYE"

<!-- box count bar --> **#68**

WRITER: Arthur Heinemann (story by Lee Cronin [Gene L. Coon])
DIRECTOR: Jud Taylor
PRINCIPALS: Kirk | Chekov
Spock | Deela
McCoy | Crewman Compton
Scott | Ekor
Sulu | Rael
Uhura

Kirk encounters a stubborn forcefield

◄ *Stardate 5710.5:* Responding to a distress call from the planet Scalos—a call accompanied by visual images of the Scalosians—the *Enterprise* discovers a beautiful city with no signs of life except mysterious, insectlike buzzing sounds. Puzzled, Kirk is even more astounded when one crewman disappears after tasting the Scalosian water. Back on board the *Enterprise*, the captain himself disappears after drinking a cup of coffee. Actually, he has also been given Scalosian water, which accelerates him to the level of the beautiful Deela, Queen of Scalos, who needs his help. The aliens have been poisoned by radiations from the core of their planet, resulting in an incredibly accelerated metabolism and male sterility. Now they plan to use all the male crew aboard ship to repopulate their planet. Kirk records a tape informing Mr. Spock of the situation. Dr. McCoy finds an antidote to the Scalosian water, and Spock then drinks the water to accelerate himself. Locating Kirk, Spock administers the antidote to the captain, staying behind in his accelerated state to undo the Scalosians' damage to the *Enterprise*. The defeated aliens are returned to their world, as Kirk watches a taped image of Deela and her ill-fated people.►

Ignoring the questions and puzzles that arise from the science in "Wink of an Eye," we are left free to appreciate the tale's mystery, suspense, and humor. "Wink of an Eye" is an enjoyable episode, in no small part due to Deela's selection of Captain Kirk—the galaxy's most notorious womanizer—as an aid in the repopulation of her planet.

Topping the list of "moments-the-network-censors-did-not-notice-but-should-have" is the sequence where Kirk and Deela adjourn to the captain's cabin to discuss the business at hand. Just as Deela has Kirk right where she wants him, there is a cut to another scene, and when we return, she is standing before the mirror combing her hair and Kirk is putting his boots back on.

Two additional sequences add elements of eeriness to the episode. Crewman Compton's death again shows us Kirk's anguish at losing someone under his command. His horror is even greater considering the bizarre manner of Compton's death, a fate similar to that almost experienced by Kirk and some of his coworkers in "The Deadly Years."

In a more upbeat sequence, Mr. Spock's super-speed tour of the *Enterprise,* in which he invisibly repairs hundreds of systems and circuits before returning to his normal metabolic rate, enables him to act out his symbolic role as the starship's scientific guardian angel.

Regardless of the enjoyable aspects of this episode, much of its effectiveness is cancelled by the lack of thought behind the acceleration's effect upon Kirk and Spock and the story's failure to convey an accurate picture of the exact rate of speed of the Scalosians vs. the *Enterprise* crew.

Captain Kirk's metabolism accelerated greatly in "Return to Tomorrow," while his body was being "possessed" by Sargon. During that adventure, McCoy mentioned that Kirk's body could only stand short bursts of such activity before serious damage resulted. During his metamorphosis in that segment, Kirk showed signs of being severely weakened by the ordeal. The Scalosian water accelerates Kirk to an incredible degree in comparison to his earlier experience, and yet he shows no such signs of weakness.

The Scalosian city, seen in the background of Deela's taped plea for help, is a reused optical painting originally created for "A Taste of Armageddon."

"THAT WHICH SURVIVES"

▭▭▭▭▭▭▭▭▭▭▭▭▭▭▭▭▭▭▭▭▭▭▭▭▭▭▭▭▭ **#69**

WRITER: John Meredyth Lucas (story by Michael Richards [D. C. Fontana])
DIRECTOR: Herb Wallerstein
PRINCIPALS:
Kirk	Losira
Spock	Lieutenant Rahda
McCoy	Lieutenant D'Amato
Scott	Ensign Wyatt
Sulu	John B. Watkins
Uhura	Dr. M'Benga

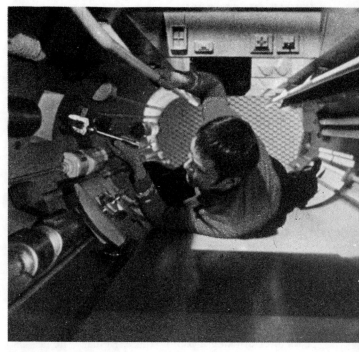

Scotty in the Jeffries tube

◄ *Stardate unknown:* Preparing to beam down to investigate puzzling geological conditions on an unexplored Class M planet, Kirk, McCoy, Mr. Sulu, and geologist Lieutenant D'Amato witness a beautiful woman's appearance in the *Enterprise* transporter room. She attacks an ensign, killing him instantly, as Kirk and company are dematerializing, helpless to assist. When they materialize, they are unable to contact the *Enterprise,* which has been hurled almost a thousand light-years away as a result of Losira's appearance. Losira's image keeps materializing aboard the *Enterprise* and on the planet. Whenever it appears, people die. A young engineering officer is killed aboard the starship, and Lieutenant D'Amato is slain on the planet's surface. Mr. Sulu narrowly escapes death after Losira's image announces that she has come for him. The landing party discovers that she can only kill the person she names. They stumble across an underground chamber, where they find that the woman, Losira, is a holographic projection materialized by a computer left behind by the Kalandans, an extinct alien race who had used the planet as a scientific outpost. Just as Kirk and company are about to be destroyed by multiple images of the projection, Spock beams down. He destroys the ancient computer, canceling out the holograms of Losira that were designed to repel everyone except the now long-dead Kalandans. ▶

Despite similarities to other "Trek" segments, "That Which Survives" is an imaginative episode, a sensitively conceived story that doesn't skimp on action.

We had seen a computer materialize the image of a human in "The Return of the Archons," but in that episode, the image of Landru is spectral rather than solid and never does any direct harm. In contrast, Losira makes her entrances by materializing as a thin, vertical line that expands horizontally into the figure of the beautiful woman, comparable to the way a televised image first appears on the picture tube on an old television set. We're not certain until the episode's conclusion that Losira is a projection rather than a living entity.

While Losira's image kills several people, its behavior

indicates that the original Losira, who programmed the computer, transferred her respect for life forms into the device. There is no malevolence in the actions of the hologram. It appears to be doing its assigned task with reluctance.

In the story outline for this episode, entitled "Survival," the image of Losira was more brutal than it is in the final version. It also manufactured illusions that caused the *Enterprise* crew to fight among themselves. Sulu saw a fellow crewman as a monster, while Uhura saw Sulu attack another crewman. Kirk was almost induced to stab himself while in his quarters.

Guest star Lee Meriwether's (Losira) television career includes recurring roles in four television series. She was Ann Reynolds in "The Young Marrieds" (1964–66); Ann McGregor, an engineer in "The Time Tunnel" (1966–67); the wife in "The New Andy Griffith Show" (1972); and the daughter-in-law on "Barnaby Jones." Ms. Meriwether, a former Miss America, also appeared in segments of "Land of the Giants" and "The Man from U.N.C.L.E." Her feature-film career includes roles in *The 4-D Man* (with Robert Lansing) and the feature-film version of *Batman,* in which she played Catwoman.

"LET THAT BE YOUR LAST BATTLEFIELD"

#70

WRITER: Oliver Crawford (story by Lee Cronin [Gene L. Coon])
DIRECTOR: Jud Taylor
PRINCIPALS: Kirk Uhura
Spock Lokai
McCoy Bele
Scott

◄ *Stardate 5730.2:* On an urgent rescue mission, the *Enterprise* intercepts a stolen Federation shuttlecraft and its thief, a humanoid named Lokai who asks for asylum. Lokai, a native of the planet Cheron, is half-white and half black. Soon after his arrival, the *Enterprise* discovers another ship following them at incredible speed. Locking on that craft's passenger, the *Enterprise* transports him aboard just as his ship explodes. The passenger is Bele, another native of Cheron who is also half-black and half-white, though oppositely colored from Lokai. He claims to be Cheron's chief officer attached to the commission of political traitors, in pursuit of Lokai. Kirk resists his undiplomatic extradition attempts, and after the near destruction of the *Enterprise,* the starship arrives at Cheron to discover a dead world: the inhabitants have killed each other with their insistent hatreds. Bele and Lokai chase each other down to their dead planet where they will continue their senseless fight. ►

Many "Star Trek" episodes are concerned with the problem of prejudice; the Vulcan concept of appreciating the existence of infinite diversity in infinite combinations (I.D.I.C.) is an eloquent statement on the issue. "Is There In Truth No Beauty?" offered a sensitive and subtle exploration of how the differences between life forms could be resolved for the benefit of all concerned. "Let That Be Your Last Battlefield," on the other hand, examines prejudice without subtlety, literally tackling the problem in "black and white." But in confining itself to this fundamental study, the episode's logic suffers. Even if the Federation has never heard of Cheron's two-toned humanoids, how could two entities as conspicuous as Bele and Lokai have crossed into Federation territory and remained unnoticed? Lokai, who "hitch-hiked" at least part of the way, would certainly have been seen, especially on Starbase 4, where he stole a shuttlecraft.

Kirk's threat to activate the *Enterprise*'s self-destruct mechanism provides the episode's most suspenseful scene, a well-directed and well-played sequence that utilizes close-ups of Kirk, Spock, Scotty, and the two aliens (this same sequence, word for word, was used in ST III: TSFS to destroy the *Enterprise*).

Al Francis's cinematography for this episode includes the highly effective transporter sequence in which the camera is on the transporter platform, rather than by the control console. This single experiment is the closest thing to a subjective (first-person) camera transporter shot to appear on "Star Trek."

Budget considerations probably accounted for some of this episode's shortcomings. For instance, we hear about concerned personnel on Ariannus and Starbase 4, but we never see (or hear) them. Stock footage, including views of destruction on Cheron and the more specialized "Trek" inventory of the shuttlecraft and *Enterprise* miniatures, abounds in this segment. The real budget saver here is Bele's spaceship: fast, streamlined, and conveniently invisible.

Guest star Frank Gorshin (Bele), one of the most famous impressionists in the world, is best known for his imitations of celebrities such as James Cagney, Kirk Douglas, and Richard Widmark. One of his first acting roles was in *The Invasion of the Saucer Men,* a humorous tale of Earth menaced by little men from outer space: television audiences will recall his wonderfully insane portrayal of the Riddler in the "Batman" TV series.

Frank Gorshin apparently had a good time appearing in "Star Trek": the third-season "Trek" blooper film shows the performer poised on the transporter platform, suddenly transforming himself into James Cagney. Another blooper sequence has Gorshin and Lou Antonio (Lokai) running down the *Enterprise* corridor eluding each other until they meet and collide with great impact.

A deadly struggle on the bridge

"WHOM GODS DESTROY"

◀▩▩▩▩▩▩▩▩▩▩▩▩▩▩▩▩▩▩▩▩▩▩▩▩▩ **#71**

WRITER: Lee Erwin (story by Jerry Sohl, Lee Erwin)
DIRECTOR: Herb Wallerstein
PRINCIPALS: Kirk   Marta
Spock   Donald Cory
Scott   Andorian
Garth of Izar   Tellarite

◀ *Stardate 5718.3:* Kirk takes the *Enterprise* to Elba II, home of an asylum for the galaxy's last insane humanoids. He has brought a new drug that, when used in conjunction with other treatments, can cure these individuals. Beaming down, Kirk and Spock are met by the colony's governor, Donald Cory—who turns out to be Garth of Izar, a brilliant former starship captain. Now an inmate of Elba II, Garth used his mysterious shape-changing power to assume Cory's appearance. Imprisoning the real governor, Garth then freed his fellow inmates and took over the asylum.

Now he seeks to gain possession of the *Enterprise*. His attempts, involving impersonation and the wiles of the beautiful inmate Marta, are unsuccessful. In a rage, Garth has Marta dragged into the poisonous atmosphere beyond the asylum dome and killed with a powerful explosive he has invented. Mr. Scott, left in command of the *Enterprise*, cannot penetrate the asylum's force field to aid Kirk. But Spock manages to escape his guards—only to discover Garth has transformed himself into Kirk's double. The

Vulcan correctly deduces which is the impostor, and after control of the asylum is restored to Cory, we see that Garth is on his way to recovery. ▶

Three plot devices, two of which are very familiar by now, are present in "Whom Gods Destroy": (1) an important person within the Federation is introduced and discovered to be mentally unbalanced; (2) a humanoid gains superhuman abilities as a result of the intervention of an alien influence; and (3) the insane asylum is taken over by its inmates (a cinematic convention first made famous in the 1919 horror classic *The Cabinet of Dr. Caligari*).

The Federation institution we glimpsed in "Dagger of the Mind" is similar to the asylum in this episode, and despite the horrible "curative" measures employed by Dr. Adams in "Dagger," the Elba II installation, as mismanaged by Garth, emerges as the more blatant "chamber of horrors."

William Shatner and Leonard Nimoy made subtle changes in their characterizations to function within the exaggerated framework of Garth's insanity. Kirk appears more vocal than usual, while Mr. Spock seems more sedate, making it apparent that he regards the behavioral aberrations of Garth and his accomplices with pity. In an extremely subtle hint, director Herb Wallerstein and Nimoy inform the audience that "Spock" is actually now Garth in disguise by having "the Vulcan" casually holding his phaser aimed directly at Kirk while speaking with the captain—something the real Spock would never do.

Spock chooses the real Kirk

In the first-draft script of "Whom Gods Destroy," Garth of *Titan* was more brutal, having thrown the asylum guards out of the dome and watched, laughing, as they suffocated. The atmosphere within the asylum was more graphic. Inmates were shown exhibiting symptoms of various mental illnesses. Garth tortured Governor Cory in a cage of the inmate's design that created an electronic simulation of hell.

The Tellarite makeup introduced by Fred Phillips for "Journey to Babel" appears in this episode in a slightly simplified version and would later appear in "The Lights of Zetar" modified in the same manner; the original appliance was cut to omit the deep-set eyes seen in "Babel." Marta's costume is a very simplified version of Vina's slave-girl outfit in "The Cage." The space suits from "The Tholian Web" are also seen here together with Dr. Adams's robe and "neural neutralizer" chair from "Dagger of the Mind."

Steve Ihnat (Garth), an exceptionally gifted actor who was equally able to portray heroes or villains, deserves much of the credit for making this episode as interesting as it is. Ihnat played Garth as a madman, logical and gentle one instant, violent and discordant the next. His film roles include appearances in *The Chase* and *In Like Flint*. On television, he was featured in the pilot film for "The Sixth Sense" and appeared in episodes of "The Outer Limits," "Voyage to the Bottom of the Sea," and "Honey West" ("A Million Bucks in Anybody's Language," where he also portrayed a villain named Garth).

Yvonne Craig (Marta) also appeared in *In Like Flint*, although the former ballerina is best known for her recurring role as Batgirl in the "Batman" TV series. Keye Luke (Governor Cory) appeared in many films in the 1930s, including the classic *The Good Earth*; he was also "Number One Son" opposite Warner Oland in the earliest *Charlie Chan* films. He is best known to television viewers as Master Po, Caine's blind, all-seeing teacher in "Kung Fu."

"THE MARK OF GIDEON"

▭▭▭▭▭▭▭▭▭▭▭▭▭▭▭▭▭▭▭▭▭▭▭▭▭▭▭▭▭▭▭▭ **#72**

WRITER: George F. Slavin, Stanley Adams
DIRECTOR: Jud Taylor
PRINCIPALS: Kirk   Hodin
           Spock   Krodak
           McCoy   Admiral Fitzgerald
           Odona

◀ *Stardate 5423.4:* Captain Kirk beams down to Gideon, a disease-free planet the United Federation of Planets is attempting to recruit as a member. Something goes wrong with the transporter, and Kirk never arrives in the Gideon council chambers. A frustrated Mr. Spock fails to secure permission from either Starfleet or the council members to beam down and search for the captain. Kirk awakens in the middle of an exact duplicate of the *Enterprise,* empty except for himself and a beautiful young woman, Odona. He discovers he is actually on Gideon, which, though disease-free, is also terribly overpopulated. Because of this, Gideon councilman Hodin lured Kirk into the starship mock-up. Now Odona, his daughter, has been infected with Vegan choriomeningitis, a virulent disease Kirk survived but still carries in his blood. Odona will die and infect others on Gideon with the disease, paving the way for a reduction in population. Mr. Spock finally locates the captain and then brings Kirk and Odona back to the *Enterprise.* Odona is cured—but happily returns to Gideon to infect other citizens of that world with the potentially fatal disease. ▶

"The Mark of Gideon" is essentially a mystery story. Captain Kirk disappears, and the *Enterprise*'s crew is not certain what has become of him. Kirk's bafflement is even greater. He believes that he has never left the *Enterprise* but that everyone else aboard her has vanished. To add to the mystery, the beautiful Odona appears on the empty pseudo-*Enterprise* with Kirk but provides no helpful information to aid Kirk in discovering what is really happening. The audience knows only that Kirk is *not* aboard the *Enterprise* and that Odona is part of some unknown plan.

But the biggest mystery about this entire episode is how the Gideons could create a duplicate of the starship *Enterprise* perfect enough to fool Captain Kirk completely. Kirk knows his ship inside out and (as he observes) is even familiar with its functional *sounds*. Even Mr. Spock refers to the mock-up as an exact duplicate of the *Enterprise.*

Another mystery in this episode is why Kirk, who thinks his entire crew has vanished without a trace, does not interrogate Odona with any severity, taking her at her word although she supplies no helpful information.

Despite these riddles, there are some excellent touches

Kirk on Gideon

in "Mark of Gideon." We have previously glimpsed the ponderous and stubborn Starfleet bureaucracy in "action," notably in "Amok Time," but here we see even Mr. Spock has a boiling point when it comes to Earthside "paper pushers" making decisions regarding a starship's priorities.

Spock is not the only one whose patience wears thin during the captain's disappearance—and if Scotty had heard Hodin describe him as a "very excitable repairman," he probably would have beamed down and punched the Gideon councilman in the nose.

The split-second glimpses of demoralized, hooded crowds pressed together outside the mock-up starship's "windows" are quite effective in depicting the planet's overcrowded conditions (Odona's description of her planet seems like a recollection of some of the larger "Star Trek" conventions).

The story outline for "The Mark of Gideon" is very different from the filmed episode. The Gideons were virtually immortal because of their ability to regenerate damaged cells within their bodies instantly. A party of

Gideons, beamed aboard the *Enterprise* took over the transporter room and forced Kirk, Spock, and other key personnel to beam down so they could function as living blood banks for antibodies that would cancel out the immortality of everyone on the planet (except for the ruling council). Using these antibodies, the Gideons then attempted to use Odona and two others to produce deadly germs.

Two unusual camera angles are used in this episode. When Krodak transports down to the *Enterprise,* we see him vanish on the starship's viewing screen. When Kirk is seated in the Gideon council room, the camera shoots up at Kirk and Hodin through a transparent tabletop.

One final mystery remains about this tale. The Gideons were obviously prepared to take extremely bizarre measures to solve their overpopulation problem—but if their planet was really so incredibly crowded that people were willing to kill to enjoy a moment's privacy, where did Hodin and his council find the space to construct the duplicate of such a large vehicle as the U.S.S. *Enterprise?*

"THE LIGHTS OF ZETAR"

▭▭▭▭▭▭▭▭▭▭▭▭▭▭▭▭▭▭▭▭▭▭▭▭▭▭▭▭▭▭▭ **#73**

WRITERS: Jeremy Tarcher, Shari Lewis
DIRECTOR: Herb Kenwith
PRINCIPALS: Kirk   Uhura
           Spock   Lieutenant Mira Romaine
           McCoy   Lieutenant Kyle
           Scott

◄ *Stardate 5725.3:* Lieutenant Mira Romaine has been assigned to the *Enterprise* to supervise the transfer of new equipment to Memory Alpha, the central library facility of the United Federation of Planets. Mr. Scott is attracted to the lieutenant, and the feeling is mutual. Then an energy storm of unknown nature destroys all the inhabitants of Memory Alpha—and the collective memory of its computer banks as well. Apparently as a result of the storm, Lieutenant Romaine is able to predict where the energy will strike next—the *Enterprise.* Despite Kirk's best efforts, the energy enters the ship and possesses the mind and body of Mira. They discover the storm is actually a collective mentality, the surviving life force of the last natives of Zetar, a dead planet. Mira's psychological attributes make her an ideal host for the "Lights," who communicate through her as though they were spirits speaking through a medium. The Zetars refuse to leave the lieutenant's body, insisting that they have a right to live, even at the expense of Mira's life. But the "Lights" are extinguished when Mira is placed in a pressure chamber, and the Zetars, accustomed to the vacuum of space and the ship's light gravity, are subjected to extremely high pressure. A recovered Mira returns to Memory Alpha to help restore the planet's heavily damaged facilities. ►

Essentially, "The Lights of Zetar" is about the "possession" and "exorcism" of Lieutenant Mira Romaine. This episode is a good example of how "Star Trek" explored topics that would later become very popular—in this case after the release of the movie *The Exorcist.* In addition to this science-and-supernatural combination, the episode also emphasizes the romance between Scotty and Mira.

Mr. Scott was clearly affected by "Mudd's Women," but it wasn't until "Who Mourns for Adonais?" that we saw him actively pursuing a specific female, Lieutenant Carolyn Palamas (his short-lived fascination for the dancer Kara in "Wolf in the Fold" can be attributed to shore leave). In "The Lights of Zetar," his attraction to Lieutenant Romaine is based on a common bond (her father, Jacques Romaine, had been a chief engineer for Starfleet). This both added to and detracted from the relationship—for Mr. Scott, an ageless individual who thought nothing of falling for the younger Lieutenant Palamas, would prob-

ably have stayed away from a woman who identified him with her father. Scotty, however, apparently does not see this, or does not care.

In the story outline for "The Lights of Zetar," Mira Romaine was Scotty's new engineering assistant and shared his fascination for machinery. After the Lights attacked Memory Seven (as it was called), they penetrated the *Enterprise* and affected the bridge crew as though they had been subjected to electrical shocks. Mira, as she was "possessed," was enveloped in glowing light. Mira had always regarded herself as a trifle strange, because of her experiences with visions and other similar phenomena. Scotty was extremely defensive about Mira's problems: when Mr. Spock questioned Mira at one point, Scotty *hit* the Vulcan. In an attempt to "short-circuit" the Lights, which could cancel out gravity and sound, the *Galileo* was steered into the storm. Mira was placed in a cryogenic chamber instead of a decompression chamber to drive the Lights out of her.

The episode's score, credited to Alexander Courage, was largely taken from "Where No Man Has Gone Before," and because of similarities in plot and pacing (both episodes deal with the possession of *Enterprise* crewmembers by alien energy forces), the music fits very well. The scenes in which the *Enterprise* first encounters the Lights and the initial "possession" of Mira utilize the same music that accompanies the *Enterprise*'s entry into the galactic barrier and the "possession" of Dr. Dehner in "Where No Man."

The "lights" penetrate the Enterprise

"THE CLOUDMINDERS"

#74

WRITER: Margaret Armen (story by David Gerrold, Oliver
Crawford)
DIRECTOR: Jud Taylor
PRINCIPALS: Kirk   Vanna
Spock   Anka
McCoy   Midro
Scott   Plasus
Droxine

◄ *Stardate 5818.4:* In quest of the crucial and rare element
zienite, which is needed to stop a plague on planet Merak
II, the *Enterprise* journeys to the zienite-rich world of
Ardana. The substance is excavated by miners—Troglytes—
who are forced to live on the harsh surface of Ardana
while the ruling class—Stratos-dwellers—reside in a luxurious city high above the planet. When the Troglytes
refuse to turn over the zienite, Captain Kirk is drawn into
their struggle for equality. Plasus, the High Adviser of
Ardana's ruling council, maintains that the Troglytes are
naturally inferior beings. While Mr. Spock is involved in a
relationship with Droxine, Plasus' daughter, Kirk befriends
Vanna, a Troglyte leader. Kirk, Vanna, and other Troglytes
enter a zienite mine, where Kirk causes a cave-in that
isolates them. He then has Plasus transported into the
mine with them. Without protective gas masks, they all
display violent, unreasoning behavior. Plasus, now aware
of the reason for the Troglytes' mental state, promises to
revise his planet's social structure—and the Troglytes
gather the needed zienite. ►

"The Cloudminders" again borrows heavily from other
sources for its story, most notably the classic science
fiction film *Metropolis*, which situated its workers in an
underground factory/city environment while the idle rich
lived in a luxurious, art deco city filled with skyscrapers,
landscaped gardens, multileveled highways, and numerous
land and air vehicles. It is no real surprise that Captain
Kirk becomes involved in the Troglytes' fight to obtain
rights equal to those of the Stratos-dwellers: Kirk has
always championed the downtrodden. Their exclusive ability to provide the zienite he needs—and their beautiful
leader—only add to his interest.

But while Kirk is becoming deeply involved with Vanna
and her cause, Mr. Spock is attracted to Plasus's daughter, Droxine. This relationship *is* quite a surprise—and
quite out of character for the Vulcan. In "Amok Time,"
when events forced Spock to discuss the *pon farr* with his
captain and closest friend, it was difficult for him to speak
of: the Vulcan matriarch T'Pau stated in no uncertain
terms that these subjects were not to be discussed in the
presence of "outworlders." In "Cloudminders," though,

Mr. Spock not only mentions his mating cycle but indicates that he is sorry that he has met Droxine between
pon farrs. Although it is reasonable for Spock to notice and
appreciate Droxine's intelligence and beauty, this does
not account for his discussion of topics other than "the
parabolic intersection of dimension with dimension."

Guest star Jeff Corey (Plasus) is not only an actor but a
director and teacher as well. He was, in fact, one of
Leonard Nimoy's acting instructors and, like Nimoy, also
directed segments of "Night Gallery." Fred Williamson
(Anka) achieved fame on the football field, where he was
known as "the Hammer," before pursuing an acting career.

Kirk supervises mining operations

"THE WAY TO EDEN"

#75

WRITER: Arthur Heinemann (story by Michael Richards [D. C. Fontana] and Arthur Heinemann)
DIRECTOR: David Alexander
PRINCIPALS: Kirk   Dr. Sevrin
            Spock   Irini Galliulin
            McCoy   Tongo Rad
            Scott   Adam
            Sulu   Mavig
            Uhura   Lieutenant Palmer
            Chekov

Spock—"we reach"

◄ *Stardate 5832.3:* Captain Kirk sights a stolen spaceship, the *Aurora*, and orders pursuit. The strain of the chase overheats the cruiser's engines, and the ship's crew is beamed aboard just before the *Aurora* explodes. The guests are a group of young idealists seeking to begin a new life on the mythical planet Eden. Their leader is a brilliant engineer named Dr. Sevrin who is also quite insane—and also a carrier of sythococcus novae, a disease deadly to those not immunized against it. Sevrin seeks to gain control of the *Enterprise* and find Eden. Among his followers are Irini Galliulin, a beautiful young woman once romantically involved with Mr. Chekov, and the son of a Catullan ambassador to the Federation. The latter's presence results in Kirk's receiving instructions to handle the group gently and to allow them free run of the *Enterprise.*

While Sevrin is placed in protective confinement, Spock begins a search for Eden—which he surprisingly discovers. Once the *Enterprise* is in orbit, Sevrin's followers arrange for his escape—and before they leave, the former engineer rigs an ultrasonic device that almost kills Kirk and several crewmembers. Stealing a shuttlecraft, the group flees to the planet below. Kirk and a landing party follow them down, only to discover that Eden's soil and vegetation are highly poisonous. One young man is already dead. The others agree to leave their Eden—except for Dr. Sevrin, who kills himself by tasting a highly toxic fruit. ▶

Recent years have seen nostalgia-minded individuals reach back into history and influence contemporary tastes in fashion and music, transplanting elements from "simpler" times into today's more complex way of life. In "Star Trek's" era, this urge to return to more tranquil surroundings is also present: it is specifically voiced by Kirk and McCoy in "The Paradise Syndrome," and here by Dr. Sevrin. Spock is the logical choice to show sympathy for Sevrin and his followers. They are seeking the same thing *he* wants: a home. But this common bond hardly accounts for the usually reticent Vulcan's participation in a "jam session" with Adam and his hippie friends.

The story outline for this episode (entitled "Joanna") featured McCoy's daughter instead of Irini Galliulin. Joanna, the doctor's only child, was mentioned in *Star Trek Writers' and Directors' Guide.* She was said to be a nursing student back on Earth, who received only an occasional letter from her father to remind her of his existence. Her appearance would certainly have added depth to McCoy's character, but for unknown reasons she was written out of the episode's final script.

Irini (Mary-Linda Rapelye) is apparently included in this adventure as a substitute for Joanna McCoy. The relationship between Irini and Pavel Chekov could have provided more insight into the young Russian navigator than it actually contributes, but it is still effective in adding substance to Chekov's character.

The space cruiser *Aurora,* which is seen in the episode's teaser, was produced by taking the miniature alien ship from "The Tholian Web" and treating it to a new paint job plus a new pair of nacelles (which appear to make use of parts from *Enterprise* and Klingon-ship plastic-model kits).

Actor Skip Homeier (Dr. Sevrin) also appears as Melakon in "Patterns of Force," and Phyllis Douglas (Girl Number Two) also appears as Yeoman Mears in "The Galileo Seven."

"REQUIEM FOR METHUSELAH"

Spock realizes the impossible is true

▭▭▭▭▭▭▭▭▭▭▭▭▭▭▭▭▭▭▭▭▭▭▭▭ **#76**

WRITER: Jerome Bixby
DIRECTOR: Murray Golden
PRINCIPALS: Kirk   Flint
            Spock   Rayna Kapec
            McCoy

◄ *Stardate 5843.7:* When an outbreak of deadly Rigellian fever strikes aboard the *Enterprise,* the starship journeys to planet Holberg 917-G in search of ryetalyn—the disease's only known antidote. Kirk, Spock, and McCoy beam down to the supposedly uninhabited planet's surface, only to discover a mysterious gentleman named Flint. Despite his initial anger over their appearance, Flint orders his robot servant to gather the crucial ryetalyn while he and his beautiful young ward Rayna Kapec entertain the *Enterprise* crewmembers. Spock notices that Flint's home is filled with rare art treasures, including an unknown Brahms waltz. Meanwhile, Rayna and the captain are swiftly falling in love.

When Flint's robot proves to be more of a hindrance than a help in gathering the ryetalyn, the landing party strikes off on its own and makes a shocking discovery—a succession of "Rayna" androids, the last of which is the Rayna Kirk loves. Flint reveals that he is an immortal who wandered the Earth for thousands of years, existing as da Vinci, Brahms, and many other important individuals. He came to Holberg to rest at last—and to ease his loneliness, he built the "Rayna" androids. He initially encouraged the present Rayna's involvement with Kirk in the hope it would accelerate her emotional development but is now violently jealous. As he and Kirk fight over Rayna, the android, sensitive and hopelessly confused by her conflicting emotions, short-circuits and dies. The landing party collects the ryetalyn and returns to the *Enterprise,* where McCoy tells Kirk and Spock that Flint, too, will soon die. In leaving Earth's atmosphere, Flint also left behind the source of his immortality. In a rare act of compassion, Spock uses a Vulcan mind touch to erase the painful memory of Rayna from Kirk's mind. ►

"Requiem for Methuselah" tells the story of a timeless individual: Flint's incredibly long life span (6,000 years in the final episode) has enabled him to gather experience and knowledge from the finest minds of history. He has read every available book, studied every art and science known to man, and developed a unique genius. His immortality, however, has also made him subject to the same loneliness felt by other long-lived beings within the "Star Trek" universe (including Apollo and Zefram Cochrane).

The story outline for this episode contained touches which recall the classic science fiction film *Forbidden Planet:* e.g., a home of futuristic design·all-purpose robot and a beautiful young woman with a very possessive guardian. In one scene, Kirk and McCoy attempted to sneak into Flint's home to look around; when Flint's robot discovered them, Rayna stopped it from attacking them. As Kirk embraced Rayna, Dr. McCoy guarded the doorway. Finally, Kirk fought a monster that was actually an illusion thrown around Flint's robot. Other portions of the outline had Kirk and his companions discovering a Michelangelo painting in Flint's studio that had not yet dried. The 8,000-year-old man was also Beethoven—Spock's favorite composer because of his music's logical, mathematical construction. Mr. Spock enabled Kirk to forget Rayna by using mental suggestion from a distance, while Kirk was in his cabin and the Vulcan was on the bridge.

Touches from other science fiction and fantasy works also abound in this episode: *Lost Horizon* featured a scene (deleted before release) in which an explorer performed an unknown work of Chopin that had been taught to him by an incredibly old pupil of the composer. A scientist in *The Island of Lost Souls* sent a visiting man to his creation, a panther transformed into a woman, to see if she was capable of falling in love. An episode of "The Twilight Zone" ("The Lateness of the Hour") featured a lonely old scientist who constructed an android "daughter" programmed to think she was human. In this episode, Rayna's surname "Kapec" was derived from the Czechoslovakian writer Karel Capek, who first coined the term "robot" in his 1921 play, *R.U.R.* Yet despite the many points of resemblance to other works of science fiction and fantasy, "Requiem" is on the whole an interesting and sensitive "Star Trek" segment.

The episode's ending, in which Spock uses his Vulcan abilities to enable the captain to "forget" is one of "Star Trek's" most sensitive moments, even though it is not clear what Spock is actually doing. Can his Vulcan gifts enable him to erase all memories of Rayna from Kirk's mind? Even if this was possible, would Spock take it upon himself to make the decision to "edit" his friend's memories? It is more likely that Mr. Spock is removing the pain of the experience rather than the captain's memories of Rayna.

Flint's residence was the same optical painting (reversed and tinted) that was used as the Rigel fortress in "The Cage." Also in the interests of economy, Flint's M-4 robot incorporated parts of the Nomad probe created for "The Changeling."

The late James Daly (Flint) was a popular television actor in the 1950s; after starring in the "Hallmark Hall of Fame" segment "Give us Barabbas," he went on to play adventurer Michael Powers in the series "Foreign Intrigue" (1953–54). His best-remembered recurring role is that of Dr. Paul Lochner on "Medical Center." Mr. Daly portrayed Flint as a brooding, secretive man, mixing equal parts of menace and tragedy in a well-executed, difficult performance. His characterization of Flint was aided by makeup (featuring a set of expressive eyebrows not unlike those of Dr. McCoy), hairstyle (similar to that of a Michelangelo statue), and costume (an excellent William Theiss design combining futuristic elements with raiment that might have been worn by Prince Hamlet).

Louise Sorel (Rayna), who also created a mysterious and tragic character (with just a hint of a 17-jewel movement) can also be seen in "Night Gallery" episodes "Pickman's Model" and "The Dead Man" (with Jeff Corey).

"THE SAVAGE CURTAIN"

 #77

WRITERS: Gene Roddenberry, Arthur Heinemann (story by Gene Roddenberry)
DIRECTOR: Herschel Daugherty
PRINCIPALS:
Kirk	Colonel Green
Spock	Zora
McCoy	Abraham Lincoln
Scott	Surak
Sulu	Genghis Khan
Uhura	Kahless
Chekov	Lieutenant Dickerson
Yarnek	

◀ *Stardate 5906.4:* While surveying the planet Excalbia, which appears to consist of nothing but a lavalike surface, the U.S.S. *Enterprise* is scanned by a powerful energy source coming from that world. Soon afterward, an entity who resembles Abraham Lincoln materializes in space, clad in traditional dark suit and stovepipe hat. The being claims to be the real Lincoln and requests to be beamed aboard. Against the recommendations of Dr. McCoy, Kirk and Spock welcome the entity aboard with a full-dress ceremony, and then accept his invitation to visit Excalbia. There, a rock creature named Yarnek appears and announces that the *Enterprise* officers will participate in a battle between good and evil, so that Excalbians can learn about these humanoid concepts. On the "good" side are Kirk, Spock, Lincoln, and Surak (the Vulcan who united the people of his planet and taught them to suppress their emotions and live in peace). On the "bad" side are Zora (a merciless criminal scientist), Genghis Khan

Kirk and Uhura contemplate Abraham Lincoln

(the tyrant of ancient Earth), Colonel Green (an unprincipled, aggressive Terran killer), and Kahless (the Klingon who set the style for his entire empire, the evil counterpart of Surak). Yarnek threatens to destroy the *Enterprise* if Kirk and Spock do not participate. After both sides conceive plots and counterplots, only Kirk, Spock, Genghis Khan, and Zora are left alive. Yarnek returns Kirk and Spock to the *Enterprise*. ▶

"The Savage Curtain" is more of a morality play than an action episode, an attempt at illustrating the I.D.I.C. concept that ultimately fails and makes the entire episode seem pointless. Unlike "Arena" and "Spectre of the Gun," there is no hint that Yarnek's people will ever meet or negotiate with the Federation. There is only the statement that Yarnek's motivations, no matter how destructive or fruitless they may seem to Kirk and company, are essential to the learning processes of his people.

The episode is memorable only because it introduces two individuals analogous (and important) to Kirk and Spock—Lincoln and Surak. Abraham Lincoln is a person who epitomizes concepts deeply appreciated by Trek's creator Gene Roddenberry and his creation James T. Kirk. Lincoln's presence on the *Enterprise* and throughout the episode enables the audience to observe Kirk behaving more like a human being than a starship captain.

Vulcans are the most impressive and interesting race introduced in "Star Trek." What little we know of them is conveyed to us by Mr. Spock (who is not a typical Vulcan). In "The Savage Curtain" we meet Surak, who personifies the Vulcan credo. Quiet and compassionate, he rejected his emotions to unify his people. This tantalizing glimpse we get of Surak is enough to make us wish that he had been featured in another episode.

The late Barry Atwater deserves a major share of the credit for bringing Surak to life. His portrayal is particularly impressive considering that Atwater is also remembered for his horrifyingly undead performance of vampire Janos Sgorzny in the 1972 TV movie *The Night Stalker*. He can also be seen in episodes of "The Outer Limits," "The Twilight Zone," "Night Gallery," and "One Step Beyond" ("The Day the World Wept," in which he portrayed Abraham Lincoln).

Lee Bergere (Lincoln) can also be seen in segments of "One Step Beyond" and "The Man from U.N.C.L.E." ("The Tigers Are Coming Affair," with Jill Ireland). In "The Savage Curtain" he portrayed a warm and intimate Lincoln, who at times conveyed the impression he regarded Kirk almost as a son.

Robert Herron (Kahless) was also actor Jeffrey Hunter's stunt double in "The Cage." Janos Prohaska (Yarnek) also appeared as alien creatures in "The Devil in the Dark" and "A Private Little War."

Director Herschel Daugherty's television career began in the 1950s and includes segments of "The Time Tunnel," "The Six Million Dollar Man," "Circle of Fear," and "Thriller." Prior to "Star Trek," Daugherty directed William Shatner in segments of "Thriller" ("The Grim Reaper") and "For the People" ("With Intent to Interference").

Chekov looks at McCoy and Scott in fulldress

"ALL OUR YESTERDAYS"

▭▭▭▭▭▭▭▭▭▭▭▭▭▭▭▭▭▭▭▭▭▭▭▭▭ #78

WRITER: Jean Lisette Aroeste
DIRECTORY: Marvin Chomsky
PRINCIPALS: Kirk   Scott
            Spock   Zarabeth
            McCoy   Mr. Atoz

Zarabeth listens as McCoy berates Spock

◄ *Stardate 5943.7:* Beaming down to the planet Sarpeidon, about to be engulfed in the explosion of its sun, Kirk, Spock, and McCoy discover a huge library. The librarian, Mr. Atoz, has supervised the transferral of his race into Sarpeidon's past by the use of a machine called the "atavachron." At the librarian's invitation, Kirk and Spock begin to examine various historical eras using the machine. When the captain hears a woman's scream, he leaps to her aid through the atavachron's portal. Spock and McCoy, attempting to follow, unintentionally enter Sarpeidon's ice age, where they meet a beautiful exile, Zarabeth. Kirk, accused of being a demon, is charged with witchcraft and imprisoned.

Meanwhile, Spock has fallen in love with Zarabeth. He finds himself growing more and more emotional, reverting to the ways of his Vulcan ancestors: for the first time in his life he eats meat and reacts adversely to McCoy's constant baiting. Zarabeth tells Spock and McCoy that they cannot return to the present without dying, but she has erroneously assumed that they were "prepared" (as she was). They not only can return, they must. The captain, meanwhile, has escaped and, with the aid of another traveler in time, returned to the library. After Atoz and several of his android duplicates fail to return Kirk to the past, they begin a search for Spock and McCoy, who have returned to the place where they entered the ice age. Guided by Kirk's voice, they return to the present. Zarabeth remains behind—alone forever in the past. Atoz leaps through the portal to a time of his own choosing, and the *Enterprise* leaves the planet. ▶

In "All Our Yesterdays," the strange events that befall Captain Kirk, Mr. Spock and Dr. McCoy are their own fault. Kirk succumbs to his usual weakness for the opposite sex by leaping before he looks. Arriving in a Sarpeidon locale resembling 17th-century England, the captain finds himself jailed on a charge of witchcraft (merely because he materializes out of thin air and converses with a disembodied spirit voice called "Bones"). Spock and McCoy, understandably concerned about the safety of the captain, follow just as incautiously—and propel themselves into the cold, lonely hell of an alien ice age.

"The Immunity Syndrome" established Spock's ability to receive telepathic impressions from the U.S.S. *Intrepid's*

doomed Vulcan crew. Apparently, his receiving capabilities are greater—and more important—than glimpsed in that segment. In "All Our Yesterdays" we are led to believe that his sudden transformation into an emotional being is a direct result of being stranded in the past, in an era when the distant Vulcans were illogical savages, fighting among themselves. The only conclusion is that at least part of Spock's ability to maintain his Vulcan decorum results from constant telepathic attachment to his father's race. Unfortunately, we never learn more about this intriguing possibility.

Spock's conversion into an emotional, woman-seeking, meat-eating primitive also provides problems for McCoy. The doctor finds himself acting as psychoanalyst for his transformed friend, and Zarabeth, who had already adapted to the idea of spending the rest of her life utterly alone, only contributes to the problem. Considering the future awaiting her, it is no wonder that she wishes the Vulcan would stay, and their farewell is as shattering to the television audience as it is for Spock and Zarabeth.

The story outline for this segment, entitled "A Handful of Dust," bore little resemblance to the completed episode. The most outstanding difference was the complete absence of Zarabeth. Kirk, Spock, and McCoy went to Sarpeidon and found the planet in ruins, except for the undamaged library containing an unnamed time-portal machine. Kirk unwittingly entered the past into a locale resembling San Francisco's Barbary Coast but escaped back to the library with the aid of another time traveler. Spock and McCoy, attempting to follow Kirk, found themselves in a desert wasteland. Spock coped with the climate but McCoy was dying from the heat when the duo was captured by mutant humanoids. While Kirk battled Mr. Atoz, his fellow time traveler aided Spock and McCoy

Mr. Atoz (Ian Wolfe) aids Kirk.

to return to the library. Their return was almost disastrous when McCoy became "stuck" in the portal, his arm in the library and the rest of him in the desert. Finally, Kirk's time-traveling benefactor destroyed the time machine to prevent further interruptions of the planet's past. The library collapsed in ruins behind our friends, who observed that all that remained was "a handful of dust."

The atavachron's monitor screen and control console were fashioned from pieces of Gary Seven's Beta 5 computer designed and constructed for the episode "Assignment Earth." The view of Kirk vanishing into the (time portal) brick wall was accomplished via split screen: two separate photographic images were combined on one piece of film, and Kirk "vanished" by stepping into the seam between them.

Mariette Hartley (Zarabeth), a regular player in both "The Hero" television series and "Peyton Place," also costarred in Gene Roddenberry's 1973 TV pilot film "Genesis II" (with Percy Rodrigues). In "The Twilight Zone" episode "The Long Morrow" she played a young woman alienated from her astronaut fiancé (Robert Lansing). More recently, Ms. Hartley has been seen in a series of commercials for Polaroid with actor James Garner and as a cohost on NBC's "Today" show.

Zarabeth's original costume revealed her belly button—which the network forced Roddenberry to change. Years later, when producing "Genesis II," Roddenberry made sure not only to show Ms. Hartley's belly button, but to give her character two!

Ian Wolfe (Mr. Atoz) also appears as Septimus in "Bread and Circuses" and certainly has the best possible name for a librarian—Mr. "A" to "Z."

"TURNABOUT INTRUDER"

#79

WRITER: Arthur H. Singer (story by Gene Roddenberry)
DIRECTOR: Herb Wallerstein
PRINCIPALS: Kirk   Chekov
Spock   Dr. Janice Lester
McCoy   Dr. Arthur Coleman
Scott   Angela
Sulu   Mr. Lemli
Uhura

◄ *Stardate 5298.5:* Dr. Janice Lester, once romantically involved with James Kirk, hates the captain because she was unable (and unfit) to become a starship commander. She lures Kirk to planet Camus II, where she has discovered an alien mechanism capable of transferring minds between bodies. Using the device, Dr. Lester transfers her consciousness into Captain Kirk's body, trapping his mind in hers. Dr. Coleman, Janice's current lover and partner, makes sure that Kirk's mind is kept sedated. But Spock becomes suspicious and, using a Vulcan mind meld, determines that Captain Kirk's mind is trapped in Dr. Lester's body. Janice, using Kirk's body, initiates court-martial proceedings against Spock and all who believe that the captain's mind is not where it belongs. But she is unable to control her emotions and during the proceedings loses her temper, arousing the suspicions of other crewmembers. When "Kirk" charges McCoy and Scotty with mutiny and imposes the death penalty, the entire crew knows something is seriously wrong. Fortunately, Kirk, with Spock's telepathic assistance, is able to reverse the effects of the mind transfer. Janice, trapped again in her own body, is unable to bear her frustration and collapses. ►

Captain Kirk has survived crises that have confined and frustrated him physically and emotionally. He has experienced his mind and body being separated into two halves (in "The Enemy Within"), but "Turnabout Intruder" provides Kirk with his most pressing and intimate problems, separating him from his friends, his command, and his own physical body.

Logically, Captain Kirk knows Spock, McCoy, Chapel, Scotty, and the other officers in his crew so intimately that he could probably cite dozens of facts that would convince these people of his identity, no matter *what* body his mind was in at the time. But the shock of transition, the drugs administered to Janice's body, and the incredible nature of this predicament combine to make things extremely difficult for Kirk—and very suspenseful for "Star Trek" fans.

Actress Sandra Smith (Dr. Janice Lester) gives an extremely dedicated and effective performance in this episode. This was the only occasion in "Star Trek" that a performer other than William Shatner portrayed Captain James T. Kirk, and Ms. Smith rose to the challenge of this unique and strenuous assignment.

Barbara Baldavin (Communications Officer Angela) also appeared in "Balance of Terror" and "Shore Leave."

"Turnabout Intruder" was the last "Star Trek" episode produced. On January 9, 1969, Sandra Smith and William Shatner were photographed for the episode's teaser against the alien machine's sculpted panels, and in front of black backdrops, footage later used to create the photographic effect of the actual mind transfer. The takes went quickly, the teaser was completed on schedule—and suddenly people who had worked together since 1966 real-

ized that it was finally all over. The familiar trips to the studio, tight deadlines, bits of business, the day-to-day routine of "Star Trek" production—all had come to an end.

Later that day, there was a cast and crew party. People drank and joked, talking about what they would do with their time and where they would work next. Good-byes were said, small talk was exchanged, and appointments were made. All left the studio smiling, knowing they had all been a part of something very special. Some even thought that maybe someday they would all be back together doing "Star Trek" again.

They were, as Mr. Spock would say, "quite correct."

Dr. Lester in Kirk's body

THIRD SEASON PRODUCTION CREDITS

PRODUCER   Fred Freiberger
CO-PRODUCER   Robert H. Justman
EXECUTIVE PRODUCER   Gene Roddenberry
ASSOCIATE PRODUCERS   Edward K. Milkis, Gregg Peters
STORY CONSULTANT   Arthur H. Singer
THEME MUSIC   Alexander Courage
ADDITIONAL MUSIC   Various
ART DIRECTOR   Walter M. Jefferies
DIRECTORS OF PHOTOGRAPHY   Jerry Finnerman, Al Francis
FILM EDITORS   Bill Brame, Donald R. Rode
UNIT PRODUCTION MANAGER   Gregg Peters
ASSISTANT DIRECTORS   Gil Kissel, Claude Binyon, Jr., Gene DeRuelle
SET DECORATOR   John M. Dwyer
COSTUMES CREATED BY   William Ware Theiss
PHOTOGRAPHIC EFFECTS   Various
SOUND EFFECTS EDITOR   Douglas H. Grindstaff
MUSIC EDITOR   Richard Lapham
RE-RECORDING MIXER   Gordon L. Day, CAS
PRODUCTION MIXER   Carl W. Daniels
SCRIPT SUPERVISOR   George A. Rutter
RECORDED BY   Glen Glenn Sound Co.
CASTING   Joseph D'Agosta, William J. Kenney
MAKEUP ARTIST   Fred B. Phillips, SMA
HAIR STYLIST   Pat Westmore
GAFFER   George H. Merhoff
HEAD GRIP   George Rader
PROPERTY MASTER   Irving A. Feinberg
SPECIAL EFFECTS   Jim Rugg
A Paramount Production in association with Norway Corp. Douglas S. Cramer; Executive Vice President in charge of production

THE LONG ROAD BACK

9
SYNDICATION

On the night of June 3, 1969, "Star Trek" fans realized the end of the original five-year mission had come—but they would not let the show become a thing of the past. Even while the series was on the air, "fanzines" had begun to appear. These publications were printed with whatever means and materials were available: loaded with fiction, art work, and articles about "Star Trek," they appeared as regularly as their amateur publishers could manage to produce them. No one was paid for their contributions to fanzines (unless one counts copies of the fanzines as payment of a kind). The rewards to the publishers, contributors, editors, and readers were new materials, stories, and illustrations about "Star Trek." After cancellation, more fanzines were introduced. Poetry and trivia tests joined the contents of these publications, along with puzzles, fan-club news, and other attractions.

"Star Trek" memorabilia began to surface—at a premium. Gene Roddenberry and Majel Barrett started a mail-order company called Star Trek Enterprises (also known as Lincoln Enterprises) through which they sold original "Star Trek" scripts, photos, and art work—even the original "Star Trek" 35mm footage, cut into sets of individual frames and mounted as slides. They were so deluged with orders that for a time fans had to wait for months to receive their material.

But above all else, what enabled the series not only to survive but even prosper was syndication.

"Star Trek" was originally marketed only to NBC's affiliate stations all over the United States—at the hours NBC specified. Now, there were countless other markets, and countless other time slots. Paramount prepared a "syndication kit," listing all the episodes in their original production order and providing additional print and publicity materials. Trade papers were called, and press releases sent to the newspapers: they were ready to distribute "Star Trek" all over the world. In its syndication brochure, Paramount also mentioned the honors the show had been accorded. "Star Trek" was credited as "the recipient of over one million letters of support and encouragement from a worldwide space-oriented populace" and called "one of the NBC television network's highest audience-response shows."

Independent stations all across the country caught on quickly, no doubt aided by the real-life space program, which had made some impressive progress since "Star Trek's" cancellation. Man had walked on the moon, and concepts that had once intrigued a few science fiction fans now interested millions across the globe. And it wasn't long before all those fans—new and old—began to gather together to celebrate the show.

10
CONVENTIONS

In June 1971, a group of East Coast science fiction fans held a modest gathering in a New Jersey public library to honor "Star Trek." Fan art was displayed, a comedy skit performed (with fans—including this writer as Mr. Sulu—playing various members of the *Enterprise* crew), and panel discussions and lectures given concerning not only "Star Trek" but other science fiction film projects and literary works as well. By definition, this gathering would have to be called one of the first "Star Trek" conventions, perhaps even *the* first, though nobody there thought of it that way. It was just a way to enjoy oneself and meet other "Star Trek" fans.

Two fans were instrumental in organizing that New Jersey gathering: Elyse Pines, a member of one of the first "Trek" fan groups, and Devra Langsam, copublisher of *Spockanalia*, one of the first "Star Trek" fanzines. After the New Jersey gathering they began to casually discuss plans to stage another get-together for "Trek" fans who had tried to keep the series from being canceled. It was a waste of time, they were told. Nobody would come: it was *over*. But Elyse and Devra kept talking, and eventually others joined their discussions. These fans became known as "the Committee." Their convention, as they envisioned it, would be of modest size. If they were lucky, a decent number of people would attend. Maybe.

At that time Elyse was attending Brooklyn College. Many of the college's mass-media students were "Star Trek" fans, and so she planned an evening at the college to honor both "Star Trek" and science fiction. I was asked to appear to give a short talk on the "Star Trek" fan movement and talk trivia. The program was to take place in Gershwin Auditorium, which could hold approximately 200 people. Waiting with friends for the events to begin, I could see people pouring into the room in a steady stream. Soon all the seats were taken . . . then the spaces in the aisles . . . then the spaces against the

walls . . . between the rows of seats . . . finally, as I started to speak, I saw people sitting on top of each other. Piles of heavy coats placed by the doors (it was early in December) finally stopped the fan influx. It was impossible to enter or leave the auditorium. Elyse, meanwhile, having finished her last class for the day, approached the building . . . only to be unable to gain entrance (fortunately, she knew of another way into the building).

There were many questions asked about the convention—including several concerning expected attendance. As Elyse and I surveyed the crowded room, a silent realization caused us to look at each other. We *had* to get to a phone as quickly as possible: if New York City was anything like Brooklyn College, the Committee would have to hire experts to prevent *overcrowding* the hotel!

The 1972 convention was a tremendous success—and a tremendous trendsetter. "Star Trek" merchandise was available everywhere. There were shirts with pictures of the "Star Trek" characters and vessels. Buttons, bumper stickers, decorative posters, and homemade duplicates of props were being sold through fan organizations, by individual fans. Overnight, dealers interested only in a quick buck had appeared with an assortment of "Star Trek" souvenirs.

The conventions also cast the members of the "Star Trek" crew (and creator Roddenberry) in a new role: guest speakers. And each succeeding convention attempted to hire more cast members than the one before. The earliest conventions were especially magical, because the fans were able to see the genuine happiness that resulted when "Trek's" performers and executives found themselves back together—if only to relive moments now past.

But the day was not far off when the *Enterprise* and her crew would fly once again.

11
ANIMATION

"Star Trek" was always an obvious choice for animation. Not only did the medium provide opportunities to present stories and characters impossible within a live-action television budget, but the show was a natural for Saturday morning's younger television viewers. But the first discussion of "Star Trek" in animated form had ended after an interested producer put forth a proposal for an action-oriented series specifically designed for those younger viewers.

Filmation Associates, a West Coast animation company, had a more constructive idea. They wanted Gene Roddenberry to be closely involved with their proposed series, which would stress all the values and character relationships that had made the original such a success. This proposal was accepted—and the new voyages of the starship *Enterprise,* with Roddenberry aboard as executive consultant and D. C. Fontana as associate producer and story editor, were under way.

Work on the series progressed: in June 1973, the series' original cast—William Shatner, Leonard Nimoy, DeForest Kelley, George Takei, Nichelle Nichols, Majel Barrett, and James Doohan—reunited for the first time since the show had been canceled to record the dialogue for three animated "Star Trek" segments, and in August Lou Scheimer, president of Filmation, appeared on a panel at a "Trek" convention. Scheimer stated: "When they [the fans] saw how much we cared, and how faithful we are trying to be to the original series, I think they realized they really have 'Star Trek' back again." Roddenberry elaborated on some of the changes made in the show's format:

We've updated the ship, mostly by taking viewer suggestions. For example, there are now two doors on the bridge of the *Enterprise,* one of which does not lead to an elevator. People used to write in and ask, "What do they do if the doors get stuck?" and we didn't have an answer. We will have a lot of alien crewmembers, not just Mr. Spock. We always wanted to have more aliens, but there are very few of them in the Screen Actors Guild.

Writers for the animated episodes included people who had provided scripts for the original "Trek" series. Fontana said when she asked for submissions she didn't get one turndown. Participants included Samuel A. Peeples, Stephen Kandel, Margaret Armen, Paul Schneider, David Gerrold, Marc Daniels (who had directed segments of the original series), Walter Koenig, science fiction superstar Larry Niven, and Fontana herself.

Working from the scripts provided by these and other writers, the series' storyboarding staff translated the tales into illustrated terms. Special-effects animation specialist Reuben Timmins coordinated the visuals involving the starship *Enterprise,* in some cases tracing over live-action footage from the original episodes to reproduce familiar views of the vessel.

Finally, seven years to the day after "Star Trek" made its debut on NBC, the first episode of the all-new animated series aired on the same network.

Episodes are again listed here in order of production.

"MORE TRIBBLES, MORE TROUBLES"

`□□□□□□□□□□□□□□□□□□□□□□□□□□□□□□□□□` #1A

WRITER: David Gerrold
PRINCIPALS: Kirk   Sulu
            Spock   Koloth
            McCoy   Korax
            Scott   Cyrano Jones
            Uhura

◄ *Stardate 5392.4:* Transporting quadrotriticale to Sherman's Planet (now in the midst of a second famine), the *Enterprise* rescues Cyrano Jones from a Klingon warship. Jones has a new cargo of tribbles, which, he says, have been altered to prevent their frequent reproduction. But even these tribbles can't resist the quadrotriticale on board the *Enterprise* and get so fat that Cyrano's tribble-eating glommer can't swallow them. The Klingons appear again and demand that Cyrano be handed over, as he has stolen the glommer from *their* ship. Kirk returns the animal but retains Cyrano, and McCoy discovers the genetically altered tribbles are actually colonies of many small ones. Some of these are beamed aboard the Klingon vessel, and Captain Koloth has his hands full as the *Enterprise* leaves.

"THE INFINITE VULCAN"

`□□□□□□□□□□□□□□□□□□□□□□□□□□□□□□□□□` #2A

WRITER: Walter Koenig
PRINCIPALS: Kirk   Keniclius Five
            Spock   Agmar
            McCoy   Lieutenant Arex
            Scott   Lieutenant Morgan
            Sulu   Lieutenant Kolchek
            Uhura

◄ *Stardate 5554.4:* On the planet Phylos, an *Enterprise* landing party discovers Keniclius Five, a cloned giant of Dr. Starros Keniclius, a Terran scientist who lived during the Eugenics Wars. The giant wishes to clone Spock to use as a galactic peacemaker, refusing to believe Kirk's claims that the galaxy is an almost totally peaceful group of civilized worlds. Keniclius clones one giant from the Vulcan, which weakens Spock to the point of death. Kirk, citing the Vulcan philosophy of life and death, makes the clone realize he is simply a copy of Spock. The replicant, using the Vulcan mind touch, saves the original's life. The Keniclius and Spock clones remain behind on Phylos to revitalize its culture.

"YESTERYEAR"

`□□□□□□□□□□□□□□□□□□□□□□□□□□□□□□□□□` #3A

WRITER: D. C. Fontana
PRINCIPALS: Kirk   The Healer
            Spock   Young Selek
            McCoy   Young Sofek
            Scott   Young Stark
            Ensign Bates Thelin the Andorian
            Sarek   Aleek-OM
            Amanda   Grey
            Young Spock Erickson

◄ *Stardate 5373.4:* Federation personnel, including Kirk and Spock, explore the planet Orion's past using the Guardian of Forever. When they return, no one recognizes Mr. Spock: for the past five years, the *Enterprise*'s first officer has been an Andorian named Thelin. Ship's records reveal that Sarek and Amanda's son was killed at the age of seven, and that the couple separated after their loss. Spock recalls that years before, during his *kahs-wan*—a Vulcan coming-of-age ritual—a distant cousin, Selek, saved his life. Spock realizes he must return through the Guardian and become Selek to rectify the distorted time line. Arriving in his home city of ShiKahr, "Selek" saves young Spock's life—but the boy's pet *sehlat*, I-Chaya, is gravely wounded. Given the choice of keeping his beloved pet alive for a short time longer or offering the *sehlat* a dignified death, young Spock chooses the latter and, in doing so, decides to live by his Vulcan heritage. "Selek" returns to the future to find the time lines restored to normal and resumes his station on the *Enterprise*.

"BEYOND THE FARTHEST STAR"

`□□□□□□□□□□□□□□□□□□□□□□□□□□□□□□□□□` #4A

WRITER: Samuel A. Peeples
PRINCIPALS: Kirk   Sulu
            Spock   Uhura
            McCoy   Transporter Chief Kyle
            Scott

◄ *Stardate 5521.3:* Pulled off-course by Questar M-17, an imploded negative star mass, the *Enterprise* discovers a strange starship inhabited by a formless and evil alien life form. The ship's builders had failed to rid themselves of the creature and attempted to destroy their vessel rather than risk bringing the malevolent entity to civilization. The creature takes control of the *Enterprise*. But Kirk and Spock, by heading directly toward Questar M-17, trick the entity into believing they are about to destroy themselves, and the creature flees. Using a slingshot effect, the *Enterprise* escapes Questar's gravity pull, leaving the alien trapped in orbit around the dead star.

"THE SURVIVOR"

▭▭▭▭▭▭▭▭▭▭▭▭▭▭▭▭▭▭▭▭▭▭▭▭▭▭▭▭ #5A

WRITER: James Schmerer
PRINCIPALS: Kirk   Carter Winston/Vendorian
Spock   Lieutenant Anne Nored
McCoy   Lieutenant M'Ress
Scott   Romulan Commander
Sulu   Gabler
Chapel

◄ *Stardate 5143.3:* Philanthropist Carter Winston, missing for five years, is discovered aboard a damaged one-man craft. In a reunion with his fiancée, Lieutenant Anne Nored (who is stationed on board the *Enterprise*), Winston states that he has changed and can no longer marry her. "Winston" is actually a shape-changing Vendorian, who assumes Kirk's appearance to bring the *Enterprise* into the Neutral Zone, where Romulan vessels quickly surround the starship. The Vendorian is a Romulan spy—but because he absorbed so many emotions and recollections from the real Carter Winston before the man died, he cannot allow Lieutenant Nored to die. The alien transforms himself into a deflector shield and saves the *Enterprise.*

"THE LORELEI SIGNAL"

▭▭▭▭▭▭▭▭▭▭▭▭▭▭▭▭▭▭▭▭▭▭▭▭▭▭▭▭ #6A

WRITER: Margaret Armen
PRINCIPALS: Kirk   Chapel
Spock   Lieutenant Arex
McCoy   Theela
Scott   Dara
Uhura   Security Officer Davison

◄ *Stardate 5483.7:* Once every 27 years, a starship has been disappearing near the Taurean system. The *Enterprise* receives signals which captivate all the starship's male personnel—visions of lovely, golden-skinned, silver-haired women. Kirk, Spock, and McCoy beam down and are captured by the women of their visions. Fitted with headbands that drain their life energies, they age rapidly. Uhura and an all-female landing party arrive and rescue the men. Theela, the aliens' leader, explains that after their race's men died, the women began to kidnap other males to draw off their life force and remain alive. Spock uses the *Enterprise* transporter which retains the crew's undamaged, molecular structure to restore the male landing party to normal. The alien women are taken to another world where they can live normal lives.

"ONE OF OUR PLANETS IS MISSING"

▭▭▭▭▭▭▭▭▭▭▭▭▭▭▭▭▭▭▭▭▭▭▭▭▭▭▭▭ #7A

WRITER: Marc Daniels
PRINCIPALS: Kirk   Sulu
Spock   Uhura
McCoy   Arex
Scott

◄ *Stardate 5371.3:* A huge cosmic cloud that "eats" planets is headed for Mantilles—home to 82 million people. The *Enterprise* is able to warn Mantilles of the approaching danger and is then pulled inside the cloud. Spock steers toward the creature's "brain"—and escape—but the cloud's antimatter villi are draining the ship's energy. Mr. Scott brings one of the villi aboard and uses it to recharge the *Enterprise*'s warp-drive engines. Spock initiates a Vulcan mind meld with the entity, informing it that as it ingests planets it is also destroying countless life forms. The cloud agrees to leave our galaxy.

"MUDD'S PASSION"

▭▭▭▭▭▭▭▭▭▭▭▭▭▭▭▭▭▭▭▭▭▭▭▭▭▭▭▭ #8A

WRITER: Stephen Kandel
PRINCIPALS: Kirk   M'Ress
Spock   Arex
McCoy   Harcourt Fenton Mudd
Scott   Lora
Chapel

◄ *Stardate 4978.5:* Captain Kirk discovers his old friend Harry Mudd selling a fake love potion to lonely miners on the planet Motherlode. Kirk rescues Mudd from the miners, but once aboard the starship Harry persuades Christine Chapel to try the love potion on Mr. Spock. Pursued by Chapel when the potion does not work, Harry steals a shuttlecraft and takes her hostage. Spock experiences a delayed reaction to the potion, as does everyone else on the vessel, and enthusiastically leads a mission to rescue Christine. After all return safely to the *Enterprise,* they discover that when the potion wears off, those affected by the formula hate each other for several hours. Mudd, back in the brig, confesses to a number of other crimes and is again sent away for rehabilitation.

"THE MAGICKS OF MEGAS-TU"

▯▯▯▯▯▯▯▯▯▯▯▯▯▯▯▯▯▯▯▯▯▯▯▯▯▯▯▯▯▯▯▯▯ #9A

WRITER: Larry Brody
PRINCIPALS: Kirk   Sulu
            Spock   Uhura
            McCoy   Lucien
            Scott   Megan Prosecutor

◄ *Stardate 1254.4:* A whirlwind of matter and energy propels the *Enterprise* into another dimension where its technology does not function. The crew is rescued by a devil-like creature named Lucien who claims that in this dimension magic functions just as surely as science does in ours. But the crew's use of mystical energy is detected on planet Megas-Tu, and they are transported to the Megans' planet. Long ago the Megans had visited Earth, where they were first regarded as sages and then persecuted as witches. Lucien became the basis for the ancients' visual concept of Satan. A magical battle between the two races ends when the aliens realize that the humans are only fighting in defense of Lucien. Impressed, they aid the *Enterprise* in returning home.

"TIME TRAP"

▯▯▯▯▯▯▯▯▯▯▯▯▯▯▯▯▯▯▯▯▯▯▯▯▯▯▯▯▯▯▯▯▯#10A

WRITER: Joyce Perry
PRINCIPALS: Kirk   Commander Kuri
            Spock   Captain Kor
            McCoy   Kaz
            Scott   Kali
            Sulu   Xerius
            Uhura   Devna
            Gabler   Magen
            Bell

◄ *Stardate 5267.2:* Exploring the Delta Triangle, an area of space in which many ships have disappeared, the *Enterprise* is attacked by Klingon vessels and trapped in the Triangle with the Klingon cruiser *Klothos*. There, Kirk discovers a weird graveyard of ships—and the descendants of the vessels' crews. Kirk and Captain Kor of the *Klothos* are taken before the Elysian Council, composed of members of many races, including humans, Klingons, Gorns, Romulans, Kzin, and Vulcans. They are told there is no way out of Elysia, where all these races have learned to live in harmony. Kirk and Kor plan to escape using the combined power of their vessels. Kor is also plotting to destroy the Federation starship (using a bomb). The Elysians inform the *Enterprise*—and the device is found and disconnected after both vessels have escaped.

"SLAVER WEAPON"

▯▯▯▯▯▯▯▯▯▯▯▯▯▯▯▯▯▯▯▯▯▯▯▯▯▯▯▯▯▯▯▯▯ #11A

WRITER: Larry Niven
PRINCIPALS: Spock   Chuft Captain
            Uhura   Kzin Telepath
            Sulu

◄ *Stardate 4187.3:* Spock, Uhura, and Sulu, aboard the shuttlecraft *Copernicus,* are carrying a Slaver stasis box, manufactured by the long-dead race that once ruled most of the galaxy. The stasis boxes, the Slavers' means of carrying information and devices, are the only remnants of their civilization—and are mutually attractive. The stasis box indicates the presence of another such box on an ice-covered planet. Beaming down, the three are taken prisoner by the Kzin—catlike, violent creatures who have a stolen empty stasis box to lure others to them and obtain the Slavers' technology. Confining our people on the Kzin ship, the Kzin Chuft Captain opens Spock's stasis box and finds a weapon. While testing it, the Chuft Captain accidentally deactivates the "police web" confining Spock and company. They escape, taking the weapon with them—but Uhura is captured. To free her, Spock agrees to fight the injured but still dangerous Kzin commander. Using the Slaver weapon, Sulu causes a nuclear explosion which throws everyone off balance and permits the Kzin Chuft Captain to recover the weapon. When he cannot furnish the proper code words, the device advises the Chuft Captain to try another setting—which causes the weapon to explode, destroying the Kzin and their ship.

"JIHAD"

▯▯▯▯▯▯▯▯▯▯▯▯▯▯▯▯▯▯▯▯▯▯▯▯▯▯▯▯▯▯▯▯▯#12A

WRITER: Stephen Kandel
PRINCIPALS: Kirk   Sord
            Spock   Em/3/Green
            Scott   Lara
            Sulu   Vedala
            Tchar

◄ *Stardate 5683.1:* The Vedala, the first race to venture into outer space, summon the *Enterprise*—specifically Kirk and Spock—to a rendezvous with other specialists to combat an imminent threat to the galaxy. Their mission: recover the stolen brainwave pattern of Alar, responsible for the transformation of the warlike Skorr into a peaceful people. Failure to recover the "Soul of Skorr" will result in a galaxy-wide holy war—a jihad. After tracking down the holy relic, Kirk and company learn that one of their number (a Skorr prince) is plotting against the group. The Vedala come to Kirk's assistance, and the mission ends successfully.

"THE AMBERGRIS ELEMENT"

#13A

WRITER: Margaret Armen
PRINCIPALS:

Kirk	Domar
Spock	Rila
McCoy	Cadmar
Scott	Lemus
Arex	Nephro
Lieutenant Clayton	

◄ *Stardate 5499.9:* Exploring the seas of Argo, an unstable planet almost completely covered by water, Kirk and Spock are attacked—and regain consciousness as water breathers. They discover an underwater race, the Aquans. The younger Aquans, convinced the surface dwellers come in peace, save their lives using ancient surgical techniques. The older Aquans believe the "air breathers" are hostile, and when Scott, learning of an impending sea-quake, beams down, the elders interpret his visit as the start of an invasion. Kirk and Spock are left on an island to die, but Rila, a young Aquan, rescues them and gives McCoy her people's medical knowledge. The younger Aquans gather the substances needed to reverse the operation on Kirk and his people, and all watch from the starship bridge as the *Enterprise*'s phasers save their city from the quake. The younger Aquans decide to live on the surface of their world once again, while the older ones remain water dwellers.

"ONCE UPON A PLANET"

#14A

WRITERS: Len Jenson, Chuck Menville
PRINCIPALS

Kirk	M'Ress
Spock	Gabler
McCoy	Computer
Scott	White Rabbit
Sulu	Alice
Uhura	Queen of Hearts
Arex	

◄ *Stardate 5591.2:* The *Enterprise* crew returns to the "Shore Leave" planet—but as Dr. McCoy attempts to conjure up a picture of the old South, the Queen of Hearts appears and screams, "Off with his head!" Uhura is taken prisoner by a robot. Kirk discovers a grave with the inscription: "The Keeper, last of his race, ceased to function, fifth day of the 12th Moon of this planet's year 7009." Kirk and Spock find the captured Uhura and the planet's computer, which resents its role of servant now that the Keeper is dead. They convince the computer it must stop its hostile actions. Spock remains with the computer, and the rest of the *Enterprise* crew enjoys another memorable shore leave.

"THE TERRATIN INCIDENT"

#15A

WRITER: Paul Schneider
PRINCIPALS

Kirk	Uhura
Spock	Chapel
McCoy	Arex
Scott	Mendant
Sulu	

◄ *Stardate 5577.3:* The U.S.S. *Enterprise* receives a mysterious transmission containing only one decipherable word—"terratin." Arriving at the signal's source world, the vessel is hit by a lightning bolt—and all living matter on the *Enterprise* starts to shrink. Beaming down to the planet, Kirk discovers a miniature city. The city's leader explains that the "attack" is actually a call for help; their planet is breaking up. Spock discovers the tiny people are the mutated survivors of an exploration party from Earth—whose forebears named this strange world "Terra Ten." The entire city is beamed aboard and the *Enterprise* people are restored to normal size.

"THE EYE OF THE BEHOLDER"

▭▭▭▭▭▭▭▭▭▭▭▭▭▭▭▭▭▭▭▭▭▭▭▭▭▭▭▭▭ #16A

WRITER: David P. Harmon
PRINCIPALS: Kirk   Arex
            Spock   Lieutenant Commander Tom Markel
            McCoy   Randi Bryce
            Scott

◄ *Stardate 5501.2:* The *Enterprise* locates the missing spaceship *Ariel* orbiting the planet Lactra VII. Her records indicate the entire crew beamed down to the planet. Following, Kirk, Spock, and a landing party encounter giant slugs, the intelligent life form of Lactra, and are put in a zoo. Spock establishes telepathic contact with a child of the slugs. The child convinces the adult Lactrans that the starship's personnel are intelligent. They free the landing party.

"BEM"

▭▭▭▭▭▭▭▭▭▭▭▭▭▭▭▭▭▭▭▭▭▭▭▭▭▭▭▭▭ #17A

WRITER: David Gerrold
PRINCIPALS: Kirk   Uhura
            Spock   M'Ress
            Scott   Arex
            Sulu   Commander Ari bn Bem

◄ *Stardate 7403.6:* The *Enterprise* is in orbit around the recently discovered planet Delta Theta III. On board— Commander Ari bn Bem. Beaming down with the landing party, Bem is imprisoned by a group of natives. Kirk, attempting to rescue him, is addressed by a female voice claiming to be a god. She orders Kirk to leave her children and her planet alone. Kirk defies her to continue his search. Bem, originally just testing Kirk's resourcefulness, now realizes his actions have placed the starship in jeopardy, and wishes to disassemble into the individual elements of which he is composed. Kirk persuades him to return to the ship, and the voice permits the *Enterprise* to leave in peace.

"ALBATROSS"

▭▭▭▭▭▭▭▭▭▭▭▭▭▭▭▭▭▭▭▭▭▭▭▭▭▭▭▭▭ #18A

WRITER: Dario Finelli
PRINCIPALS: Kirk   Kol-tai
            Spock   Demos
            McCoy   Supreme Prefect

◄ *Stardate 5275.6:* While delivering medical supplies to the planet Dramia, Dr. McCoy is arrested and charged with causing a plague on Dramia II 19 years before. The warrant has been approved by the Federation and Kirk is concerned because Dramian justice is swift. He and Spock journey to Dramia II to find only ruins and scattered, desperate survivors of the plague, including Kol-tai, whose life was saved years ago by McCoy. The Dramian plague then strikes the *Enterprise*. Only Spock is immune, and he frees McCoy from prison to find a cure for the disease. Using Kol-tai's blood as the basis for an antidote, Bones is vindicated and honored by the Dramians and the entire Federation.

"THE PIRATES OF ORION"

▭▭▭▭▭▭▭▭▭▭▭▭▭▭▭▭▭▭▭▭▭▭▭▭▭▭▭▭▭ #19A

WRITER: Howard Weinstein
PRINCIPALS: Kirk   Captain O'Shea
            Spock   Freighter Officers
            McCoy   Orion Commander
            Scott   Orion Science Officer
            Chapel   Orion Ensign
            Arex

◄ *Stardate 6334.1:* On the way to a Federation ceremony, an epidemic of choriocytosis strikes the *Enterprise*. To Terrans it is not a serious danger, but in Vulcans it causes suffocation after three days, and Spock has the disease. While Spock is given a dose of synthetic Strobolin— the disease's only antidote—to slow its progress, Kirk arranges to pick up a supply of the drug from the S.S. *Huron*. But on its way to the *Enterprise*, the *Huron* is attacked by Orion pirates who steal her cargo. Kirk attempts to bargain with the pirates, but to protect their planet's neutrality, the Orions decide to destroy themselves. With Scotty's assistance, the attempt fails, the Orions are captured, and Spock's life is saved with the recovered Strobolin.

"PRACTICAL JOKER"

▭▭▭▭▭▭▭▭▭▭▭▭▭▭▭▭▭▭▭▭▭▭▭▭▭▭ #20A

WRITER: Chuck Menville
PRINCIPALS: Kirk   Arex
            Spock   M'Ress
            Scott   Computer
            Sulu   Romulan Commander
            Uhura

◄ *Stardate 3183.3:* On a routine survey mission, the *Enterprise* is attacked by Romulan warships who claim the Federation vessel has crossed into their territory. The starship successfully evades the enemy vessels by entering a cloudlike energy field. However, strange things then begin to happen: drinks spill, a food machine throws fruit at Scotty, and even Spock is not spared, getting a "black eye" after looking through a viewer. The energy cloud is alive—and has possessed the main computer system. After the entity returns the *Enterprise* to the Neutral Zone, Kirk tricks the Romulans into following his ship through the cloud. The creature leaves the *Enterprise*—and invades the Romulan vessels.

"HOW SHARPER THAN A SERPENT'S TOOTH"

▭▭▭▭▭▭▭▭▭▭▭▭▭▭▭▭▭▭▭▭▭▭▭▭▭▭ #21A

WRITERS: Russell Bates, David Wise
PRINCIPALS: Kirk   Uhura
            Spock   Arex
            McCoy   Ensign Dawson Walking Bear
            Scott   Kulkukan

◄ *Stardate 6063.4:* The *Enterprise* is captured by a highly advanced starship piloted by Kulkukan, an ancient astronaut who visited Earth centuries before and was worshiped as a god. Kulkukan beams Kirk, McCoy, Scott, and Ensign Walking Bear aboard his vessel: there, they find themselves in a city constructed in styles reminiscent of many ancient Terran cultures. While Spock attempts to free the *Enterprise* from Kulkukan's energy field, Kirk discovers the purpose of the city and frees the interplanetary specimens Kulkukan gathered during his travels. Concluding that these humans do not intend to worship him, Kulkukan leaves.

"THE COUNTER-CLOCK INCIDENT"

▭▭▭▭▭▭▭▭▭▭▭▭▭▭▭▭▭▭▭▭▭▭▭▭▭▭ #22A

WRITER: John Culver
PRINCIPALS: Kirk   Arex
            Spock   Commodore Robert April
            McCoy   Dr. Sarah April
            Scott   Karla Five
            Sulu   Karla Four
            Uhura

◄ *Stardate 6770.3:* Commodore Robert April, the first captain of the *Enterprise,* and his wife Sarah, the ship's first medical officer, are aboard the starship once again to journey to Commondore April's retirement ceremonies. When an alien craft speeds by them, Kirk attempts to stop the other vessel with a tractor beam—which results in the *Enterprise* being pulled straight into a nova. Both vessels arrive in a universe where everything is reversed: even time flows backward, so everyone on the *Enterprise* begins to get younger. The explorer who drew the *Enterprise* into this universe offers to return the starship to its own continuum. But the *Enterprise* personnel have all become children. Commodore April, now a healthy young man of 30, resumes command. After they reach normal space, April and his wife place all the *Enterprise* crewmembers into the ship's transporter, which materializes them in their normal states. The Aprils elect to return to their actual age. Considering April's performance, the Federation Council decides to review the mandatory retirement age.

Given the limited scope of most animated television series, the Filmation "Star Trek" episodes were highly successful, both in visual terms and story content. The episodes realistically depicted the crew of the starship *Enterprise* and, despite deadlines and budget limitations, made effective use of exotic humanoid and nonhumanoid characters, backgrounds, and effects sequences. Special mention must go to actors James Doohan and Majel Barrett, who provided many of the voices for aliens and "guest stars" throughout the series, and to Hal Sutherland, who directed all the episodes.

The "Star Trek" animated series ran for 22 episodes, originally telecast through October 12, 1974, and continued in NBC reruns through September 1975. The series won an Emmy Award for best children's series of the 1974–75 television season.

But as faithful as the animated shows were, they simply could not substitute for live-action "Star Trek"—and even while the series was being produced, discussions were under way to bring back the real thing.

12

THE SECOND TELEVISION SERIES

Even at the first "Star Trek" Committee convention in 1972, rumors were heard of a new live-action "Star Trek" production. The next few years were filled with such rumors, but it wasn't until 1974 that Gene Roddenberry began discussing "Star Trek's" return with Paramount. Finally, after months of negotiations, Roddenberry moved back into his old offices on the Paramount lot, and *Star Trek II*—a movie—was planned for release in Christmas 1975, budgeted at approximately $3 million. But Roddenberry's first-draft script for the picture, dealing with a living computer that restored Kirk and his crew to the age they were when they completed their original five-year mission, was rejected by Paramount.

The release date of the movie was postponed until spring 1976.

Other writers, including Ray Bradbury, Harlan Ellison, and Theodore Sturgeon began submitting ideas. None of these were deemed suitable either. Roddenberry and Jon Povill then submitted a time-travel story—which was also rejected.

The starting date of *Star Trek II* was moved up to July 15, 1976.

In early 1976, *Star Trek II* was made a television movie: writers asked to submit material included Howard Burke, Chris Knopf, Will Loren, and Howard Rodman. All their ideas were rejected.

In April 1976, *Star Trek II* was again scheduled as a theatrical feature film, with Gene Roddenberry as producer.

The budget for the film was raised to the neighborhood of $6–8 million dollars, and Jon Povill became Roddenberry's assistant. In July, he compiled a list of screenwriters including Peter Benchley, Robert Bloch, Paddy Chayefsky, Francis Ford Coppola, James Goldman, Ernest Lehman, George Lucas, Lorenzo Semple, Jr., and Robert Towne. All those names were rejected in favor of two young British writers, Allan Scott and Chris Bryant. Povill also

compiled a list of prospective directors, including Francis Ford Coppola, William Friedkin, George Roy Hill, Norman Jewison, George Lucas, Steven Spielberg—and Robert Wise. None of them was available, and Phillip Kaufman was chosen as the director.

In September the studio became openly enthusiastic about *Star Trek* when approximately 400,000 letters were received in Washington urging NASA to rename the first space shuttle the *Enterprise*. Later that month the *Enterprise* was unveiled at ceremonies attended by the cast of the original "Star Trek" television series, and the September 21 edition of *The New York Times* carried this full-page ad taken out by Paramount Pictures:

WELCOME ABOARD . . . SPACE SHUTTLE *ENTERPRISE* . . . Paramount Pictures and the thousands of loyal fans of "Star Trek" are happy that the United States of America's new space shuttle has been named after "Star Trek's" starship, the *Enterprise*. (It's nice to know that sometimes science fiction becomes science fact.) Starship *Enterprise* will be joining the space shuttle *Enterprise* in its space travels very soon. Early next year, Paramount Pictures begins filming an extraordinary motion picture adventure—*Star Trek*. Now we can look forward to two great space adventures.

Scott and Bryant finished their story outline for the motion picture, which Paramount accepted. The script concerned the disappearance of Captain Kirk, the resignation of Mr. Spock, and the discovery of an invisible "Planet of the Titans."

But . . .

The first-draft script, which included input from Roddenberry, executive producer Jerry Isenberg, and Kaufman, was finally rejected by Paramount.

In the middle of June 1977, *Star Trek* was again scheduled as a television project, this time called "Star Trek—Phase II." Gene Roddenberry was to be the executive producer of this new television *series,* conceived as the foundation of Paramount Television Service, an attempt to start a fourth television network to rival NBC, ABC, and CBS. Television stations that joined the Paramount Television Service would be affiliates, and would be provided with the new "Star Trek" television series and other programming produced especially for the fourth network.

Coproducers Harold Livingston and Robert Goodwin were hired to work with Roddenberry. Paramount, enthusiastic about their plans for their network, wanted the first episode to air the following spring. This meant that work had to start immediately. Joe Jennings was hired as the new series' art director, Jim Rugg was in charge of special effects, and Walter M. Jefferies was retained as the series' creative consultant. On July 25 construction began on the *Enterprise* sets.

The exterior and interior designs of the U.S.S. *Enterprise* were updated. NASA technical adviser Jesco von Puttkamer joined the "Star Trek" family, and in other departments discussions began regarding optical effects necessary for the new series.

The original cast was approached and, with one major exception, signed on for a second five-year mission. Leonard Nimoy was engaged in a successful run of *Equus* on Broadway and did not want to leave the play. Roddenberry decided the series would have to be done without him.

The *Writers'/Directors' Guide for "Star Trek II"*, dated August 12, 1977, stressed the changes in the *Enterprise* and her crew. Here are some excerpts:

Following its first mission, the Enterprise has been completely refit . . . the details of the vessel . . . are vastly more sophisticated . . .

To command this second five-year mission, Captain James T. Kirk has refused an admiral's star and managed to recruit many of the original crew. An exception to this is Mr. Spock, who has returned in high honor to Vulcan to head the Science Academy there. In fact, all of our original crew have found themselves to be very nearly legends in their own time . . . Chekov is now a full lieutenant and commands the starship security division. "Bones" McCoy, Scotty, Uhura, and Sulu are at their familiar stations. We'll also see Yeoman Janice Rand again; our former head nurse is now Dr. Christine Chapel . . .

A young Vulcan named Xon is the new science officer, a 22-year-old Vulcan who looks something

Decker (Stephen Collins) and Ilia (Persis Khambatta): the new crewmembers as they appeared in ST-TMP

like a young Michael York with pointed ears. . . . A genius, even by Vulcan standards, he is as competent as Spock in all fields of science. He lacks knowledge, however, in one very important area—the human equation. Unlike Spock, Xon is a full Vulcan. He realizes that the reason that Spock performed so well on board the *Enterprise* was that he could understand emotional human nature. In order to perform as well as Spock, he knows he is going to have to eliminate his Vulcan revulsion at emotional displays. He is, in fact, going to have to reach down within himself and find the emotions that his society has repressed for thousands of years so that he will have some basis for fully understanding his human associates . . . Whereas Spock was engaged in a constant battle to repress his emotions, Xon will be engaged in a constant struggle to release his buried emotions to be more humanlike for the sake of doing a good job . . . We'll get humor out of Xon trying to simulate laughter, anger, fear, and other human feelings. As a full Vulcan, Xon is even stronger than Spock. He can endure lack of water and high temperatures for very long periods. All his senses are particularly keen. He has strong Vulcan mind-meld abilities.

First Officer of the *Enterprise* is Commander Will Decker. In his youthful thirties, Decker comes very near to worshiping Kirk and would literally rather die than fail him . . . When not absorbed in his task of keeping the *Enterprise* at top fitness, Will Decker is a very humorous man. He particularly enjoys playing the "too perfect," soulless marionette of an officer. The joke can be confusing because Will can almost become that kind of officer when Kirk's welfare or the safety of the ship is involved. We can see that Jim Kirk is very much in the process of training the young commander for the responsibilities of starship command someday. We will see that future captain begin to happen during this five-year mission.

At the navigator's station will be Lieutenant Ilia, a young female of Planet 114-Delta V, which has recently joined the Federation. The Deltan race is much older than humans, with brains much more finely evolved in areas of art and mathematics. These abilities make her a superb navigator . . . Her face is breathtakingly beautiful. But like all Deltans, she is completely hairless. Ilia's intelligence level is second only to the science officer, and she has also the *esper* abilities common on her planet. Unlike the mind meld of Vulcans, it simply is the ability to sense images in other minds. Just as Vulcans have a problem with emotions, Ilia has a problem that accompanies her aboard the starship. On 114-Delta V, almost everything in life is sex-oriented—it is a part of every friendship, every social engagement, every profession. It is simply the normal way to relate with others there. Since constant sex is *not* the pattern of humans and others aboard this starship, Ilia has totally repressed this emotion drive and social pattern.

The first script set for production was a two-parter called "In Thy Image." Robert Collins was signed to direct; David Gautreaux was cast as Lieutenant Xon, Persis Khambatta as Lieutenant Ilia, Stephen Collins as Decker, and production was all set to start November 30.

But . . .

As work was finishing on the sets and costumes, Paramount abandoned their plans for a fourth network.

On November 11, "Star Trek II" became *Star Trek—The Motion Picture*—with a multimillion-dollar budget. The story and sets from "In Thy Image" were to be retained (although they would both undergo many revisions). Robert Wise was hired to direct—and Leonard Nimoy agreed to return as Spock.

The stage was set for "Star Trek's" leap to the big screen.

13

STAR TREK— THE MOTION PICTURES

"Star Trek" had been successful for many reasons, not least of which was its conception of the future. In the centuries to come, "Trek" told us, we will use the tools of science to explore far beyond our own world. But no matter how far we travel, we will still retain our basic human nature, and it will be as men (and women) that we react to the riddles, discoveries, and dangers we encounter in outer space. In the infinite face of the universe, we will all have our own ideas of happiness, will all wish to *attain something*, be it knowledge, position, companionship, self-awareness, or a combination of these goals. This attainment was important throughout the television series (as seen in the Vulcan concept of I.D.I.C.), and serves as the central theme in *Star Trek—The Motion Picture*.

"STAR TREK—THE MOTION PICTURE"

ST:TMP

STORY: Alan Dean Foster
SCREENPLAY: Harold Livingston
DIRECTOR: Robert Wise
PRODUCER: Gene Roddenberry
PRINCIPALS: Kirk Rand
Spock Chekov
McCoy Decker
Scotty Ilia
Sulu Klingon Captain
Chapel Sonak
Uhura Chief De Falco

For James T. Kirk, who upon returning from his initial tour of duty aboard the *Enterprise* was promoted out of his command chair to a desk job, attainment will come only when he returns to the bridge of a starship. He has no wish to be "a chairbound paperpusher," and when a huge destructive alien cloud is detected heading toward Earth, Kirk gets his return ticket to the *Enterprise*. To aid him, he recruits all of the starship's original crew—except Spock, who has returned to Vulcan. Even the recalcitrant and semiretired Dr. McCoy is "drafted" (through a little-known reserve-activation clause) to rejoin his former captain.

Kirk's attainment of his goal displaces the ship's new captain, Willard Decker. But despite initial friction between the two, Kirk soon recognizes Decker's ability and urge to command, and in turn Will comes to accord the admiral the kind of respect and admiration he gave to his late father—Matthew Decker, who sacrificed his life in "The Doomsday Machine."

Meanwhile, Spock, on the planet Vulcan, has been attempting to purge himself of the last remnants of his human half. The product of two different systems, Spock has been seeking his identity throughout his entire life. But his attainment of the Vulcan state of *kolinahr*—the shedding of all emotions—fails when he detects the questioning presence of an awesomely powerful entity . . . the same creature threatening Earth. Something inside him is drawn to that concentrated logic and knowledge. The Vulcan masters testing Spock realize this, and he is told his answer lies elsewhere. As the *Enterprise* continues toward its rendezvous with the energy cloud, Spock rejoins his former shipmates, determined not to have any emotional attachments. McCoy suspects him of returning to serve his own ends more than those of the mission. The doctor is also skeptical of Kirk—is the captain's main concern the job at hand, or is he really here to regain control of the *Enterprise?*

Penetrating the giant cloud, ship's navigator Ilia, a Deltan female with whom Decker had once been romantically involved, is seized by the strange creature—which then returns a probe, an exact duplicate of the Deltan navigator, to question the humans aboard the *Enterprise*. The probe reveals that the cloud—V'ger—is heading toward earth to find its Creator and join with it. Decker, playing on the probe's memories of his and Ilia's relationship, attempts to discover more about V'ger.

With the cloud only hours away from Earth, Spock steals a space suit and attempts to communicate with V'ger using the Vulcan mind meld. The contact nearly kills him. Brought back aboard the *Enterprise*, Spock relates that V'ger is a living machine that comes from a machine planet across the galaxy. But for all the cloud's awesome power, it, too, simply wishes to attain self-knowledge—to have its Creator answer the most basic questions of existence. Spock now realizes neither knowledge nor total logic can help him attain what he seeks most—happiness. He is both Vulcan *and* human, and must find his own unique path.

Upon reaching Earth, V'ger begins signaling the Creator and, after failing to receive a response, concludes that the carbon-based units infesting the planet are somehow interfering and must be destroyed. Kirk tells the Ilia-probe he knows why the Creator has not responded, but will only reveal that information to V'ger directly. Journeying to the heart of the vast entity, Kirk, Spock, McCoy, Decker, and the Ilia-probe discover an old Earth satellite—*Voyager* (V---GER)—transformed by the machine planet's inhabitants into a device truly capable of fulfilling its original programming: "collect all data possible and return that information to the Creator."

V'ger, however, does not simply want to transmit its findings. It wants to touch the Creator physically. Absorbing both the Ilia-probe and Decker—who tells Kirk that this union represents the attainment of his deepest desires—V'ger, now complete with newfound emotions, resumes its exploration of the universe. Human, alien, and machine elements have been drawn together, interacted, learned, and formed a new life form. Kirk, Spock, and McCoy return to the *Enterprise* to give the ship a proper shakedown.

About the only things people seem to agree on about *Star Trek—The Motion Picture* are that it was expensive to

The crew of the starship Enterprise—together again in ST-TMP

Admiral James T. Kirk returns home

postproduction. Special effects are intended to be seen in short "takes," intercut with reaction shots so that the film's characters are seen most of the time and the effects serve to enhance the story. In this movie the opposite is true. Some unknown individual(s) decided that since the effects caused most of the expenses of the production, then it should be the effects—and not the people—up there on the screen during most of the movie.

Throughout the "Star Trek" television series individual "Trek" adventures had a high degree of action. This was necessary not only to attract the attention of viewers but to provide sufficient "cliffhangers" so that they would not change channels between acts. "Star Trek" fans came to expect action along with the adventure. In *ST—TMP* there is very little action. Two sequences that would have provided some (the "zapping" of a security guard and Kirk endangered by a threat to short-circuit his life-support suit after he had left the ship) were edited out of the film.

The return of symphonic motion-picture scores had been no surprise to the discerning ears of most "Star Trek" fans; composers such as Alexander Courage, Fred Steiner, Sol Kaplan, Gerald Fried, and George Duning consistently produced extremely fine music that became an integral part of the television series. For *Star Trek—The Motion Picture*, Jerry Goldsmith composed melodies that reflect the main themes of *Star Trek—The Motion Picture*. Goldsmith's expansive score shows us Kirk's reattainment of the *Enterprise*, Spock's attempts to achieve

produce, is visually attractive, and has a fine musical score. Beyond that, it was an epic achievement to some—and a colossal disappointment to many others.

Every "Star Trek" fan has seen this film at least once. To hear them talk, it would seem that two different productions were being discussed . . . and maybe that wouldn't be so far from the truth: some see what is in the movie, and others cannot help noticing what is *not* present.

The story itself is an all too familiar one to "Trek" fans: a transformed space probe had met its creator in "The Changeling," a giant object threatened to engulf the galaxy in "The Immunity Syndrome," and a huge weapon threatened the starship *Enterprise* in "The Doomsday Machine." The film's "punch line" is all too obvious: it comes as a surprise to no one when V'ger is revealed to be a *Voyager*.

Some of the characteristics associated with "Star Trek" are also present—the theme of exploration and communication with other forms of existence, but the relationship between Kirk, Spock, and McCoy is not only lacking, it seems to have been deliberately buried. The *Enterprise* is better than her old self in terms of design and features, but she is as colorless as her crew's new uniforms.

Many of the film's problems seem to have occurred in

Spock—void of emotion

fulfillment, Decker and Ilia's wish to attain happiness together at last, the Ilia-probe's attempts to understand its human memories, and V'ger's epic attempt to attain the ability to perceive and appreciate its identity.

To a large extent *ST-TMP* is a futuristic version of a "police procedural," a story that concerns itself mostly with the mechanics of a police investigation. Such a treatment is bound to be interpreted as "cold": Mr. Spock's determination to purge his emotions intensifies this effect, and so does the design of the ship and most of the wardrobe.

The blandness of the *Enterprise* interior, the manner in which V'ger's "identity" is revealed, the often seemingly endless effects sequences—all work against "Star Trek" fans expectations. Beneath this, however, the basic "Trek" format is well represented, thanks to the participation of Gene Roddenberry. We start with a menace, something different and frightening, and end with something not so different from ourselves after all. Communication and understanding reveal the unknown entity to be a potential friend, and certainly a means of extending and sharing our understanding of the universe. In a time when most science fiction films were dealing with "shoot 'em up" situations, this quality makes *Star Trek—The Motion Picture* one of the most daring and worthwhile science fiction films of the late 1970s.

As the box-office figures for *Star Trek—The Motion Picture* started to mount up, it became increasingly apparent that there would be another *Star Trek* movie produced: the question was whether it would be a theatrical or a television movie, and what it would be about.

At first, as with any project concerning "Star Trek," the rumors ran rampant. Everybody and his brother had been signed to appear in the film, which would feature everyone who had ever appeared in the *Star Trek* television series. The movie would be about eight hours long. It would be seen on television in the form of a miniseries.

When the first official announcements about the film were made, the question heaviest on the minds of "Trek" fans was the list of people working on the film. Gene Roddenberry was listed as the production's executive consultant. The executive producer was Harve Bennett, familiar to "Star Trek" fans due to his association with "The Six Million Dollar Man," "The Bionic Woman," and other television series. The name of writer Jack B. Sowards was *not* known. What kind of a *Star Trek* movie would these individuals produce?

Director Nicholas Meyer was a known quantity, having made his directorial debut with *Time After Time*, a film well regarded within the science fiction community. But did he, like the others involved in the production, know anything about "Star Trek"? Would there be any concern about keeping within the existing parameters of the "Star Trek" universe?

Many fans of "Trek" reached the conclusion that since Mr. Spock was rumored to die in the film, efforts to remain faithful to earlier "Star Trek" productions had been abandoned. They were wrong: fidelity to the original was a vital concern of the new team. Nicholas Meyer stated: "I said it should be like Captain Horatio Hornblower in outer space . . . when I first spoke to Bill Shatner about my idea, he said, 'That's interesting; that was also Gene Roddenberry's original take on it.' "

The filmmakers' concern is evident in the final product. *Star Trek II—The Wrath of Khan* is an excellent motion picture no matter how you look at it, a direct, accurate expansion on earlier "Trek" productions.

As is any motion picture, *STII* was produced within very definite budget and time restrictions. These restrictions, however, were much larger than those for a television series. As a result, that much more of what we always wanted to see in the series is present in this movie. This is especially true of the story, which, although essentially an expanded television episode, permits much greater development of plot and character.

"THE WRATH OF KHAN"

STORY:	Harve Bennett and Jack B. Sowards	
SCREENPLAY:	Jack B. Sowards	
DIRECTOR:	Nicholas Meyer	
PRODUCER:	Robert Sallin	
PRINCIPALS:	Kirk	David Marcus
	Spock	Terrell
	McCoy	Saavik
	Scotty	Khan Noonian Singh
	Chekov	Kyle
	Sulu	Beach
	Uhura	Preston
	Carol Marcus	

The movie opens on board the U.S.S. *Enterprise*. All the familiar crew—Spock, McCoy, Uhura, Sulu, and Scotty—are at their usual stations, with the exception of James T. Kirk. In the captain's chair is a Vulcan/Romulan woman—Saavik. Answering a distress call from the unarmed freighter *Kobayashi Maru,* she takes the *Enterprise* across the Neutral Zone—only to be surrounded by Klingon warships. The distress call was a fake. Hopelessly outnumbered, Saavik watches helplessly as Spock, McCoy, and the bridge crew go down . . . and the simulator's doors open to reveal Admiral James T. Kirk. Saavik was undergoing a test of her command abilities—a test, Kirk states, to see how she would respond in a no-win scenario. After the test, Spock wishes Kirk happy birthday. Kirk, feeling the world has passed him by, considers it nothing of the sort. Both Spock and McCoy urge him to regain command of a starship—his first, best destiny—before he really does get old.

Saavik (Kirstie Alley) with her mentor

Meanwhile, searching for a lifeless planet on which to test the Genesis device, the U.S.S. *Reliant*'s Captain Terrell and First Officer Pavel Chekov have beamed down to supposedly uninhabited Ceti Alpha VI—only to be captured by Khan Noonian Singh, a genetic superman from late 20th-century earth. Khan and his followers had been marooned on Ceti Alpha V—at the time a lush, fertile planet—by Captain James T. Kirk 15 years ago. Six months after their arrival, neighboring Ceti Alpha VI exploded, altering his planet's orbit and changing it into an inhospitable desert wasteland. Khan's wife was among those who died in the destruction and its aftermath—and he has vowed revenge on Kirk. He then introduces Chekov and Terrell to Ceti Alpha's only remaining life form—the Ceti Eel, a parasite that enters its victims through the ears and then wraps around their cerebral cortex, rendering them extremely susceptible to suggestion.

Aboard the *Enterprise,* Admiral Kirk is accompanying Spock and his cadets on a training voyage when he receives a message from Dr. Carol Marcus, an old and very special flame. Though her transmission is garbled (blocked at the source, Uhura says), he understands enough to realize someone is threatening Project Genesis, a Federation-sponsored research project of surpassing secrecy and importance that she and her son head. Kirk assumes command of the *Enterprise* and proceeds at warp five to Regula I, home of the Genesis project. En route, he plays Spock and McCoy a tape of Carol's Genesis proposal to the Federation. The project is literally life from lifelessness, involving a molecular reorganization of mat-

ter that can be an awesomely powerful tool for creation—or destruction.

The presentation is interrupted when sensors detect the presence of the U.S.S. *Reliant.* Reporting to the bridge, Kirk is repeatedly unable to establish contact with the ship and, growing suspicious, orders a yellow alert. Too little, too late. *Reliant* attacks, cripples the *Enterprise,* and then establishes two-way visual contact.

It is Khan—who, with the unwilling aid of Terrell and Chekov, has seized control of the *Reliant.* He now plans to destroy the *Enterprise* and his most hated enemy. But he agrees to spare Kirk's ship and crew if the admiral surrenders himself and all material relating to Project Genesis. Stalling for time, Kirk agrees to deal . . . while Spock, punching up the code for *Reliant's* command console, orders that ship to lower its shields. The *Enterprise* attacks, and Khan is driven off.

Left with only impulse power, the ship proceeds to Regula I, where a landing party of Kirk, McCoy, and Saavik discover a deserted base—and the mutilated corpses of several Genesis scientists. Khan has been here, and apparently learned nothing. Saavik's tricorder reveals Chekov and Terrell, locked inside storage lockers. In the Regula transporter room, Kirk notices the controls have been set for deep within the planetoid—and remembers that the second phase of the Genesis project was to be tested underground. Contacting the *Enterprise,* he reaches Spock, who informs him that "by the book," the ship will not have main power for six days or auxiliary power for two. They cannot even beam the landing party back aboard. Kirk acknowledges, and the five beam down to the transporter's preset coordinates.

They discover an empty chamber and the Genesis device. While examining their surroundings, Kirk is attacked by one of the project's young scientists. When Carol appears and calls the young man David, Kirk realizes that he has been fighting his son. A worse surprise is yet to come. Chekov and Terrell both draw their phasers. Though still under Khan's direct control, rather than kill Kirk, Terrell commits suicide. Chekov collapses in agony, and Khan beams aboard the Genesis device.

The stranded landing party explores the Genesis Cave—a small-scale sample of what the device is capable of. While relaxing, Saavik asks the admiral how he performed on the *Kobayashi Maru* test—and Kirk reveals that he was the only cadet to ever beat the no-win scenario . . . by reprogramming the simulator. "I don't like to lose," Kirk states, and, flipping open his communicator, orders Spock to beam them back on board.

They had been communicating by code earlier—so that what was two days became two hours. The *Enterprise* lures *Reliant* into the Mutara Nebula, where neither sensors nor screens function and the two ships will be evenly matched. Kirk and Spock together outwit Khan—but the madman is determined to have his revenge. He

Khan

Maru test. Kirk, who has never actually coped with death before, must realize that his youth is a thing of the past. He starts out by experiencing his midlife crisis, depressed because half his life is gone. He ends by realizing that half his life lies ahead, and that it can be just as exciting (or more so) than his previous experiences.

Both Kirk and McCoy must bear the loss of their friend Spock. Together these three formed one mind, with Kirk furnishing the impulse, Spock the logic, and McCoy the modulation.

In the television episodes, we saw Kirk repeatedly devising solutions to dire threats. Many of these took the form of bluffs: the "corbomite device" of "The Corbomite Maneuver," the "godfather" imitation in "A Piece of the Action," the harmless sugar pill of "Mudd's Women." All of these were really variations on "Hey . . . your shoelace is untied," on a colossal scale. And they have always worked. Kirk, as he confides to his son in this movie, has never actually taken the *Kobayashi Maru* test without changing the programming so that he can win; never, that is, until in communicating this fact to his son, Kirk realizes that he has just taken the test and passed, with flying colors.

Of the three principals, Spock has the best of times coping with his loss, although he loses the most . . . his life. As McCoy once pointed out to the Vulcan, Spock is not afraid to die because he's more afraid of living. Things have changed for Spock somewhat since McCoy's observation in the episode "Bread and Circuses," but Spock is still holding a good deal of his true self in check. He remains stoic and ready to defend his loyalties, obliga-

triggers the Genesis device—and without warp speed, the *Enterprise* will be unable to escape the deadly Genesis wave.

Spock leaves the bridge and proceeds to Engineering, where a horrified Scotty watches him enter the highly radioactive reaction chamber to restore the ship's warp drive. He is successful, the *Enterprise* escapes, and on the bridge a jubilant crew is celebrating . . . until McCoy summons Kirk to Engineering. A visibly burned and weakened Spock tells Kirk this is his solution to the *Kobayashi Maru* test, the no-win scenario . . . and then dies. The *Enterprise* proceeds home—leaving behind Spock's body on the Genesis planet.

Star Trek II—The Wrath of Khan is, most of all, a story of the acceptance of loss, as expressed by the *Kobayashi*

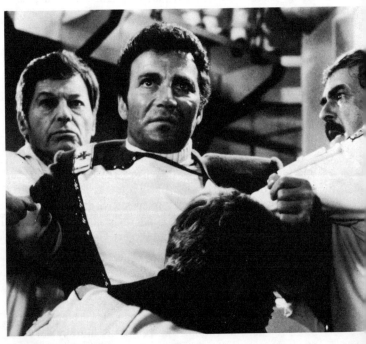

A shattering discovery

tions, and friendships to the ultimate degree. It is painfully clear by the end of the story that he is thoroughly prepared to die, as he had always been throughout the original "Star Trek" TV episodes. In "The Galileo Seven" Dr. McCoy could not believe that Spock was actually prepared to leave someone behind to die. Spock's answer to McCoy's observation that "life and death are seldom logical" was "attaining a desired goal always is."

More than once in the series Spock demonstrated his willingness to die to protect what he loved. He took the poison thorns meant for Kirk in "The Apple," risked death to obtain lifelong happiness for his ex-captain Pike in "The Menagerie," and subjected himself to unknown perils to kill the monsters of "Operation: Annihilate!" Spock is wrong; he has taken the *Kobayashi Maru* test on several occasions—and passed each time.

The movie's special effects were also first-rate: science fiction's state-of-the-art technical effects house, ILM, (Industrial Light and Magic) handled practically everything for Bennett.

STII's *Enterprise* is the same one used during the production of *Star Trek—The Motion Picture*. Constructed by another company for the different demands of the first "Trek" feature film, the *Enterprise* is filled with complex circuitry. For shots in which the starship had to photograph smaller, ILM constructed other, smaller miniatures of the *Enterprise*, minus the complicated insides of the big one.

The U.S.S. *Reliant* is a starship of a slightly different variety, designed and constructed especially for *Star Trek II*. Constructed from vacu-formed plastic, the *Reliant* is much lighter than the *Enterprise*. Its interior wiring is also simpler than the *Enterprise*'s, since it contains only the workings to permit it to do exactly what was required of it in the *Star Trek II* script. The ship, which contains most of the design features of the *Enterprise*, is a more consolidated version of her sister ship. The vessel is a newer design, which is why her registration number is higher than that of the *Enterprise*.

Project Genesis came about as the result of the film's art director, Michael Minor. Minor, a science fiction fan and a follower of the original "Star Trek" television series (who also created the Melkot for "Spectre of the Gun" and some miscellaneous decorative artwork used during third-season episodes), recalled a word used in an episode of the series: "terraforming." Mentioning the con-

Watching Genesis—life from lifelessness

cept to executive producer Harve Bennett, Minor found his idea instantly accepted. Once Project Genesis became part of the script, it became necessary to bring it to life on motion picture film. We first see the potential of Project Genesis in the tape Kirk runs for Spock and McCoy. Though this tape runs only slightly over one minute in length, it took a crew of ten artists almost six months to achieve. Alvy Ray Smith and Loren Carpenter headed the team that produced the tape, first conceived of by ILM visual-effects supervisor Jim Veilleux. The final tape was produced as an animation drawn directly into a computer using a light-sensitive pen and a special screen.

Another integral component in *STII*'s success is composer James Horner's score. Director Nicholas Meyer wanted his film to feel like a high-seas adventure. Although Starfleet is a military organization, and the *Enterprise* is certainly the futuristic equivalent of a warship (a "ship of the line," as Admiral Hornblower would call it), his prime concern was that the audience feel the thrill of the ship's mission: a distinct switch from other recent science fiction films, which accentuated military pomp in their scores.

Horner felt that the opening portion of Alexander Courage's TV series theme should be retained in his score. This questing melody, which suggests the essence of exploration that drives Kirk, is called "Where No Man Has Gone Before." Its presence in the film's opening credits is executive producer Harve Bennett's musical statement of his intention to preserve and present as many points of the original "Star Trek" format as possible.

In addition to the presence of Courage's theme, Horner's music is exciting and free, plainly suggesting a tall ship sailing to parts unknown. In contrast to this theme of vastness and expansion is the claustrophobic and uncertain flavor present in the Mutara Nebula theme. This portion of the film was intended by Bennett and Meyer to resemble a World War II submarine warfare situation in which each ship is equally matched against the other due to a lack of working sensor equipment and extreme weather conditions. Horner's music carries this illusion across to the audience.

The film's epilogue and end credits are filled with hope, indicating that Kirk's career has resumed and the *Enterprise* will sail on.

The decision to kill Mr. Spock in *Star Trek II* greatly concerned fans: could there be a "Star Trek" without the *Enterprise*'s Vulcan first officer? The thinking behind Spock's death was not to create a situation that would make future "Treks" impossible. The intent was to do something new, something that had never been attempted before. This was the boldest exploration attempted where "Star Trek" was concerned. A concept based on sending the *Enterprise* "where no man has gone before" now directed one of its principals into "the undiscovered coun-

try" (a Shakespearean reference to death originally part of the title of *Star Trek II*). But there was never any doubt in Leonard Nimoy's mind that Spock would return to clear the way for further "Star Trek" adventures with the original crew of the *Enterprise*. And when plans for *Star Trek III* were announced, Nimoy was indeed participating—as the film's director. *Star Trek III* evolved with the direct purpose of bringing about Spock's return while serving as a sequel to the events of *Star Trek II*.

"THE SEARCH FOR SPOCK"

WRITER:	Harve Bennett	
DIRECTOR:	Leonard Nimoy	
PRODUCER:	Harve Bennett	
PRINCIPALS:	Kirk	Saavik
	Spock	David Marcus
	McCoy	Sarek
	Scotty	Rand
	Sulu	T'Lar
	Chekov	Maltz
	Uhura	Valkris
	Kruge	

Following the events that resulted in the death of Mr. Spock and the formation of the Genesis planet, the *Enterprise* is en route to Starfleet's Earth Spacedock for repairs. Investigating an unauthorized presence within the sealed quarters of Mr. Spock, Kirk discovers Dr. McCoy—and is shocked when Mr. Spock's voice and sentiments come from the lips of the physician.

At Spacedock is the U.S.S. *Excelsior* (NX-2000), a huge starship, the first to be equipped with the experimental "transwarp drive." In the shadow of that vessel Kirk learns the *Enterprise* is to be decommissioned rather than repaired.

Kirk is entertaining Uhura, Sulu, and Chekov in his San Francisco apartment when he is visited by Sarek, Spock's father. Sarek, searching for his son's *katra*, Spock's living spirit, initiates a mind meld with Kirk, but does not find it.

Kirk replays the taped records of Spock's last minutes of life and discovers that the Vulcan's *katra* is in the keeping of Dr. McCoy. Kirk realizes he must return to the Genesis planet to recover Spock's body for the sake of his two closest friends. Starfleet's Admiral Morrow, however, denies Kirk permission to return to the Genesis planet. Kirk decides to go anyway.

Rescuing McCoy, who had been put into protective medical custody, Kirk beams aboard the *Enterprise* with Uhura's aid. Aboard their starship, Kirk, McCoy, Scotty, Sulu, and Chekov embark on their journey, to be joined later by Uhura. Mr. Scott, assigned to the *Excelsior*, sabotaged that vessel's transwarp drive to prevent the *Enterprise* from being overtaken. After his skill makes it possible for the *Enterprise* to clear the Spacedock's outer doors, the starship has clear sailing to the Genesis planet.

Kirk is not the only conspirator within Federation space. Klingon Commander Kruge has obtained a copy of the top-secret file on Project Genesis. Extremely warlike even by Klingon standards, Kruge wants to obtain the secrets of Genesis, which he believes will bring his empire ultimate power. He heads for the Genesis planet in his Klingon *Bird of Prey* ship.

Meanwhile, the Federation vessel U.S.S. *Grissom,* in orbit around the Genesis planet, is awaiting word from Dr. David Marcus and Lieutenant Saavik, who are exploring the planet's surface. Their tricorder registers life-form readings, which appear to be nothing more than microbes that adhered to Spock's casket. The casket, however, is empty: only the Vulcan's burial robe is found.

Saavik and David discover a Vulcan child: Spock, his body's cells regenerated by the effects of the Genesis wave, is alive and rapidly aging along with the Genesis planet. The *Grissom,* meanwhile, has been destroyed by Kruge's ship, and the Klingon has sent a landing party to the surface of the planet.

Arriving at the Genesis planet, the *Enterprise* encounters Kruge's vessel. Scott's preparations, which automated the *Enterprise*'s systems so that the skeleton crew could run the entire vessel, did not include taking the ship into a combat situation. Kirk can only listen helplessly as he learns that Klingons are holding Spock, David, and Saavik prisoner. David is killed—and in order to save his loyal crew, Kirk agrees to surrender the *Enterprise.*

But in truth, he has decided that rather than turn the ship over to the Klingons, he will destroy it. Kirk, Chekov, and finally Scotty verify the self-destruct order. With Sulu and McCoy, they beam down to Genesis as a Klingon party beams aboard *Enterprise*—and from the planet's surface watch both explode. As Kirk agonizes over what he's done, McCoy puts the *Enterprise*'s loss in persepective by noting that once again, Kirk has turned death into a fighting chance for life.

Leonard Nimoy directs his commanding officer

The Admiral then contacts the *Bird of Prey*, telling Kruge he has Genesis.

After most of the others are beamed aboard the orbiting Klingon vessel, Kirk finds himself stranded on the surface of the unstable Genesis planet, locked in battle with Kruge. Kruge is killed, and Kirk tricks Maltz into beaming him and Spock aboard the *Bird of Prey*. Aboard the vessel, the *Enterprise* crew have defeated the only surviving Klingon, and Kirk heads the ship to Vulcan.

Sulu lands the vessel safely. They are joined by Sarek, who asks the Vulcan high priestess T'Lar to attempt the *fal-tor-pan*, a legendary and dangerous procedure that can restore Spock's *katra* to his living body.

The refusion, as dangerous for McCoy as it is for Spock, is successfully completed. Spock, who will have to be assisted in his mental and emotional recovery, recognizes Jim Kirk as the *Enterprise* executive officers gather and welcome their friend and colleague back to life.

Star Trek II—The Wrath of Khan was conceived as a follow-up to the television series episode "Space Seed." *Star Trek III—The Search for Spock* was developed to resolve the Vulcan's fate as seen in the previous feature film. When *Star Trek II* and *III* are considered as a single, two-part entity, the entire adventure has much in common with the "Star Trek" television series' only two-part episode, "The Menagerie."

Each introduces and resolves a major threat to Mr. Spock's continued existence: in "The Menagerie" he must clear himself of all charges against him to resume his career in Starfleet, and in *Star Trek III* he must return from death.

Each also concentrates on Mr. Spock's unique nature, and his place within the "Star Trek" continuity. In each, we learn how essential Spock's presence is to the "Trek" universe.

We know Spock is logical. His apparently *il*logical behavior in "The Menagerie" is the result of his loyalty to Captain Pike. Appealing to Captain Kirk, Spock pleads: "Captain . . . Jim . . . Please—don't stop me. Don't let *him* [Mendez] stop me. It's your career and Captain Pike's life!" Just as Spock risks his career for Captain Pike, Kirk is willing to risk all he has attained for his first officer in *Star Trek III*. In *TSFS*, Admiral Morrow tells Kirk: "Jim! Your life and your career stand for rationality, not intellectual chaos. Keep up this emotional behavior and you'll lose everything. You'll destroy yourself!" Morrow refuses Kirk's request to travel to Vulcan, saying, "Jim . . . You are my best officer, and if I *had* a best friend, you'd be that too. But I am commander, Starfleet, so I don't break rules." Here, Kirk's response could come from Spock's lines in "The Menagerie": "Don't quote rules, Harry! We're talking about loyalty. And sacrifice . . ."

This loyalty and friendship—this human compassion—is

Kirk and McCoy—on the run

at the core of "Star Trek," seen in I.D.I.C., the Prime Directive, and especially between the *Enterprise*'s captain, first officer, and physician.

Both "The Menagerie" and *Star Trek II* and *III* illustrate the burdens of command, the loneliness and demands placed upon the *Enterprise*'s captain—also a recurring theme in "Trek." In "The Menagerie," Dr. Phillip Boyce consoles Captain Christopher Pike regarding the crewmen who died on their (unseen) mission to Rigel VII:

BOYCE
Sometimes, a man will tell his bartender things he'll never tell his doctor. What's been on your mind, Chris, the fight on Rigel VII?

PIKE
Shouldn't it be? My own yeoman and two others dead, seven injured.

BOYCE
Was there anything you personally could have done to prevent it?

And, later:

BOYCE
Chris, you set standards for yourself that no one could meet. You treat everyone on board like a human being, except yourself. And now you're tired . . .

PIKE

You bet I'm tired. I'm tired of being responsible for two hundred and three lives. I'm tired of deciding which mission is too risky, and which isn't, and who goes on the landing party and who doesn't. And who lives . . . and who dies . . .

This discussion bears a close resemblance to the talk McCoy gives Kirk in the admiral's apartment in San Francisco, at the start of *Star Trek II*. From "The Menagerie":

PIKE

The point is . . . that this isn't the only life available. There's a whole galaxy of things to choose from.

BOYCE

Not for you. A man either lives life as it happens to him . . . meets it head-on and licks it or turns his back on it and starts to wither away.

PIKE

Now you're beginning to talk like a doctor, bartender.

BOYCE

You take your choice. They both get the same two kinds of customers . . . the living . . . and the dying.

And from *Star Trek II*:

BONES

Dammit, Jim, what the hell's the matter with you? Other people have birthdays. Why are we treating yours like a funeral?

KIRK

Bones, I don't want to be lectured.

BONES

What the hell *do* you want? This is not about age, and you know it. It's about you flying a goddamn computer console when you wanna be out hoppin' galaxies.

The two-part "Menagerie" and *Star Trek II* and *III* owe their similarities not only to plot but to the determination of Harve Bennett to preserve the original "Star Trek" ethos established by Gene Roddenberry. This ethos and the relationship between Kirk, Spock, and McCoy, are the central elements behind "Star Trek's" success— and the central inspirations of *Star Trek III—The Search for Spock.*

Star Trek II and *III*, while popular with "Star Trek" fans, are certainly not comedies. Both have their share of funny moments, although their central themes involve vengeance and loss, including the ultimate loss: death. In *Star Trek II*

we took the Kobayashi Maru test in the form of Spock's death. And in *Star Trek III* we shared Kirk's loss of David and the U.S.S. *Enterprise.*

Leonard Nimoy and Harve Bennett wisely decided that *Star Trek IV* should be an enjoyable motion picture, dealing with victories rather than defeats. The damage done to the "Star Trek" continuity because of what had happened to Mr. Spock and the starship *Enterprise* would be repaired— and Nimoy and Bennett were determined to have a good time doing it.

"THE VOYAGE HOME"

STORY:	Leonard Nimoy & Harve Bennett
SCREENPLAY:	Steve Meerson & Peter Krikes and
	Harve Bennett & Nicholas Meyer
DIRECTOR:	Leonard Nimoy
PRODUCER:	Harve Bennett

PRINCIPALS:		
	Kirk	Amanda
	Spock	Dr. Gillian Taylor
	McCoy	Admiral Cartwright
	Scott	Klingon Ambassador
	Sulu	Dr. Nichols
	Uhura	Federation President
	Chekov	Saratoga Captain
	Sarek	Bob Briggs
	Saavik	

A gigantic alien probe moving through space is sending out transmissions of incredible power—transmissions that completely cripple Starfleet vessels *Shepard* and *Yorktown*. The probe's destination: Earth.

Within the council chambers of the United Federation of Planets in San Francisco, the Klingon ambassador demands Admiral James T. Kirk be brought to justice for his creation of the Genesis device. Kirk is eloquently defended by Ambassador Sarek of Vulcan—but the President of the Federation Council is in agreement with the Klingon ambassador. Kirk must return to Earth and stand trial for his crimes.

Unaware of these occurrences, Kirk and his crew (McCoy, Scotty, Sulu, Uhura, Chekov, and Saavik) have been on the planet Vulcan repairing their captured Klingon Bird of Prey (rechristened the *Bounty* by Dr. McCoy), and awaiting the recovery of their former shipmate Spock, who has been undergoing extensive retraining of his mind following the successful completion of the fal-tor-pan (refusion of mind and body). He is able to answer a series of complex intellectual problems put to him by a computer, but does not know how to respond to the inquiry "how do you feel?" Amanda, his mother, reminds Spock that he has been (once again) trained" . . . in the Vulcan way, so you may not understand feelings. But as my son," she says, "you have them. They will resurface."

Spock disguised as a human.

Meanwhile, the mysterious probe has reached Earth, where, having received no response to any of its transmissions, it creates a cloud cover around the planet that neutralizes all its power systems—and leaves the home world of the United Federation of Planets completely defenseless. In the headquarters of Starfleet Command, the President of the U.F.P. Council initiates emergency evacuation plans. As storms of ever-increasing magnitude devastate the planet, Ambassador Sarek advises the President to transmit a planetary distress signal warning all ships away from Earth—while there is still time to do so.

On Vulcan, Kirk and his crew (joined once again by a seemingly-recovered Spock), decide to return to Earth to stand trial for their theft and destruction of the *Enterprise.* Saavik remains behind.

As they approach Earth, they are puzzled by the lack of any Federation escort—until Uhura receives the Council President's distress signal. Picking up the probe's transmissions and learning they are being directed towards Earth's oceans, Spock concludes they are intended to be received by a form of life other than man. The transmissions are the songs sung by humpback whales—a species long-since extinct on Earth of the 23rd Century. There is one slim chance, however: if they can bring a whale from the past into their time, it may be able to establish contact with the probe. Over Dr. McCoy's strenuous objections, Kirk decides to attempt the journey through time.

Using the slingshot effect first discovered aboard the Enterprise, the *Bounty* whips around the sun, warping out of its own era and into the 20th Century. But the trip has taken its toll: the ship's dilithium is de-crystallizing—and unless some way can be found of reversing the

process, they will not have enough power to return to their own time.

Uhura detects whalesong coming from San Francisco. Landing their cloaked ship in Golden Gate Park, Kirk splits up the crew to better accomplish their objectives. He and Spock will attempt to locate the whales; McCoy, Scotty, and Sulu will find a factory to manufacture plexiglass for a whale tank; and Uhura and Chekov will infiltrate a nearby naval base's nuclear reactor to siphon off the high-energy photons needed to recrystallize the dilithium.

Kirk and Spock journey to the Cetacean Institute in Sausalito, where they meet its assistant director Dr. Gillian Taylor and her two special charges—George and Gracie, the only humpback whales in captivity. Spock enters the whales' tank and mindmelds with Gracie to inform her of their intentions. Kirk is somewhat less successful in communicating with Dr. Taylor: after she informs him that the whales are to be released the next day into the open sea (where they will be at the mercy of the whale-hunter's ships), he attempts to convince her that he can take George and Gracie someplace where they won't be hunted. He informs her he is actually from the 23rd Century and hopes to return the whales to his time. But when he refuses to give Gillian any proof, she refuses to help him. She leaves Kirk in a seemingly-deserted area of Golden Gate Park—and he tells her that if she changes her mind, this is where he'll be.

Meanwhile, McCoy and Scotty, posing as visitors from Edinburgh, have been receiving a tour of Plexicorp from one of its scientists, Dr. Nichols. After seeing the company has the plexiglass they will need to construct the whale tank, Scott offers Dr. Nichols an enticing deal. In exchange for a few thousand dollars worth of materials, he will give Dr. Nichols the formula for transparent aluminum, a discovery that will make him "wealthy beyond the dreams of avarice". Nichols agrees to the deal—just as Sulu is receiving some first-hand instructions on how to handle the controls of a Huey 205 helicopter.

Chekov and Uhura have discovered the nuclear energy they need access to is located aboard the aircraft carrier *Enterprise.* They beam in and attach Scott's jury-rigged photon collector to the reactor room walls. At last, the job is finished, and Uhura beams back aboard the Bounty with the collector. Chekov, however, is captured by naval personnel. Attempting to escape, he falls and is gravely injured.

Gillian returns to the Institute and discovers the whales have been released a day early to avoid a publicity crush. In desperation, she returns to Golden Gate Park—in time to witness a Huey 205 lowering huge sheets of plexiglass into what looks like thin air. Kirk was telling the truth! The next minute she finds herself aboard the *Bounty,* where she informs Kirk that the whales are already gone.

Uhura discovers Chekov is hospitalized in Mercy Hospital in critical condition. He is not expected to survive.

With the help of Dr. Taylor, Kirk and McCoy are able to locate and treat Chekov, and following a madcap chase through the hospital, all return safely to the *Bounty*. Gillian provides Kirk with the frequency of the radio transmitters attached to George and Gracie, and convinces him to let her return to the future with them. The ship reaches the whales just as a whaling ship is about to harpoon them. The *Bounty* de-cloaks, scaring the hunters away, and beams the whales aboard. Next stop: the 23rd Century.

The *Bounty* repeats its slingshot maneuver around the sun and returns to its own time. Disabled by the probe, the vessel crashlands in San Francisco Bay, near Starfleet Command Headquarters. The crew abandons ship—and Kirk is able to release the whales before the ship sinks.

They communicate with the probe, apparently to its satisfaction. The mysterious entity departs. The threat to Earth is ended.

Summoned before the United Federation of Planets Council, Kirk and his shipmates are exonerated of all charges save one, a charge directed at Kirk alone: disobeying orders of a superior officer. He is demoted to Captain, and returned to that duty "for which he has repeatedly demonstrated unswerving ability: the command of a starship."

Sarek admits to his son that he now approves of Spock's Starfleet career, and of his choice in shipmates. Spock requests that his father relay a message to Amanda: "Tell her I feel fine."

As the film ends, Kirk and his crew shuttle toward their new vessel: a starship designated *"Enterprise NCC-1701-A."*

It began ominously, with the sinking feeling that we had seen it all before. First an exterior view of space, then a strange sound and the sight of an enormous object entering the picture, an alien creation of great power. It destroys space vessels and heads toward Earth, where its power threatens to end all life on the planet.

The opening of *Star Trek IV* is identical to that of *Star Trek—The Motion Picture,* but here the resemblance ends. In that first film, the crew was there to react to the threat—with occasional dialogue, arguments and open-mouthed stares. In *Star Trek IV* the opening threat is a vehicle, whose appearance sends Kirk and company back in time, giving them the chance to be themselves and to save the world. The movie's title, "The Voyage Home," is appropriate not only in terms of the film's plot, but also represents the restoration of the interplay and the spirit of adventure that have endeared the original "Star Trek" cast to an ever-growing and consistently loyal audience.

"Star Trek's" first experience with time travel was in "The Naked Time." Though that episode was originally designated "part I" of an unknown and unproduced story possibly concerning time travel, the capability was not explored again until "Tomorrow Is Yesterday," the tale that introduced the technique of whipping by the sun to achieve time travel.

In "Tomorrow Is Yesterday," "City on the Edge of Forever," "Assignment Earth," and "All Our Yesterdays," the other "Star Trek" episodes dealing with time travel, it was vital to avoid revealing the presence of time travelers in the past. Aside from concerns regarding time paradoxes, this

Spock, Kirk, and McCoy on board the Klingon Bird of Prey.

is directly associated with the Prime Directive of Starfleet Command: the "non-interference" directive. While some fun was had at Kirk's expense in "Tomorrow Is Yesterday" (he was interrogated in a scene that resembled Chekov's interrogation in *Star Trek IV*), none of the previous "Star Trek" time travel tales was as comedy-oriented as *Star Trek IV*. It is possibly because of this comedy element that some liberties with the Prime Directive were taken in the film.

Many things were altered by the appearance of Kirk et al in our century, but none of these—with the exception of Scotty giving someone the formula for transparent aluminum—seems to be anything that will "make waves" in the flow of time. It is probable that somewhere during the scripting of the film more attention was paid to this problem, but it was discovered that any attempts to explain these things away would not contribute to the story and might detract from the comedy elements of the adventure. We must assume that no one will miss two whales, that Gillian has no one who will notice she's gone (and no future offspring who might have made it into the history books), that Chekov's appearance on the (aircraft carrier) *Enterprise* will be filed away and forgotten, that the garbage men in Golden Gate Park will remain silent, that the man on the bus will recover from the Vulcan neck pinch, and that the crew of the whaling ship will not discuss what they saw. Of course, the individual who would be most grateful for the crew's "interference" would be the little old lady who grew another kidney, thanks to one of Dr. McCoy's miracle pills.

But one point must be remembered above anything else when discussing *Star Trek IV—The Voyage Home*. It is possible, when recalling any film, to find holes but in a movie as fast-paced and enjoyable as this one, what counts is the experience one has while watching it. *Star Trek IV* passes that test with flying colors.

The ability to enjoy this movie is something that is not confined to "Star Trek" fans, according to the film's glowing reviews and record-smashing box office figures. Leonard Nimoy, Harve Bennett, Nicholas Meyer, and everyone else who worked on *Star Trek IV* have taken the positive and entertaining elements of Gene Roddenberry's universe and successfully presented them to a brand-new audience. *Star Trek IV* has brought the concept of I.D.I.C. and the other ideas regarding the unity of living creatures into the world of reality, and indicates that, at least, the world finally seems united in its appreciation of "Star Trek."

"There is a texture to the best 'Star Trek' hours that verges on tongue-in-cheek but isn't . . . it's as though the characters within the play have a great deal of joy about themselves, a joy of living . . . you play it with the reality you would in a kitchen-sink drama written for today's life."

* * *

Those are the words of William Shatner, reflecting on the combination of drama and humor he feels is so important to "Star Trek." Harve Bennett has referred to this quality as "tap dancing"—the ability to bring to even the most dramatic moments of a production that certain sense of joy. As co-writers of the original story for *Star Trek V*, Shatner and Bennett were determined to bring those elements of "Star Trek's" success to the fore.

Indeed, the appeal of *Star Trek V* is not so much in its plot as in the relationship between the characters, and the fun that results from their interplay. It's all in the lines—and what's *between* the lines as well.

"THE FINAL FRONTIER"

TFF

STORY:	William Shatner and Harve Bennett and David Loughery
SCREENPLAY:	David Loughery
DIRECTOR:	William Shatner
PRODUCER:	Harve Bennett

PRINCIPALS:	Kirk	Sybok
	Spock	Caithlin Dar
	McCoy	St. John Talbot
	Scotty	General Korrd
	Sulu	Klaa
	Chekov	Vixis
	Uhura	

Nimbus III, the "Planet of Galactic Peace" in the Neutral Zone, has been jointly colonized by the United Federation of Planets and the Klingon and Romulan empires. To this world comes Sybok, an openly emotional Vulcan who can eliminate anyone's deepest emotional pain, replacing it with an almost messianic devotion to the Vulcan and his cause. Sybok is searching for God, and for his quest he requires a starship.

Meanwhile, Kirk, Spock, and McCoy are taking shore leave in Yosemite National Park. Rescued by Spock from a fall down a mountainside, Kirk tells his friends that he wasn't afraid of dying because they were with him; he has always believed that he would die while he was alone.

Back on Nimbus III, Sybok and his followers have captured the planet's capital, Paradise City, and three consuls. To free Sybok's captives—the UFP representative St. John Talbot, Romulan Caithlin Dar, and the famed retired Klingon general Korrd—Starfleet will send him the starship he needs.

The shore leaves of Kirk and his crew are abruptly ended by a priority call from Starfleet. Despite Kirk's protests that the *Enterprise* is not fully operational (even the transporter and turbolifts aren't functioning), he and his starship are ordered to Nimbus III.

Arriving on Nimbus III, Kirk, Spock, McCoy, and sev-

Kirk makes a dangerous climb.

Preparing for the trip to Nimbus III.

eral others attempt a rescue, only to become Sybok's captives. Spock recognizes Sybok as his half brother (Sarek's son by a Vulcan priestess), who had left home years before. After "treating" the officers of the *Enterprise* crew, Sybok takes command of the vessel.

Locked in the brig, Kirk, Spock, and McCoy learn that Sybok is heading the *Enterprise* toward the Great Barrier at the center of the galaxy—a wall that no starship has ever penetrated.

With Scotty's aid, the three escape, reach an emergency transmitter, and contact Starfleet. Or so they think. . . . In reality, a pursuing Klingon ship has intercepted their message.

On the *Enterprise,* Sybok recaptures our friends and makes each confront his greatest pain.

McCoy sees himself shutting off the machine that kept his terminally ill father alive and in agony. Sybok's powers relieve the doctor of his guilt.

Spock witnesses his own birth, and Sarek's initial rejection of him.

Only Kirk resists Sybok's efforts. "I don't want my pain taken away. I *need* my pain," he exclaims, stating that it is part of the man he is. Hearing this, Spock and McCoy both reject Sybok.

Sybok guides the starship safely through the Great Barrier. Still confined, Kirk and company watch the ship penetrate a black cloud and approach the single planet hidden at the center of the galaxy. Is this really the world known as "Sha Ka Ree" to Vulcans, "Vorta Vor" to Romulans, "Quie'Tu" to Klingons, and "Eden" to Terrans?

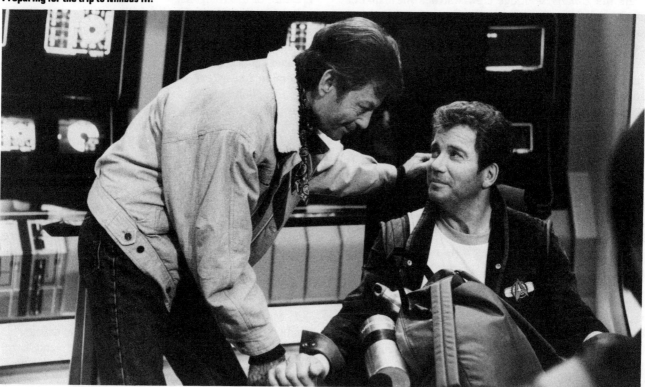

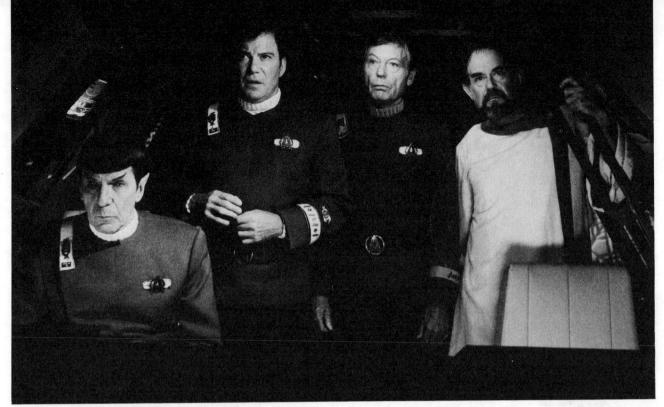

Spock, Kirk, McCoy, and Sybok on their way to the God planet.

Sybok voluntarily surrenders control of the *Enterprise*. Kirk decides to explore the planet and, with Spock, McCoy, and Sybok, travels there in the shuttlecraft *Copernicus*. Scotty continues to work to repair the ship's transporter.

As the *Enterprise* bridge crew watches the explorers' journey on the main viewscreen, the unattended defense station posts an unheeded warning: KLINGON VESSEL IN QUADRANT.

Down on the planet, huge rock formations erupt, forming a primitive cathedral around the explorers. A shaft of energy appears and assumes a variety of forms, which each observer sees as his own image of God.

"You are the first to find me," the being announces, explaining that the *Enterprise* will carry his power "to every corner of creation." Sybok is awestruck—but Kirk, characteristically, dares to ask what *God* needs with a starship. When the being inquires "Who is this creature?" Kirk challenges it further. "Who am I? Don't you know? Aren't you God?" Furious, the creature attacks Kirk. Realizing that he's been lured to the planet by this evil being, Sybok attacks. The two struggle furiously—then disappear beneath the ground.

A photon torpedo fired from the *Enterprise* blasts the cathedral to bits, but the creature reappears in a more terrifying form. Kirk, Spock, and McCoy flee to the shuttlecraft, but the energy-being disables the *Copernicus*. The transporter, not yet fully operational, can initially retrieve only Spock and McCoy.

Before Scotty can rescue Kirk, the Klingon ship attacks the *Enterprise*, and the shields are raised. Separated from his friends, Kirk now sees the possibility of death as very real.

Trapped atop a rocky pinnacle, Kirk sees the Klingon Bird of Prey swoop down. Who will reach him first—the creature or the Klingons?

Transported in the nick of time aboard the Klingon vessel, Kirk is led to its bridge, where he finds Spock in the command chair! Realizing that Korrd still outranked the Klingon captain Klaa, the Vulcan persuaded the Klingon general to take action so that Kirk could be rescued.

A reception held aboard the *Enterprise* celebrates the recovery of the hostages. The three consuls—realizing that the Federation and the Klingons have worked together to save them—return to Nimbus III to begin planning for a lasting peace.

Later, Kirk, Spock, and McCoy return to Earth and finish their shore leave together at Yosemite.

In the 1940 film version of *The Thief of Baghdad*, the young thief releases a genie from a bottle. As the creature prepares to kill him, the youth expresses his doubts that the genie could ever have fit into that small bottle. "What? You dare doubt?" the genie angrily roars. "If I'm going to die in a moment," the thief answers, "I can dare *anything.*" The genie voluntarily reenters the bottle, which the thief promptly corks. This is the stuff of which "tap dancing" is made. The films of Douglas Fairbanks, Sr., and Errol Flynn have it, as do *Raiders of the Lost Ark* and its sequels.

Successful "tap dancing"—requiring a delicate balance

of wit and seriousness stopping short of parody—is present in *Star Trek IV,* directed by Leonard Nimoy. Following that film's successful reception, director William Shatner intended *Star Trek V* to showcase this elusive quality. Tap dancing is indeed present when Kirk doubts the creature is God because it hasn't heard of *him,* and in Spock's first words to Sybok after twenty years ("You are under arrest for violating seventeen counts of the Neutral Zone Treaty"). But the film crosses the fine line separating tap dancing from parody, particularly when Scotty knocks himself unconscious, and in the running gag of an *Enterprise* on which *nothing* works.

Laurence Luckinbill is fine as Sybok. But had actor David Warner, at once charming and terrifying as Jack the Ripper, been cast as Sybok, he would have provided the character and the film with additional tension, strength, and dimension. Instead, Warner appears in a minor role.

Star Trek V may be remembered for two things. First, in it we learn that Dr. McCoy "killed" his father. Second, it has Captain Kirk asking, "Excuse me—excuse me, but what does *God* need with a starship?"

"THE UNDISCOVERED COUNTRY"

▯▯▯▯▯▯▯▯▯▯▯▯▯▯▯▯▯▯▯▯▯▯▯▯▯▯▯▯▯▯ **TUC**

STORY: Leonard Nimoy and Lawrence Konner & Mark
               Rosenthal
SCREENPLAY: Nicholas Meyer & Denny Martin Flynn
DIRECTOR: Nicholas Meyer
PRODUCER: Ralph Winter & Steven-Charles Jaffe

PRINCIPALS: Kirk   Chancellor Gorkon
               Spock   General Chang
               McCoy   Chancellor Azetbur
               Scotty   Federation President
               Sulu   Admiral Cartwright
               Uhura   Klingon Ambassador
               Chekov   Colonel Worf
               Lieutenant Valeris   Martia
               Ambassador Sarek

Aboard the starship *Excelsior,* Captain Sulu learns of the accidental destruction of Praxis, the key energy-production facility of the Klingons. Learning that his people have only fifty years of oxygen remaining following the disaster, the Klingon chancellor proposes rechanneling their military budget into programs that will save the Klingon race.

After preliminary peace talks between Spock and Chancellor Gorkon of the Klingon High Council, a top-secret meeting of the Federation High Command is called. There, Kirk and company learn of plans to dismantle the Klingon and Federation military forces. Despite Kirk's protests that the Klingons are not trustworthy, he is assigned to rendezvous with Gorkon's battle cruiser and escort the

Captain Hikaru Sulu of the U.S.S. *Excelsior.*

Chancellor to a peace summit. Aboard the *Enterprise* is a new crew member, the Vulcan Lieutenant Valeris.

"It has been said," observed Khan Noonian Singh, "that social occasions are only warfare concealed"—an accurate description of the dinner Kirk arranges to introduce Gorkon and his party to the *Enterprise* officers. Only Gorkon appears courteous and eager for peace, and although he *wants* to trust him, Kirk is still dubious. Gorkon's daughter, Azetbur, is doubtful, but polite. His chief of staff (General Chang) and military adviser (Brigadier Kerla) seem to the *Enterprise* crew unfriendly and barbarous.

Soon after the Klingons return to their ship, photon torpedoes are fired at Gorkon's vessel. Two helmeted assassins board the ship, and in the chaos caused by zero-gravity conditions, they shoot Gorkon, and everyone else within range. Kirk is both horrified and mystified; although all the *Enterprise* torpedoes are accounted for, the ship's data banks show that two *were* fired.

When Chang orders his ship to confront the *Enterprise,* Kirk surrenders and prepares to beam aboard the Klingon vessel. Spock, without Kirk's knowledge, swiftly affixes a patch of viridium to the Captain's jacket, enabling the Captain to be tracked and retrieved if necessary.

On board, Kirk and McCoy find the Chancellor dying. Gorkon regains consciousness long enough to prove his sincerity to Kirk, then dies. Kirk is now doubly stunned—Gorkon's peace overtures were genuine, and Chang arrests both Federation officers, charging them with assassinating the Chancellor.

Wishing to avoid further hostilities, the President of the Federation—with Ambassador Sarek's counsel—decides not to interfere with the Klingons' plans to try Kirk and McCoy for murder. Spock, although ordered back to Earth, falsely states that the *Enterprise*'s warp drive is nonfunctional, keeping the starship in the area.

On the Klingon world Kronos, Kirk and McCoy are tried, found guilty, and sentenced to spend the rest of their lives in the dilithium mines on the penal asteroid archipelago of Rura Penthe (Nicholas Meyer called it Rura Penthe in homage to the 1954 Buena Vista film *20,000 Leagues Under the Sea*).

Spock realizes that his friends' only hope is for him to unmask the true assassins. He deduces that a cloaked Klingon Bird of Prey, fired the torpedoes from beneath the *Enterprise*, and that someone aboard the *Enterprise* then altered the computer records.

With the aid of Martia, a shape-changing Chameloid, Kirk and McCoy escape to a place on the surface of Rura Penthe where Spock can beam them up. But Kirk realizes that their "escape" is really a death trap, engineered by the same conspirators who killed Gorkon. As they are about to die, they are beamed back to the *Enterprise*—just as Kirk was about to learn who is behind the plot.

Enterprise crewmen Burke and Samno, who, it is discovered, assassinated Gorkon, are found dead. Using that discovery, Kirk exposes their killer, Lieutenant Valeris. Spock and Valeris mind-meld, and through her, Kirk learns the names of those who have organized the conspiracy to sabotage the peace talks—UFP admiral Cartwright, Klingon general Chang, and Romulan ambassador Nanclus.

With Chang pursuing in his cloaked ship, Kirk rushes toward Camp Khitomer, where the peace conference is about to start—and where an attempt will be made to assassinate the Federation president. Kirk draws Chang's ship into attacking the *Enterprise*, as Spock and McCoy rig a special photon torpedo to home in on the cloaked vessel's ionized fuel trail. After it is fired, the explosion is monitored by Sulu, who uses the weapons of the *Excelsior* to destroy Chang's ship.

Kirk races into the auditorium at Khitomer, saving the President, while Scotty disposes of a hidden Klingon assassin. Azetbur and Kirk confer, confirming that a new era of peace is about to begin. And the *Enterprise* heads into space on what may be its final cruise with Captain Kirk commanding its familiar crew.

Star Trek VI is an excellent way to end the series. The story provides us with the first details of the events leading to the improved relations between the Federation and the

Kirk, McCoy, and Chang try to save Chancellor Gorkon.

Klingon defense attorney Colonel Worf.

Klingon Empire and serves as a fine bridge into "Star Trek: The Next Generation." The screenplay's greatest irony is that the conspirators, rather than sabotaging the attempt at peace, succeed only in proving that Klingons, Romulans, and the Federation can work together.

On this voyage, save for the absence of Christine Chapel, no recurring member of the crew is omitted or neglected. Of all the *Enterprise*'s original crew, Mr. Sulu has gained the most. No longer aboard the *Enterprise*, he has officially gained a first name (Hikaru) and his own starship to command—the U.S.S. *Excelsior*. Christopher Plummer, as General Chang, and David Warner, returning to the "Star Trek" universe as Chancellor Gorkon, both deliver stunning performances, and Michael Dorn is great in a cameo appearance as one of Worf's (from "Star Trek: The Next Generation") ancestors.

The subtitle of this (the last?) "Star Trek" original-series film, *The Undiscovered Country,* comes from Shakespeare's *Hamlet* and is an allusion to death. Back in 1969 when the television series was canceled, NBC thought "Star Trek" was dead. Following the release of *Star Trek II* in 1982, we thought Mr. Spock was dead. Is this movie the death of the original "Star Trek" continuity? Maybe, but in the "Star Trek" universe, death is often easily overcome.

INDICES
THE VOYAGES OF THE U.S.S. ENTERPRISE

LIVE ACTION

INDEX OF PRINCIPALS

KEY: Principal (Actor)—Episode appearance(s)

Abrom (William Wintersole)—#52
Adam (Charles Napier)—#75
Adams, Dr. Tristan (James Gregory)—#11
Agmar (voice of James Doohan)—#2A
Akaar (Ben Gage)—#32
Akuta (Keith Andes)—#38
Alden, Lt. (Lloyd Haynes)—#2
Alexander (Michael Dunn)—#67
Alice in Wonderland (Marcia Brown)—#17
    (voice of Nichelle Nichols)—#14A
"Alice" Series (Alyce and Rhea Andrece)—#41
Amanda (Jane Wyatt)—#44, TVH
    (voice of Majel Barrett)—#3A
Anan 7 (David Opatoshu)—#23

Elaan of Elas

Andorian (Richard Geary)—#71
Andrea (Sherry Jackson)—#10
Anka (Fred Williamson)—#74
Apella (Arthur Bernard)—#45
Apollo (Michael Forest)—#33
Appel, Ed (Brad Weston)—#26
April, Commodore Robert—#22A
April, Dr. Sarah—#22A
Arex, Lt. (voice of James Doohan)—#2A, 6A, 7A, 8A,
    13A–17A, 19A–22A
Atkins, Yeoman Doris (Carolyn Nelson)—#40
Atoz, Mr. (Ian Wolfe)—#78
Ayelborne (Jon Abbott)—#27
Azetbur, Chancellor (Rosana DeSoto)—TUC

Bailey, Lt. Dave (Anthony Call)—#3
Balok (Clint Howard) (voice of Vic Perrin [puppet voice:
    Ted Cassidy])—#3
"Barbara" Series (Colleen and Maureen Thornton)—#41
Barris, Nilz (William Schallert)—#42
Barrows, Yeoman Tonia (Emily Banks)—#17
Barstow, Commodore (Richard Derr)—#20
Bates, Ensign—#3A
Beach (Paul Kent)—TWOK
Behan, Johnny (Bill Zuckert)—#56
Bele (Frank Gorshin)—#70
Bem, Cmdr. Ari bn (voice of James Doohan)—#17A
Benton (Seamon Glass)—#4
Berkeley, Ensign (Larry Anthony)—#11
Bilar (Ralph Maurer)—#21
Boma, Lt. (Don Marshall)—#14
Bonaventure, Ruth (Maggie Thrett)—#4
Boyce, Dr. Phillip (John Hoyt)—#1,16
Brent, Lt. (Frank da Vinci)—#7
Briggs, Bob (Scott DeVenney)—TVH
Brown, Dr. (Harry Basch)—#10
Bryce, Randi (voice of Majel Barrett)—#16A

Caretaker (Oliver McGowan)—#17

Trelane—the squire of Gothos

Carlisle, Lt. (Arnold Lessing)—#37
Carstairs, Ensign—#53
Carter, Dr. (Ed McReady)—#54
Cartwright, Admiral (Brock Peters)—TUC
Centurion (John Warburton)—#9
Chandra, Captain (Reginald Lalsingh)—#15
Chang, General (Christopher Plummer)—TUC
Chapel, Nurse Christine (Majel Barrett)— #7, 10, 28, 29, 34, 37, 40, 44, 45, 47, 48, 50, 51, 57, 58, 59, 60, 67, 5A, 6A, 8A, 15A, 19A, ST:TMP
Chekov, Ensign Pavel Andreivich (Walter Koenig)— #30, 32, 33, 34, 38, 39, 40, 41, 42, 43, 44, 45, 46, 47, 48, 49, 50, 52, 53, 55, 56, 57, 58, 59, 60, 61, 62, 64, 66, 67, 79, 5A, 6A, 8A, 15A, 19A, ST:TMP, TWOK, TSFS, TVH, TFF, TUC
Childress, Ben (Gene Dynarski)—#4
Christopher, Captain John (Roger Perry)—#21
Claymare (Peter Brocco)—#27
Clayton, Lt.—#13A
Cloud William (Roy Jensen)—#54
Cochrane, Zefram (Glenn Corbett)—#31
Cogley, Samuel T. (Elisha Cook, Jr.)—#15
Coleman, Dr. Arthur (Harry Landers)—#79
Colt, Yeoman, J.M. (Laurel Goodwin)—#1, 16
Compton, Crewman (Geoffrey Binney)—#68
Cory, Donald (Keye Luke)—#71
Crater, Nancy (Jeanne Bal/Francine Pyne)—#6
Crater, Professor Robert (Alfred Ryder)—#6
Cromwell (Don Keefer)—#55

D'Amato, Lt. (Arthur Batanides)—#69
Dar, Caithlin (Cynthia Gouw)—TFF
Dara (voice of Nichelle Nichols)—#6A
Daras (Laura Norland)—#52
Darnell, Crewman (Michael Zaslow)—#6

Darvin, Arne (Charlie Brill)—#42
Davison (voice of Nichelle Nichols)—#6A
Davod (Chuck Courtney)—#52
Daystrom, Dr. Richard (William Marshall)—#53
Decius (Lawrence Montaigne)—#9
Decker, Commodore Matthew (William Windom)—#35
Decker, Captain Will (Stephen Collins)—ST:TMP
Deela (Kathie Brown)—#68
Dehner, Dr. Elizabeth (Sally Kellerman)—#2
DePaul, Lt. (Sean Kenney)—#19, 23
DeSalle, Lt. Vincent (Michael Barrier)—#18, 25, 30
Dickerson, Lt. (Arell Blanton)—#77
Dionyd (Derek Partridge)—#67
Don Juan (James Gruzaf)—#17
Drea (Leslie Dalton)—#50
Droxine (Diana Ewing)—#74
Drusilla (Lois Jewell)—#43
Durr (Kirk Raymone)—#32

Earp, Morgan (Rex Holman)—#56
Earp, Virgil (Charles Maxwell)—#56
Earp, Wyatt (Ron Soble)—#56
Ed (Charles Seel)—#56
Ekor (Eric Holland)—#68
Elaan (France Nuyen)—#57
Eleen (Julie Newmar)—#32
Elliott, Crewman (John Copage)—#35
Em/3/Green (voice of David Gerrold)—#12A
Eneg (Patrick Horgan)—#52
Eraclitus (Ted Scott)—#67
Evans, Crewman (Lee Duncan)—#57

Farrell (Pete Kellett)—#39
Farrell, Lt. John (Jim Goodwin)—#4, 5, 12
Federation President (Kurtwood Smith)—TUC
Fellini, Colonel (Ed Peck)—#21
Ferris, High Commissioner (John Crawford)—#14
Finney, Lt. Cmdr. Benjamin (Richard Webb)—#15
Finney, Jamie (Alice Rawlings)—#15
Finnegan (Bruce Mars)—#17
First Lawgiver (Sid Haig)—#22
Fisher, Technician (Edward Madden)—#5
Fitzgerald, Admiral (Richard Derr)—#72
Fitzpatrick, Admiral (Ed Reimers)—#42
Flavius (Rhodes Reason)—#43
Flint (James Daly)—#76
Fox, Ambassador Robert (Gene Lyons)—#23
Freeman, Ensign (Paul Baxley)—#42

Gabler (voice of James Doohan)—#5A, 10A, 14A
Gaetano, Crewman (Peter Marko)—#14
Galliulin, Irini (Mary-Linda Rapelye)—#75
Galloway, Lt. (David L. Ross)—#12, 23, 28, 54
Galt (Joseph Ruskin)—#46
Galway, Lt. Arlene (Beverly Washburn)—#40

Garrison, CPO (Adam Roarke)—#1, 16
Garrovick, Ensign (Stephen Brooks)—#47
Garth of Izar (Steve Ihnat)—#71
Gav (John Wheeler)—#44
Gem (Kathryn Hays)—#63
Gill, John (David Brian)—#52
Giotto, Lt. Cmdr. (Barry Russo)—#26
Gorgan (Melvin Belli)—#60
Gorkon, Chancellor (David Warner)—TUC
Goro (Richard Hale)—#58
Gossett (Jon Kowal)—#4
Grant, Crewman (Robert Bralver)—#32
Green, Colonel (Phillip Pine)—#77
Green, Crewman (Bruce Watson)—#6A
Grey (voice of Majel Barrett)—#3A

Hacom (Morgan Farley)—#22
Hadley, Lt. (William Blackburn)—#49
Haines, Ensign Jana (Victoria George)—#46
Hanar (Stewart Moss)—#50
Hansen, Cmdr. (Gary Walberg)—#9
Hansen, Lt. (Hagan Beggs)—#15, 16
Harold, Lt. (Tom Troupe)—#19
Harper, Ensign (Sean Morgan)—#53
Harrison, Dr. (John Bellah)—#7
Haskins, Dr. Theodore (Jon Lormer)—#1, 16
Healer, the (voice of James Doohan)—#3A
Hedford, Commissioner Nancy (Elinor Donahue)—#31
Hendorff (Mal Friedman)—#38
Hengist (John Fielder)—#36
"Herman" Series (Tom and Ted LaGarde)—#41
Hodin (David Hurst)—#72
Holliday, Doc (Sam Gilman)—#56
Humbolt, Chief (George Sawaya)—#1, 16

Ilia, Lt. (Persis Khambatta)—ST:TMP
Isak (Richard Evans)—#52

Jackson, Crewman (Jimmy Jones)—#30
Jaegeer, Lt. Karl (Richard Carlyle)—#18
Jahn (Michael Pollard)—#12
Jamal, Yeoman Zahra (Mauriska)—#29
Janowski, Mary (Pamelyn Ferdin)—#60
Jaris (Charles Macaulay)—#36
Joaquin (Mark Tobin)—#24
Johnson, Elaine (Laura Wood)—#40
Johnson, Lt. (David L. Ross)—#66
Johnson, Robert (Felix Locher)—#40
Jones, Cyrano (Stanley Adams)—#42, 1A
Jones, Dr. Miranda (Diana Muldaur)—#62
Jordan, Ensign (Michael Zaslow)—#41
Josephs, Lt. (James X. Mitchell)—#44

Kahless (Robert Herron)—#77
Kalo (Lee Delano)—#49

Kalomi, Leila (Jill Ireland)—#25
Kang (Michael Ansara)—#66
Kapec, Rayna (Louise Sorel)—#76
Kaplan (Dick Dial)—#38
Kara (Marj Dusay)—#61
Kara (Tania Lemani)—#36
Karidian, Anton (Arnold Moss)—#13
Karidian, Lenore (Barbara Anderson)—#13
Kartan (Dave Armstrong)—#29
Keel (Cal Bolder)—#32
Keeler, Edith (Joan Collins)—#28
Keeper, The (Meg Wyllie[voice of Malachi Throne])—#1, 16
Kelinda (Barbara Bouchet)—#50
Kelowitz, Lt. Commander (Grant Woods)—#14, 19, 25
Kelso, Lt. Lee (Paul Carr)—#2
Keniclius Five (voice of James Doohan)—#2A
Khan, Genghis (Nathan Jung)—#77
Kirk, Aurelan (Joan Swift)—#29
Kirk, Captain James T. (William Shatner)—#2–79, 1A–10A, 12A–22A, ST:TMP, TWOK, TSFS, TVH, TFF, TUC
Kirk, Peter (Craig Hundley)—#29
Klaa (Todd Bryant)—TFF
Klingon Ambassador (John Schuck)—TVH, TUC
Klingon Captain (Mark Lenard)—ST:TMP
Kloog (Mickey Morton)—#46
Kodos (Arnold Moss)—#13
Kolchek, Lt.—#2A

Speck's wife T'Pring

Koloth, Captain (William Campbell)—#42
   (voice of James Doohan)—#1A
Kol-tai (voice of James Doohan)—#18A
Komack, Admiral (Byron Morrow)—#34
Kor, Commander (John Colicos)—#27, 10A
Korax (Michael Pataki)—#42
   (voice of David Gerrold)—#1A
Korby, Dr. Roger (Michael Strong)—#10
Korob (Theo Marcuse)—#30
Korrd, General (Charles Cooper)—TFF
Kovas, Magda (Susan Denberg)—#4
Krako, Jojo (Vic Tayback)—#49
Kras (Tige Andrews)—#32
Krasnowsky, Captain (Bart Conrad)—#15
Krell (Ned Romero)—#45
Krodak (Gene Dynarski)—#72
Kruge, Commander (Christopher Lloyd)—TSFS
Kryton (Tony Young)—#57
Kulkukan (voice of James Doohan)—#21A
Kyle, Lt. (John Winston)—#21, 24, 30, 33, 35, 38, 39,
   48, 73, 4A, TWOK

Lal (Alan Bergmann)—#63
Landon, Yeoman Martha (Celeste Yarnall)—#38
Landru (Charles Macaulay)—#22
Lang, Lt. (James Farley)—#19
Lars (Steve Sandor)—#46
Latimer (Reese Vaughn)—#14
Lawton, Yeoman Tina (Patricia McNulty)—#8
Lazarus (Robert Brown)—#20
Leighton, Martha (Natalie Norwick)—#13
Leighton, Dr. Thomas (William Sergeant)—#13
Lemli, Mr. (Roger Holloway)—#51, 75, 79
Leslie, Lt. (Eddie Paskey)—#2, 13, 20, 22, 25, 54, 60
Lester, Dr. Janice (Sandra Smith)—#79
Lethe (Suzanne Wasson)—#11
Lincoln, Abraham (Lee Berger)—#77
Lincoln, Roberta (Teri Garr)—#55
Linden, Don (Mark Robert Brown)—#60
Lindstrom, Crewman (Christopher Held)—#22
Lindstrom, Space Command Representative (William
   Meader)—#15
Linke, Dr. (Jason Wingreen)—#63
Lipton, Sergeant (Lincoln Demyan)—#55
Lokai (Lou Antonio)—#70
Lora (voice of Majel Barrett)—#8A
Losira (Lee Meriwether)—#69
Lucien (voice of James Doohan)—#9A
Luma (Sheila Leighton)—#61
Lumo (Peter Virgo, Jr.)—#58
Lurry, Mr. (Whit Bissell)—#42

M'Benga, Dr. (Booker Marshall)—#45, 69
McCoy, Dr. Leonard (DeForest Kelley)—#3–9, 11–26,
   28–70, 72–79, 1A–10A, 13A–16A, 18A, 19A, 21A,
   22A, ST:TMP, TWOK, TSFS, TVH, TFF, TUC

McGivers, Lt. Marla (Madlyn Rhue)—#24
McHuron, Eve (Karen Steele)—#4
M'Ress, Lt. (voice of Majel Barrett)—#5A, 8A, 14A,
   17A, 20A
"Maisie" Series (Tamara and Starr Wilson)—#41
Makora (David Soul)—#38
Mallory, Ensign (Jay Jones)—#38
Maltz (John Larroquette)—TSFS
Mara (Susan Howard)—#66
Marcus, Dr. Carol (Bibi Besch)—TWOK
Marcus, Claudius (Logan Ramsey)—#43
Marcus, Dr. David (Merritt Butrick)—TWOK, TSFS
Markel, Lt. Cmdr. Tom (voice of James Doohan)—#16A
Marple (Jerry Daniels)—#38
Marplon (Torin Thatcher)—#22
Marta (Yvonne Craig)—#71
Martia (Iman)—TUC
Martine, Angela (Barbara Baldavin)—#9, 17, 79
Marvick, Dr. Lawrence (David Frankham)—#62
Masters, Lt. Charlene (Janet MacLachlan)—#20
Matson, Lt. (David Troy)—#13
Matthews (Vince Deadrick)—#10
Mavig (Deborah Downey)—#75
Maximus (Max Kelven)—#43
Mea 3 (Barbara Babcock)—#23
Mears, Yeoman (Phyllis Douglas)—#14
Megan Prosecutor (voice of James Doohan)—#9A
Melakon (Skip Homeier)—#52
Mendant (voice of James Doohan)—#15A
Mendez, Commodore Jose (Malachai Throne)—#16
Merik, Captain R.M./Merikus (William Smithers)—#43
Metron (Carole Shelyne)—#19
Midro (Henry Evans)—#74
Miramanee (Sabrina Scharf)—#58
Miri (Kim Darby)—#12
Mirt (Jay Jones)—#49
Mitchell, Lt. Cmdr. Gary (Gary Lockwood)—#2
Montgomery, Crewman (Jerry Catron)—#35
Moreau, Lt. Marlena (Barbara Luna)—#39
Morgan, Lt.—#2A
Morla (Charles Dierkop)—#36
Mudd, Harcourt Fenton (Roger C. Carmel)—#4, 41, 8A
Mudd, Stella (Kay Elliott)—#41
Mulhall, Dr. Anne (Diana Muldaur)—#51

Natira (Kate Woodville)—#65
Nesvig, Colonel (Morgan Jones)—#55
Noel, Dr. Helen (Marianna Hill)—#11
Nona (Nancy Kovack)—#45
Nored, Lt. Anne (voice of Nichelle Nichols)—#5A
Norman (Richard Tatro)—#41
Number One (Majel Barrett)—#1, 16

O'Connel, Steve (Caesar Belli)—#60
Odona (Sharon Acker)—#72
O'Herlihy, Lt. (Jerry Ayres)—#19